The Rise of Viagra

MEIKA LOE

The Rise of Viagra

How the Little Blue Pill Changed Sex in America

New York University Press • *New York and London*

NEW YORK UNIVERSITY PRESS
New York and London
www.nyupress.org

Library of Congress Cataloging-in-Publication Data
Loe, Meika, 1973–
The rise of Viagra :
how the little blue pill changed sex in America / Meika Loe.
p. cm.
Includes bibliographical references and index.
ISBN 0–8147–5200–4 (cloth : alk. paper)
1. Sildenafil—Social aspects—United States.
2. Sex—United States.   I. Title.
RC889.L64   2004
616.6'922061—dc22   2004005125

New York University Press books are printed on acid-free paper,
and their binding materials are chosen for strength and durability.

Manufactured in the United States of America

10 9 8 7 6 5 4 3 2 1

To Gramps,
    master of the printed word,
        role model,
            friend

Contents

Acknowledgments

Like Viagra, this book has been a collaborative endeavor. In volunteering their time, energy, space, colleagues, and advice, the following individuals and institutions have made this book what it is.

There would be no project without the generosity and assistance of my informants—the doctors, consumers, pharmacists, pharmaceutical representatives, and senior women who took time out to talk with me about Viagra and what it means to them. Additionally, the twelve original members of the "Working Group" helped me to realize where I stood in relation to my project. Thank you all for trusting me to represent your views fairly and honestly. Your influence is on every page of this book.

My academic mentors at the University of California at Santa Barbara read this work over and over, and supported and encouraged its development over the years. Beth Schneider grounded me, and assisted tremendously in guiding and organizing my fieldwork, my writing, and my calendar. Laury Oaks always provided consistent, indispensable feedback and nudged my thinking in new directions. Mitch Duneier's passion for ethnographic methods encouraged me to capture this emergent phenomenon. Constance Penley's lesson that consumption is production forms a basis for this project. And Sarah Fenstermaker's theoretical lens and wisdom inform this work as a whole. These individuals use their own research to promote positive social change, and this continues to inspire me.

My colleagues at the University of California at Santa Barbara were invaluable for their thoughtful feedback at all stages of the game. For help in writing, chapter by chapter, my sincere appreciation goes to Mary Ingram, Lisa Torres, Michele Wakin, Hazel Hull, Lyn Gesch, and Christopher Kollmeyer. Additionally, the gender studies proseminar participants at UCSB were essential in helping me organize, analyze, and theorize my data. I must thank Juliet Williams, Joanna Davis, Susan

Dalton, Tricia Drew, Rachel Luft, Rani Bush, and Sara Jones for going out of their way to advise and encourage me in the field and at my computer.

This project changed shape as I met and had stimulating conversations with inspiring people along the way. Ilene Kalish and the production staff at NYU Press as well as my generous reviewers at Duke University Press and Routledge helped me enormously in revising this book for a general audience. For their guidance, I also thank Leonore Tiefer, Christine Williams, Paula Treichler, Carol Tavris, Peter Conrad, Peter Nardi, Jodi O'Brien, Verta Taylor, Michael Kimmel, Ken Plummer, Harvey Molotch, Howard Becker, Jack Sutton, Chris Bobel, Jennifer Reich, Heather Hartley, Jennifer Fishman, Laura Mamo, Annie Potts, Amy Allina, and Rafael Peres. Gratitude goes to Jessica Kinstlinger for her generous hospitality in Boston, and to the Woodrow Wilson Foundation, the University of California at Santa Barbara, and Colgate University, for making this project possible. My favorite librarians, Sherri Barnes and Ellie Bolland, have been extremely helpful.

Most recently, I'm indebted to my supportive colleagues at Colgate University for advice and encouragement in the last stages of writing. This includes my research assistants, Meg Lyons and Laura Lyman, who were terribly dedicated to the end. Special thanks go to Carolyn Kissane, Mary Moran, Diane Williams, Christopher Henke, Ellen Kraly, Adam Weinberg, Don Duggan-Has, Carolyn Hsu, Marilyn Thie, Warren Blumenfeld, Karen Luciani, Molly Ames Baker, Don LaFrance, Vige Barrie, Tim Sofranko, and Charlie Melichar.

And finally, this project would not have been possible without the family members and friends who have believed in me and this project from the beginning, helping with my day-to-day stresses, asking after me, talking about this project with their friends and doctors, sending me articles, doing the dishes night after night, and helping me to keep this project in perspective. This book is dedicated to you—how lucky I am to have you all in my life!

The Rise of Viagra

"*I never had a problem before those goddam Bob Dole ads.*"

From Cartoon Bank

Preface

Bob Dole, Bill Clinton, Bazooms, and Me

STRANGE, YOU SAY. A woman has written a book about Viagra. I wonder how she got interested in that. . . . Well, I'll tell you. After all, you should always know where an author is coming from. I'm from California, but my academic interest in men and sex goes back to a place I call Bazooms: a food establishment where waitresses wear short shorts and tight tank tops and hula-hoop in between orders.[1] In the early 1990s, Bazooms was the second-fastest-growing restaurant chain in the United States. This, coupled with its controversial reputation, was enough to get me intrigued, and my burgeoning sociological eye and general curiosity resulted in a job. So, in the 1990s I was working as a Bazooms girl. As it turned out, Bazooms was a fascinating and disturbing place to learn about how sexual and gender expectations are both taught and reinforced by our social institutions.

At Bazooms, you are practically handed a script when you walk in the door. Inside, the floor is a stage, and numerous performances take place. As a Bazooms girl I was taught to smile, flirt, flaunt it, and glory in being the center of attention. I also learned, indirectly, that the Bazooms customer—male, of course—is expected to joke, ogle you, flirt, and generally act boisterous while consuming pitchers of beer, buffalo wings, and televised sporting events. After all, Bazooms is a guy's fantasy (actually, six guys in Florida came up with the idea), and Bazooms girls are supposed to help that fantasy along. This is what you'd expect from a sports bar named after breasts, right?

Well, I discovered that like any rich cultural site, Bazooms was not always the perfectly choreographed "fun" place it appeared to be. Sometimes men and women did not act as they were expected to act. At times, the "Bazooms girls" were visibly unhappy on the job. Many times, in the backroom they would bad-mouth the Bazooms customers. Even more surprising to me, some male customers were visibly uncomfortable at Bazooms. For example, one of my customers asked to be seated in the corner and proceeded to hide behind his sunglasses and hat. Later, he quietly commented that he felt ashamed and awkward in the restaurant, "like one would feel in an adult bookstore." He was clearly out of his element, as were other customers I spoke with. All of these over-the-top Bazooms moments, including the "failed" gendered performances, the parents who brought their kids to Bazooms, and the sexualized encounters that went too far—all of these moments made the research site and the business all the more complex, fascinating, and human.

As a budding sociologist I went into the job reminding myself to make note of institutionalized sexism, sexual harassment, and the general social inequality in evidence at Bazooms. All of these problems were real, important, and vexing, and I did end up writing about them, hopefully exposing the gendered power imbalances and the sexual status quo that Bazooms promotes. But it was the image of the embarrassed male customer seated in the corner that stayed with me for years, reminding me of how complex masculinity, and men, really can be.

Fast forward to 1998. Something unexpected occurred in America. President Clinton was caught, literally, with his pants down. Soon after "Monicagate," former Republican presidential nominee Bob Dole appeared on the scene, talking about sexual dysfunction. Let's pause here for a second. Put yourself back there in 1998—the media was reporting regularly about HIV, breast cancer, and the lurid details of the Starr Report. There was a national debate about the definition of sex and "sexual relations." Jokes about cigars invaded public consciousness. In this permissive "sex talk" atmosphere, it was no wonder that Bob Dole publicly confessed his prostate cancer and Viagra use on *Larry King Live*. Soon afterwards, Dole was selling erectile dysfunction (ED) and, by association, Viagra, on television screens across the country.

Before 1998, with the startling exception of Anita Hill's 1991 testimony about soon-to-be Supreme Court Justice Clarence Thomas, no American could have foreseen a moment when the country would be transfixed by the sexual lives of our most powerful politicians. But we were. We were glued to the television, mesmerized, watching their public confessions, laughing and joking out of sheer discomfort. One man couldn't get it up and the other couldn't stop getting it up; both stories were alarmingly personal and downright embarrassing. The vulnerable man was suddenly in the spotlight and male shame was big news. I was reminded again of the self-conscious Bazooms customer, chomping down greasy fries and hiding in the corner. This time, though, male shame was center stage for all of us to see.

As we now know, in the battle between adultery (extreme potency) and impotency there was only one clear winner. Dole may have lost the presidential election, but this time he returned victorious, wearing red, white, and blue and talking confidently to the camera. While Clinton was held to blame for his actions, Dole was blameless—he was a victim of prostate cancer and, consequently, ED. While Clinton spent months denying his situation, Dole spoke bluntly to television audiences about his problem. And while Clinton's dilemma appeared to worsen over time, Dole had a clear solution to his problem—Viagra. Clinton was repeatedly humiliated and then shown the door. Dole, former senator, veteran, and the new spokesperson for the little blue pill, was the one bringing respectable sexuality back to America and American politics.

The contrast between these two versions of male sexuality deserves a second look. Against the backdrop of America's Puritan ethic, Bob Dole's pursuit of sexual arousal was embraced in 1998. After all, he was a U.S. veteran, speaker of the House, a survivor of prostate cancer, and a married man. With his Republican family values, Bob Dole was advocating sexual relations in a sanitized, controlled, normal, and non-controversial (read: penetrative heterosexual) way. Clinton, on the other hand, seemed to fit perfectly with negative stereotypes of out-of-control male sexuality. Let's just put it this way—in 1998, Pfizer would never have wanted Clinton selling Viagra.

Six years and billions of dollars later, Pfizer Pharmaceuticals, manufacturer of Viagra, is perhaps the most triumphant player involved in this scenario. As Clinton and Dole have faded away, Pfizer has succeeded in keeping male sexual problems and potency in the spotlight. In the process, our sexual status quo has shifted dramatically. We live in a culture where ads for "male enhancement" are commonplace, and currently, three drugs—Viagra, Levitra, and Cialis—compete for the erectile dysfunction market. Today, the image promoted by Pfizer Pharmaceuticals (Viagra), Bayer and GlaxoSmithKline (Levitra), and Lilly ICOS (Cialis) of normal, respectable, potent sexuality encompasses everyone from seventy-five-year-old Bob Dole and sixty-something Mike Ditka with ED to thirty-nine-year-old Rafael Palmeiro, a Latino pro baseball player known for his high and consistent batting average. These product spokesmen have simple messages for male audiences: "live life again," "step up to the plate," "are you ready?" and "stay in the game." But underneath this simple marketing message lies a complex web of issues concerning health and medicine, masculinity and femininity, and product promotion in the twenty-first century.

For me, the bookends of the 1990s were Bazooms and Viagra. From where I stand today at the beginning of the twenty-first century, these two American success stories are both fascinating and troubling. As two of America's most profitable and powerful corporations, in their respective industries, both have had, and continue to have, a tremendous impact on American culture. Bazooms has continued to expand nationally and globally, and recently unveiled its own male-fantasy-based airline. Pfizer Pharmaceuticals continues to market Viagra globally and has intensified its efforts to produce a "female Viagra" while amassing profits in the billions. Of most concern for me is the fact that both promote their own versions of an idealized man, one in which there is no room for variation, vulnerability, or insecurity. And one in which the measure of a man's worth—and presumably all men are sexually active and heterosexual—is in the realm of his sexual performance.

At this point, I hope you are not expecting this book to deliver a simple story about a blue pill. Five years ago, when I began this project, I never imagined how much one could learn about one's culture from a pill. What I did learn when I began talking with people is that Viagra is embedded in stories, and the people and the culture behind these stories are complicated. This book is an attempt to do justice to the complexity of the Viagra phenomenon, from its multifaceted cast of characters—a mixture of doctors, marketers, consumers, and critics—to its sometimes uplifting, often surprising, and troubling storyline. This time, the quiet, self-conscious guy is central to the story, along with his significant others, his doctor, his pharmacist, the local pharmaceutical sales representative, the pills in the medicine cabinet, and more. Women are also crucial to this story—and, not surprisingly, they have a lot to say, particularly as women's sexual problems become part of the Viagra discourse. In the process of relaying the story of Viagra, I hope that this book will reveal what the Viagra phenomenon says about our culture and why sex in America will never be the same again.

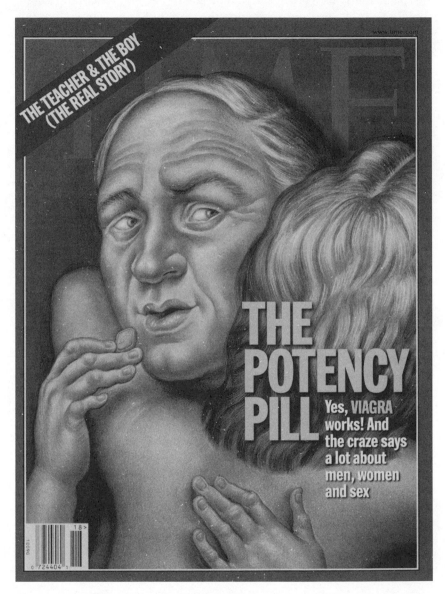

Reproduced by permission from Time Magazine, copyright Time Inc.

1
Introducing Viagra

THE TOP AMERICAN NEWS STORY OF 1998 was President Clinton's affair with Monica Lewinsky. The second was Viagra. This "story" was summarized this way in an article entitled "The Pill That Thrills" in the *San Francisco Chronicle*:

> Viagra, an innocent looking little blue pill, proved that big things do come in small packages, lifting the spirits of millions of men who suffer from impotence. After its approval in March, the drug also raised a host of ethical questions, ranging from HMOs that wondered whether to pay for it to a 70-year-old New York man whose reignited taste for friskiness made him dump his 63-year-old lover, claiming "It's time for me to be a stud again."[1]

In just two sentences, we see the makings of a cultural phenomenon. We first notice the marketing—a pill designed to look small and innocent is packaged with promises of "big things," "lifted spirits," and "thrills." This tiny commodity is linked not only to expansive promises but also to massive networks of potential consumers, "millions of men who suffer from impotence." Viagra is said to raise spirits as well as "a host of ethical questions," including how to define medical necessity and requirements for insurance coverage. Finally, the product is linked to traditional gender stereotypes about suffering men, Viagra "studs," and women who are their victims (i.e., jilted lovers and wives). Clearly, the Clinton affair and the little blue pill not only changed the way people talked about sexuality but also raised important questions about manhood, quality of life, power, and morality.

It is clear that the approval of this small pill elicited "big things" in 1998, including big medical markets, big ethical issues, big body parts, and, obviously, big news. Interestingly, big profits and big corporations are not mentioned by the *San Francisco Chronicle*, although Viagra became the fastest-selling drug in history, eventually grossing over a billion dollars in its first year.[2] In 2002, the company that makes Viagra, Pfizer Pharmaceuticals, became the fifth most profitable corporation in the United States.[3]

This "master story" about Viagra is a familiar one. We have all been exposed to Viagra stories similar to this one. But a journalist would tell this story differently from a consumer, a doctor, a marketer, or a critic. Put together, the context out of which Viagra emerged, and the "noise" it created, made Viagra both a medical breakthrough and a cultural phenomenon. This book takes a close look at this phenomenon by analyzing the stories told about Viagra, stories that reveal cultural norms and ideals related to medicine, gender, health, and aging, as well as fascinating cultural contradictions. Because the stories we tell shape and reflect our realities, Viagra offers a window onto American culture, revealing much about the society we live in and reflecting some potentially troubling social trends.

This book suggests that Viagra is what people and institutions make it. My focus is the people who construct both the product and the demand for it—not just those at Pfizer Pharmaceuticals but also doctors, patients, partners, critics, journalists, and even comedians, all with a different stake in the product and what it means. This book joins the important and growing field of "grounded" research in cultural studies and medical sociology dedicated to examining how consumers use commodities to achieve various ends.[4] A select group of medical sociologists has listened to and collected patients' experiences with medicine and medicalization. These studies center on people's experiences with HIV/AIDS, fetal surgery, fertility, obstetrics, and cosmetic surgeries.[5] Thus far, I know of no (non-Pfizer-funded) published research studies taking into account consumers' experiences with Viagra.[6] Social-scientific analyses of Viagra tend to focus on Pfizer and other medical institutions as the primary actors in the Viagra phenomenon, which unfortunately obscures the multiplicity of individuals and groups that shape and are shaped by Viagra.[7] In the process, the opportunity to learn how medical knowledge, practices, and solutions are created is lost, and Pfizer appears to have the final word. But the story of Viagra, while largely orchestrated by Pfizer, is also dependent on large constellations of people and institutions, as well as social, economic, and political happenings at the end of the twentieth century.

How Did We Get Here?

From the beginning, Viagra was a joke. You must have heard them. Viagra has been a big boon to stand-up comedians. Did you hear about the guy who took Viagra and got it stuck in his throat? He got a stiff neck. New Viagra eye drops make you look hard. In nursing homes, Viagra keeps male patients from rolling out of bed. Did you hear about the first death from an overdose of Viagra? A man took twelve pills and his wife died. Viagra is now being compared to Disneyland—a one-hour wait for a two-minute ride.

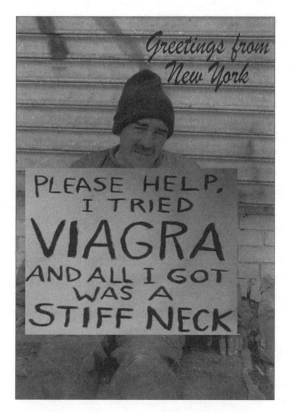

This postcard, purchased on the streets of New York in 2000, exemplifies how Viagra humor has proliferated in mainstream culture.

Most of us are familiar with these one-liners. In 1998, they were delivered by our favorite talk show hosts and comedians.[8] They were repeated by our friends, our relatives, and even our doctors. And they circulated over e-mail for years, it seemed. In our puritanical culture, the availability of a new erection pill and the social ramifications of this were, shall we say, slightly uncomfortable to talk about. But the idea of men of all ages taking pills and having erections as a result was easy to laugh about. And so we did. Because just like the news of Clinton's affair months earlier, the existence of such a pill seemed both ludicrous and deeply serious, both enabling and frightening. Unlike news of Clinton's affair, the Viagra phenomenon "penetrated" people's daily lives in bedrooms and boardrooms. Viagra humor was one way to cope with the newness and awkwardness of Viagra in our lives, and all that went with it—including acknowledgment of erectile difficulties, awareness of medical risk, the idea of seniors as sexual beings, and the acceptance of sex for pleasure's sake.

Actually, whether we felt like it or not, by 1998 Americans had already begun to transition into a new era in sex, medicine, and technological innovation. Numerous social changes at the end of the twentieth century paved the way for the emergence of a product like Viagra. These changes made it possible for many of us to see ourselves and our sex lives as "dysfunctional." And they began the chain reaction that has resulted in industries and institutions dedicated to what we now call "sexual medicine" and "male enhancement."

How did we get here? I believe that Viagra's emergence in the late twentieth century can be distilled down to five shifting sets of social circumstances: (1) medical expansion, (2) scientific and technological innovation, (3) pharmaceutical deregulation and expansion, (4) cultural and demographic shifts in gender and aging, and (5) increasing scientific and popular attention to sexuality and sexual dissatisfaction. Together, these factors made the Viagra phenomenon possible.

Expanding Medicine

First, Viagra was enabled by the rise of medicine. Sociologists Peter Conrad and Joseph Schneider argue that medicine now exercises increasing authority over areas of life not previously under its purview.[9] Disorders once treated as psychological are now treated as mainly organic. As one psychiatrist explained to me, "the pendulum has swung to the biological extreme. Everything is now located in the body, instead of the mind."[10] New medical categories are under construction, older diagnoses are expanded, and medical solutions such as pills, creams, and devices proliferate. Medicalization has been so successful that sometimes devices and pharmaceuticals appear to be the only options for treatment. In this context, patients don't leave the doctor's office without a prescription, and health insurers cover more medical treatments and fewer psychological referrals.[11]

In recent years, some scholars have begun to make visible the connection between "social problems" and "medical problems."[12] These "medicalized social problems" are similarly seen as harmful, widespread, and treatable. Such research exposes a society where previously nonmedical life events (e.g., childbirth, baldness, depression, PMS, and menopause) are redefined as medicalized social problems. In the case of Viagra, medical expansion transforms unacceptable erectile performance into a subject for medical analysis and treatment.[13] Clinical psychologist Leonore Tiefer aptly points out that this has occurred over a period of time, with the help of medical expansion "advocates" such as urologists, medical corporations, mass media, and entrepreneurs.[14]

One pharmaceutical product that has attracted significant media attention in recent years as a result of its association with medical expansion is Ritalin. In his book *Running on Ritalin,* medical ethicist Lawrence Diller analyzes the relationship between escalating Ritalin consumption and use and expanding diagnoses for ADD.[15] Diller points out that the reliance on Ritalin relieves all sorts of adults—doctors, patients, teachers, and policymakers alike—from having to pay attention to children's social environments, which may worsen as a consequence. The research of sociologists Peter Conrad and Deborah Potter pushes this issue further, exploring the expansion in the late twentieth century of hyperactive disorder (ADD) to include a wider range of troubles and age criteria (ADHD). This successful "diagnostic expansion" can be attributed to claims made by researchers, journalists, medical professionals, and the public at large. The Viagra case builds on such research by continuing to pose questions about diagnostic expansion and increased medicalization. The Viagra case also exposes how "fact" construction and dissemination can be undertaken by corporations, how diagnostic expansion can work hand in hand with market expansion, and how medical expansion can be synonymous with increased profitability.

Thus, this study poses new, crucial questions about the intersections among medicine and capital, corporations and science.

It is important to point out that the medicalization of impotence, and the cultural valuation of pills and potency, existed well before Viagra. Viagra did not just appear out of the blue, but came in response to a long-standing search for new biotechnological remedies for rehabilitating erections.[16] In 1998, Viagra joined the ranks of a growing collection of medical and technological solutions to the problem of impotence, solutions that sometimes require surgery (prosthetics), injection or insertion into the penis (with products such as Caverject and MUSE), or vacuum pumping. Additionally, Viagra relied upon a constellation of tools and new medical devices dedicated to measuring and testing sexual dysfunction in men and women, including rigiscan devices, probes, and 3-D video glasses.[17] Pfizer relied on the expanding network of standardized medical treatments to claim "improvement" upon earlier technologies, arguing that their pill is easier to use, more efficient, and the most "natural."[18] In 1998, the existence of an erection pill appeared necessary and normal in the context of previous, less efficient technologies, the proliferation of pills as solutions for everyday problems, an aging population, and a visible and growing sexual marketplace.

In the age of medical "progress," scientific knowledge and medical answers are generally unquestioned as the best, most efficient, most legitimate solutions. Technology, as an applied science, is similarly constructed and championed. However, the history of science, medicine, and technology is also a history of attempting to solve social problems and control populations.[19] In twentieth-century America, biotechnology was deployed to solve social problems, seen as large-scale sexual-morality problems, such as infertility, teenage pregnancy, venereal disease, and HIV/AIDS.[20] It is in this context of medical and biotechnological hegemony, along with U.S. government deregulation of the pharmaceutical industry, that late-twentieth-century American society witnessed the rapid expansion of pharmaceutical power and the rise of the pharmacology of sex.[21]

Technological Innovation and Enhancement

The latter half of the twentieth century witnessed expanding technological innovation, yielding products such as the birth control pill, contraceptives, and abortion options that created a separation between reproduction and sex. The development of new reproductive technologies in the mid-twentieth century was a clear precursor to the pharmacology of sex. For example, in the 1950s the oral contraceptive pill was constructed as one answer to women's needs.[22] Social scientist Elizabeth Watkins, in her book *On the Pill: A Social History of the Birth Control Pill,* tracks the way the combination of media, medical researchers, physicians, and manufacturers seduced the public into seeing "the pill" as the ideal "techno-fix" to solve individual and social problems related to fertility control without knowing the hazards of the drug. Incidentally, Lynne Luciano, author of *Looking Good: Male Body Image in Modern America,* points out that the invention of the first birth control pill (Enovid, released in May 1960) had not-so-beneficial effects on men. Wives had sharp increases in passion as a result of being freed from pregnancy fears. Instead of being delighted, many husbands were dismayed. When women assumed sexually dominant roles, egos and erections began to collapse. One thing the pill did for women was to remove the biological basis for the sexual double standard (chastity), turning women into "critical consumers of male performance." After Masters and Johnson's research was made public in the 1960s, orgasm became the "new female status symbol," and sexual performance and pleasure became the responsibility of the individual.[23]

The new oral contraceptive served as both a catalyst and a barometer of changes in social attitudes about science, technology, and medicine, and it illuminated ideas about gender, sexuality, and science as applied to women's lives.[24] Most importantly, Watkins suggests that "although Americans expressed skepticism toward medical science and its products, for example, the pill, they continued to embrace a culture of 'modern' medicine and technology after the 1960s"—a culture that was rapidly expanding and changing.[25] This cultural embrace of medicine, science, and, now, pharmacology, as "progress" has led directly to the Viagra phenomenon.

In the past twenty years, there has been growing scholarship reflecting social concern about the merging of technology and medical science to create "postmodern" bodies. Scholars addressing these issues are both intrigued and troubled by the many options available for controlling our bodies through surgeries, implants, hormones, drugs, appliances, reproductive technologies, and, more recently, cosmetic surgeries.[26] Viagra belongs to this large collection of twentieth-century "technologies of sex," or tools used for the discipline and control of "inappropriate" bodies.[27]

The Rise of "Big Pharma"

As a direct consequence of the Reagan era, during which the U.S. administration celebrated and supported deregulation and market expansion while devaluing safety nets, pharmaceutical and FDA regulations were significantly loosened.[28] The pharmaceutical industry is now the most profitable industry in the United States, grossing four hundred billion dollars worldwide.[29] After its merger with Warner-Lambert in 2001 (and, later, Pharmacia), Pfizer Pharmaceuticals became the most powerful pharmaceutical company in the world and the fifth most profitable company in the United States. According to the nonprofit organization Public Citizen, the drug industry's dominance of Fortune 500 profitability measures has been growing rapidly in recent decades. In the 1970s and 1980s, profitability of Fortune 500 medicine merchants (measured by return on revenues) was two times greater than the median for *all* industries in the Fortune 500. By 2000 it had jumped to eight times the median.[30] And in 2001 Pfizers profits surpassed the profits of Fortune 500 companies in home building, apparel, railroad, and publishing industries combined.

In this context, where the average cost of developing a new drug is estimated to be in the hundreds of millions, industry is in a better position to fund research than is the government, and as a consequence, 70 percent of the money for clinical drug trials in the United States comes from industry rather than the National Institutes of Health (NIH).[31] Critics, including Marcia Angell, former editor of the *New England Journal of Medicine,* have argued that the shift from the academic to the commercial sector has given the industry too much control over clinical drug-trial design, data analysis, and publishing.[32] This context of increasing pharmaceutical consolidation and commercialization of medicine provides an important backdrop to the Viagra phenomenon.[33]

According to medical journalist Philip J. Hilts, the current era in medicine might be described as the pharmaceutical era, because that is the chief way we treat disease now. Getting a prescription is the most likely outcome of a visit to the doctor, and about three billion prescriptions are written annually in the United States alone.[34] The average number of prescriptions per person has increased 14 percent annually for the last three years.[35] Prescription drugs are an accepted part of our day-to-day lives as Americans. As of 2001, one-quarter of all Americans took multiple prescription drugs every day, and almost half of all Americans take at least one prescription drug daily.[36] In addition, there are some twenty thousand medical experiments conducted every year in the country, and probably more than ten million people are subjects.[37] According to the *Los Angeles Times*, Americans spent one hundred billion dollars for prescription drugs in 1998, an 84 percent increase in five years.[38] Much of this increase is due to recent direct-to-consumer (DTC) advertising, the rising costs of drugs, and an aging populace that demands more drugs.

Pharmaceutical industries are more visible and profitable than ever, particularly after the prohibition on DTC advertising was eliminated six months before Viagra was approved by the FDA.[39] DTC marketing contributes to the era of the "blockbuster drug"—the largest revenue makers for the pharmaceutical companies. Interestingly, FDA's "fair balance" rule requires that any claim linking a specific drug to a specific action be accompanied by mention of the drug's limitations and side effects. It is much more common for drug marketers to avoid such warnings by purchasing "reminder ads," which feature the name of a drug without saying what it's for, and "help-seeking ads," which mention a condition and may flash the company name but won't name the drug.

The first blockbuster drug appeared in 1987 with the advent of an early antidepressant, Prozac.[40] Viagra, which five years after its debut continued to net over a billion dollars a year, is a model blockbuster drug and one of the first to be associated with DTC advertising.[41] Today, as a result of changes in marketing and deregulation, highly profitable, billion-dollar, "blockbuster" lifestyle medicines that improve quality of life, but not necessarily health, have proliferated and are now included under the medical umbrella.

Baby Boomer Society

An aging population, changing gender roles, and recent political movements have all contributed to the Viagra phenomenon. Social analysts have pointed to the "graying of America" resulting in an increase in the proportion of the population becoming elderly. Much of this aging population is attributed to the coming of age of the baby boomers, totaling seventy-six million people. In 2000, thirty-four million people in the United States were over sixty-five.[42] By the year 2030, it is estimated that eighty million people will be over sixty-five, and the percentage of very elderly people, eighty-five and older, will nearly double. Currently, average life expectancy is seventy-five years. By 2050, average life expectancy in the United States is predicted to be eighty-two years.[43] Consequently, the aging population, coupled with the gender gap in mortality, means that many women are living longer, without their spouses and with the potential to date and begin their sexual lives again. As people live longer lives, there is increased pressure to remain sexually active later in life.

In general, ideas about "normal" masculinity, femininity, and sexuality have shifted in the past thirty years in response to demographic, political, and technological trends. The availability of the "the pill" as of 1970, coupled with social movements such as women's liberation, gay liberation, and the sexual revolution, has led to the social critique of traditional sex roles and to revised sexual attitudes and behaviors.[44] Perhaps in response to such movements, especially the push for gender equality, major demographic shifts have become visible, such as the increased numbers of women in the paid workforce; the later age of marriage; the decline in fertility and childbirths; and the rise in divorce rates.[45] Clearly these recent demographic shifts have changed notions about the family as well as gender roles. Most notably for our purposes, with women's new social roles and opportunities in the second half of the twentieth century, some men have understandably felt increasingly vulnerable and confused as their traditional roles have changed.

Political movements have played a part in rendering sexuality more visible and more acceptable in America. Today, the successful marketing of products, from porn to jeans, increasingly depends on titillation and a sexualized marketplace.[46] Homosexuality is increasingly more socially accepted.[47] America is the world's largest producer of "adult entertainment," which is estimated to be a ten-billion-dollar industry. According to sociologist Charles Winick, the sexual content of American culture changed more in the past two decades than in the previous two centuries.[48] Even socially accepted ways of talking about sex have changed in recent times. According to one Pfizer spokesperson, "As someone training to be a journalist [in 1998], I remember that we were not allowed to use the terms penis or ejaculation. Instead, we had to use 'organ of sexual response.' But two things changed this: President Clinton had an affair, and Viagra was launched."[49] By 1998, sexual desire and satisfaction were popular topics of discussion for all Americans, even scientists.

Paying Attention to Sex

As sexuality has moved into mainstream culture, it has been increasingly subject to social and scientific attention, and as a result, control. The latter half of the twentieth century saw a number of scholars publishing data about sexual behavior. Following ground-breaking studies by Alfred Kinsey in the 1950s, Masters and Johnson in the 1960s, and Shere Hite in the 1970s,[50] a team of sociologists interested in the factors that influence sex in America launched *The National Health and Social Life Survey* in 1994. In all of these cases scientific facts, seen as certain truths, have contributed to the shaping of (universal) standards for sexuality. For example, Kinsey established that homosexuality was "normal" for 10 percent of the population,[51] Masters and Johnson supported the idea of sexual orgasm as normal for both men and women, and Hite suggested that women were sexual beings in their own right. All of these findings were used to create "normal" standards of sexual behavior as well as categories for sickness and sexual deviance.

In the most recent national survey on sexuality, data on sexual function, dysfunction, and dissatisfaction have provided a foundation for future medical diagnoses and solutions. *The National Health and Social Life Survey* asked one yes-or-no question about sexual problems, and it read like this:

> During the last twelve months has there ever been a period of several months or more when you lacked interest in having sex; were unable to come to a climax; came to a climax too quickly; experienced physical pain during intercourse; did not find sex pleasurable; felt anxious about your ability to perform sexually; or (for men) had trouble achieving or maintaining an erection or (for women) had trouble lubricating?[52]

The proportion of people reporting one or more problems varied from 5 to 25 percent, with the exception that one out of every three women said that she was uninterested in sex for a period of months (compared with one out of six men). Additionally, one out of every five women reported that sex provided little pleasure (compared with one out of every ten men). Interestingly, researchers found that sexual problems were most prevalent in young women and older men. The problems most commonly reported for women were lack of interest in sex, inability to achieve orgasm, finding sex not pleasurable, difficulty lubricating, experiencing pain during intercourse, and anxiety about performance. The problems most commonly reported for men included climaxing too early, performance anxiety, and lack of interest.[53]

Authors of the study based on the national survey estimated that such problems were largely interactional and social, but such "theories" quickly disappeared when the data from the national sex survey were reanalyzed and republished in *JAMA*, the official journal of the American Medical Association. In 1999 answers to this single survey question were reanalyzed to produce a "summary statistic" of total prevalence of "sexual dysfunction," not "sexual problems," which amounted to 43 percent of women and 31 percent of men.[54] Such statistics and dysfunction nomenclature are now found in countless mainstream media reports and Pfizer documents, reflecting near-epidemic proportions of organic and "fixable" sexual dysfunction in America. Today, the fields of sexual medicine and sexual pharmacology are ever growing.

By the time Viagra was approved for the public, Pfizer was able to produce, maintain, and respond to extensive medical and commercial infrastructures that supported the blockbuster drug. Pfizer directly and indirectly helped to establish thousands of "masculinity clinics" nationwide dedicated to diagnosing and treating sexual dysfunction, supported wide-ranging scientific research related to sexual problems, and paid for high-profile celebrity spokesmen such as Bob Dole, professional baseball player Rafael Palmeiro, NASCAR racecar driver Mark Martin, international soccer star Pele, and the rock band Earth, Wind, and Fire.[55] Today, Viagra continues to enjoy high visibility in the mainstream media. The little blue pill has appeared in numerous popular television shows such as *Sex in the City, Law & Order, Mad about You*, and *Ally McBeal*, each of which has featured storylines about Viagra. Even as I write this, two new high-budget feature films starring Jack Nicholson and Anthony Hopkins include Viagra storylines associated with masculinity and aging. And sports fans can now expect to see ads centered around erectile dysfunction.

At a glance, this historical moment may look no different from that of previous centuries, when sex was managed and controlled to preserve those in power and to punish those deemed to have deviant bodies.[56] In this study, I argue that the project of managing sex has expanded infinitely at the turn of the century, enrolling an even more diverse array of institutions, tools, experts, and even consumers.[57] At the center of this phenomenon is the pharmaceutical corporation, the primary architect of Viagra, sexual pharmacology, and, potentially, our sex lives.

Troubling over Normal

Sociologists care about normal. We care about how individuals internalize society's norms; how normality and abnormality are defined, and by whom; how and why particular social groups and individuals are sanctioned for being different from the norm; how social norms shift in relation to historical, economic, political, and cultural change; and how social norms reflect and perpetuate social inequalities. So when a product appears or an event occurs that pushes us to reflect upon, and maybe even change, our collective conceptions of "normal," sociologists take notice.

Viagra's debut is a perfect opportunity to examine the construction of social norms, ideals, and expectations, particularly because it renders visible many taken-for-granted social assumptions. I noticed this fixation on "normal" when I started talking with people about Viagra. I found consumers asking themselves, "Am I normal?" Urologists and Pfizer marketers told me they were dedicated to bringing their patients "back to normal." And critics were asking, "Who defines normal?" Interestingly, all of this discussion about "normal" went beyond erections and implied questions about the definition of normal masculinity, normal femininity, normal sexuality, normal aging, normal bodies, and normal medicine.

For example, since Viagra's debut, "normal sex" in America is more and more narrowly defined and difficult to achieve. Then again, normal sex is a seeming requirement for normal personhood. Pharmaceutical ads and medical experts tell us that erectile dysfunction, especially the "mild" form, is common for millions of men (reportedly "half of all men over forty"), but not normal. Likewise, female sexual dysfunction is constructed as common for millions of women (reportedly 43 percent of all women), but not normal. Normal for males, as defined by Pfizer Pharmaceuticals and its experts, is having a consistently hard and penetrative penis, feeling eighteen again, and never having to worry about occasional problems with erections. More recently, we have heard that normal for women means sexually desirous, easily aroused, fully lubricated, and orgasmic. With such elevated standards, normal sex in the Viagra era probably requires medical or pharmaceutical intervention.

When something comes to be seen as normal it is then unquestioned, or institutionalized, and this can be a problem. For example, the area of sexual problems is becoming institutionalized as a medical specialty. But fixing women's sexual problems becomes complicated when medicine's "normal body" is white, male, middle-class or above, and heterosexual. Such problem solving becomes even more complex when norms within science and medicine are shifting as corporate ties intensify. Today, it is normal to see an advertisement for a drug like Viagra on television or to visit a doctor who may be promised a regular trip to Hawaii for prescribing Viagra. As a sociologist and a human being who cares about the construction of standards by which Americans live and are taught to measure their worth, I am concerned about the Viagra phenomenon for all of the reasons listed above. Thus, the primary question that drives this inquiry is drawn from this concern with the construction of "normal sex." Specifically, I ask, How are normal bodies, sexualities, and medical practices defined today, and how do social institutions and groups play a role in this process?

Comparing Prozac and Viagra

Before the pharmaceutical success of Viagra, there was another drug that appeared to take the world by storm: Prozac. Both are blockbuster drugs, among the most prescribed in the nation today, with Prozac topping the list. Both are considered the "first in their classes," with Viagra as the first PDE5 inhibitor, and Prozac as the first in a long line of SSRIs.[58] Both set scientific "gold standards" for their time, spawning copy-cat drugs that built upon and attest to their popular success and cultural staying power.[59] In addition, both have life-enhancement or "quality-of-life" goals. In general, neither is used to treat life-threatening conditions; rather, they are designed to alleviate conditions of discomfort and personal suffering. Most importantly, both products reveal much about social ideals and insecurity in America.

In an age of identity politics, both Viagra and Prozac have been claimed as tools for the construction of new and improved identities (masculine and feminine, respectively), in a way that a pill for, say, allergies, would not. Unlike blockbuster products that promise to treat balding or allergies, both pills have elicited concerns by various social groups, in part due to the vision of the world each promises. For example, Claritin does not threaten to rupture social norms and agreements by treating allergy problems. Why not? Because allergies are not seen as central to the construction of self or identity, while erections and depression are. Prozac promises brightened spirits, fewer mood swings, and general contentedness, and is used to treat a largely female patient base diagnosed with clinical depression.[60] Viagra promises erections for men diagnosed with erectile dysfunction. Together, these products treat both genders and what are believed to be their highly stigmatized problems (depression and impotence), but they also promise to lift the stigma of illness by granting these problems medical solutions. Viagra and Prozac aid in the construction of flexible, efficient, self-controlled, "normal" identities at the turn of the twenty-first century. But the vision of the world is different for each pill: Viagra promises to restore sexual potency to the male populace, and Prozac promises to restore consistency, focus, and contentedness to, mostly, women's lives; in sum, these pills are designed to produce potent men and happy women. To a social analyst, this sounds like a recipe for restoring traditional gender roles and power relationships.

On a symbolic level, Prozac and Viagra are controversial, in part, because they appear to reinforce long-standing gender stereotypes and thus social inequalities. This becomes painfully obvious when one looks at the recent promotion of each product. Eli Lilly, the producer of Prozac, does not promote its product by depicting a muscular forty-something woman racecar driver driving through a roadblock marked with the words "clinical depression." Instead, it promotes its recent Sarafem product (Prozac, but purple) by depicting "moody" and then smiling women in grocery stores and at home. The product brand name and image are all traditionally gendered, even down to the color of the pill. In contrast, Pfizer's blue Viagra seemingly promises power, as epitomized by its powerful celebrity spokesmen, who exist in a culture invested in male potency. Advertisements depict well-respected and successful male athletes, politicians, and newly empowered office workers and party-goers. Because Viagra offers symbolic forms of "empowerment" for primarily white, middle-class, heterosexual men, this product invites social critique for at least symbolically reinforcing male privilege and power.

Prozac and Viagra epitomize the gendering of medicine and medical illness. Each plays on gender-based insecurities and offers a way to restore masculine and feminine ideals, specifically potency and contentedness. On a macro level, such products restore a gender status quo, reinforcing gender ideals and insecurities. The message we receive from Eli Lilly and Pfizer is not new. Women should care about emotions. Men should care about sex. We are practically from separate planets, Venus and Mars. The role of pharmaceutical companies in perpetuating "normal" gender identities and, in turn, power asymmetries becomes especially problematic when tens of millions of Americans are literally "buying into" such products and messages, netting their creators billions of dollars annually.

Why Study Viagra?

Following Viagra's debut, I watched different groups emerge with varying stakes in the drug. The fact that one product and its related marketing campaigns, jokes, and stories touched so many lives intrigued me. How could one product speak to so many of us, and in so many ways? And how could one product have such staying power in our culture? Even today casual references to Viagra are commonplace in the mainstream media and in everyday language. For instance, we hear about "Viagra markets," which, translated, means economic markets experiencing a vigorous, surging, or highly profitable phase. And when we hear about "Viagra for the Brain," as in *Forbes* magazine's recent story on Alzheimers drugs, we see software ads claiming to "enhance your performance without a pill."[61]

When I decided to talk to people about what Viagra meant to them, I never could have imagined the wild ride I was about to embark on, one that took me back and forth between two sexual dysfunction "hotspots," Los Angeles and Boston.[62] I attended medical meetings; visited "masculinity clinics," doctors' offices, men's support groups, senior citizen organizations, and pharmacies; and collected "Viagra stories" from over seventy women and men, some as young as seventeen and others as old as eighty-nine. I collected hundreds of media reports linked to Viagra in major newspapers, in magazines, and on television, and monitored several Viagra-related internet chat groups.

The majority of my research began one year after the FDA approval of Viagra in the United States, roughly from January 1999 through October 2003. By this time, the initial hype, sensationalism, and public joke sharing had died down, and Viagra was well known and generally well respected as an effective drug with consistent sales.[63] At the time of my interviews, Viagra was still in the media spotlight, but for new reasons. Other news stories at this time included medical reports refuting what were believed to be hundreds of Viagra-caused deaths, and media sensationalism focused on the recreational use of Viagra. As a female scholar interested in women's sexuality, I was particularly intrigued by reports about Viagra being tested on and used by women for the purposes of increasing female arousal and desire.

Once submerged in the Viagra phenomenon, I began to see that the public release of Viagra had both created and made visible a cultural crisis of widespread proportions. Millions of primarily white, middle- and upper-class, American men now visited their doctors to ask for medical assistance with erections, but most doctors were not prepared or trained to talk about sex with their patients. For the first time in history, patients were asking their doctors for particular pharmaceutical products they saw marketed through direct-to-consumer advertisements. Most male consumers I spoke with told me that they made appointments with doctors for an annual exam after seeing or hearing ads for Viagra and wanting to try the product. Many hadn't visited their doctors for some time. Usually as the doctor was leaving, the patient would ask to try Viagra. Doctors corroborated these stories, agreeing that the discomfort of asking for an erection pill led patients to wait until the last possible minute.

Who are these Viagra users? Early Pfizer ads led us to imagine white, middle- and upper-class, heterosexual men, forty years old and older, as the target demographic for Viagra. If nothing else, these were men with generous health coverage or a willingness to spend ten dollars on a pill. Mainstream news articles and my own conversations with doctors, consumers, pharmacists, and marketers confirmed this narrow patient demographic but also suggested that a significant group of Viagra users departed from this patient profile. The Viagra users who were not accounted for by Pfizer were young men in their twenties and thirties, gay men, working-class men, disabled men, members of racial minority groups, men involved in sex work, and even women. To get more information on this issue, I contacted Pfizer to ask for their information on the demographics of Viagra users. A representative from the company's research division claimed that they do not collect such information. In the end, the individuals I ended up interviewing, all of whom had used or considered using Viagra, sufficiently represent the range of Viagra users in America, which is wider than Pfizer advertising may let on. They vary in gender, age, sexual orientation, socioeconomic status, and ethnic backgrounds, but the majority are white, middle- and upper-class, able-bodied, heterosexual men over forty years of age.

What most Americans were exposed to in early 1999 was a limited public face of Viagra. Former presidential hopeful Bob Dole was on television advertising widespread erectile dysfunction and implying Viagra was the solution. In a year when presidential infidelity was constructed as scandalous, Dole made erections legitimate and important again, under the right circumstances. Health insurance controversies abounded as doctors and insurers prescribed and set normative standards for sex. Feminists asked why Viagra was covered by health insurance and yet birth control pills were not. *Dear Abby* columns featured complaint letters from Viagra users' wives. And stories and jokes about masculinity, sexuality, and impotence regularly circulated the internet, talk shows, and comedy clubs.

As I became intrigued by the social implications of Viagra and increasingly grounded in this cultural phenomenon,[64] I began asking questions about social problems, masculinity, medicine, and sexuality. How did the construction of a sexually dysfunctional populace occur? How did Viagra come to be promoted as the solution? Who played a part in this orchestration? How did Viagra's presence in the bedroom and in the boardroom shift the ways we think about and "do" sexuality and gender? How did Viagra construct and complicate contemporary social ideas about aging, technology, and medicine? What did Viagra reveal about social inequality and masculinity "in crisis"? And on a personal level, how did men and women make sense of Viagra in their lives? In answering these questions, I found multiple truths, revealing the diversity of men's and women's lives in relation to this product. There is no single narrative to be "discovered" about Viagra, but rather multiple perspectives and partial truths.[65] All of these stories and truths contribute to the Viagra phenomenon and, in turn, to the society we live in.

Plan of the Book

Each chapter of this book is concerned about the construction of normal in our everyday lives, whether in relation to bodies and sexualities, marketing practices, or medical terminology and treatments. If certain language, practices, and identities are now taken for granted in our culture, how did they come to be this way, and how are they regularly reinforced, resisted, or reinvented? Or, to the contrary, what if a cultural consensus around what constitutes normal cannot be achieved? The story of the Viagra phenomenon is about consensus and deviation. As you will soon learn, following the Viagra phenomenon means traveling the bumpy, curvy, multilane highway to "normal."

This book begins with the social, historical, economic, and political factors that created fertile ground for the Viagra phenomenon, which enabled the rise of the social problem erectile dysfunction, Pfizer's "branding" of ED, the construction of a sexually dysfunctional male populace, and the diverse constructions of manhood in relation to Viagra by male patients and their doctors. The analysis then shifts to focus on the "other half" of the sexually dysfunctional couple and populace—women. I call this "phase two" of the Viagra phenomenon, to represent the subsequent search for the "female Viagra." The book explores senior women's efforts to make sense of their bodies, desires, and (recently deceased) husbands in the Viagra era, and then moves to the realm of science, where the competition among experts to define and treat women's sexual problems ensues.

More specifically, chapter 2 introduces the most crucial events, people, and contexts that led to the rise of erectile dysfunction and the introduction of Viagra in the late 1990s. Along the way, the medical model became standard for understanding and treating erection problems. In part, this story is about medical accidents, as well as the new intimacies that have been formed and normalized among medicine and capital, corporations and science.

Chapter 3 explores the ways in which doctors and patients actively make sense of Viagra and Viagra-bodies in terms of "trouble" and "repair." For some men, Viagra can be understood as both a cultural and a material tool used to achieve normal (and extranormal) manhood. For other men, Viagra may be more of a problem than a solution.

Chapter 4 shifts the focus to reveal women aged sixty-five to eighty-six discussing the impact the Viagra phenomenon has had on their lives and beliefs. This chapter reveals senior women using Viagra to make sense of masculinity and femininity, sexual pleasure and wifely duty in their lives. For these women, Viagra provides an impetus to tell sexual stories as well as to critique manhood, marriage, health, and gender.

Chapter 5 returns to the Viagra "big picture" to explore the rise of female sexual dysfunction (FSD) and the ongoing competition among experts, marketers, journalists, and critics to understand women's sexual problems and to search for a "female Viagra." At annual medical conferences, rodent studies, outdated sexuality research, and gendered stereotypes and biases contribute to medical understandings of women's sexual problems. In contrast to the seeming success of "phase one" of the Viagra phenomenon, research on women's sexual "dysfunctions" has become bogged down in the face of expert confusion, problematic assumptions, and organized critique.

Chapter 6 revisits what experts, critics, marketers and distributors, and consumers can teach us about social change in the Viagra era, and about the general social implications of the Viagra phenomenon. In that chapter I return to questions raised here about social problems and their creation by corporations, medicalization and its continuing expansion, and the ways in which gender and sexuality are "done" by institutions and individuals. This chapter also discusses many of the unanticipated consequences of the Viagra phenomenon and what they mean for American society.

The book is divided into "phase one" and "phase two" of the Viagra phenomenon, both overlapping in important ways. In both phases, pharmaceutical companies and urologists take the helm in attempting to bring both men and women "back to normal" in a sexualized culture. New products and services promising to treat such dysfunction multiply yearly. Meanwhile, it is increasingly difficult to separate sexual-medicine "experts" from pharmaceutical marketers, and medical education from pharmaceutical marketing. On the consumer level, despite constant messages suggesting otherwise, consumers wonder if they and their partners are normal in terms their sexuality, the aging process, and gender ideals. They may experience forms of performance anxiety in each of these realms, and many turn to Viagra or Viagra-like products to bolster their confidence in an "oversexed age."[66] Or they may view sexual medicine more critically, as a double-edged sword—both dangerous and promising—or as a symbol of social pressures that are unattainable and unfair. In the chapters that follow, you'll get an up-close and personal look at life in the Viagra era.

Reproduced by permission from the *British Medical Journal*, May 2003

2

The Rise of Erectile Dysfunction

AS A PFIZER PHARMACEUTICALS sales representative,[1] one of the first things you learn is that erectile dysfunction is a disease.[2] Training manuals counsel that one of the greatest ED myths is that the problem "is all in your mind." A training chart that Pfizer representatives must memorize reveals that "up until the 1970s, erectile dysfunction was deemed 90% psychogenic," or mental, "and 10% organic," or physical. Conversely, the "current medical consensus on erectile dysfunction is 10–30% psychogenic, and 70–90% organic." Today, none of this information sounds strange to us; Pfizer's PR teams and sales representatives have succeeded in converting these "medical facts" into cultural common sense. In fact, most sexual dysfunction reporting takes this organic, or biological, causality "consensus" for granted. But do these sales representatives understand what changed after the 1970s and how these changes created fertile ground for Viagra's debut?

Today, with Viagra offered as a solution, assertions about impotence as an "organic" problem are almost everywhere, with medical practitioners, many of whom were paid researchers or consultants for Pfizer Pharmaceuticals, monopolizing mainstream discussions about impotence.[3] But this wasn't always the case. For most of the twentieth century, sexual problems were attributed to psychological, emotional, relational, and social factors.[4]

Today, most sexual problems are seen as "correctable" physiological problems. How, why, and when this shift towards an "organic model" took place is rarely questioned. What explains the shift in terminology from "impotence" to "erectile dysfunction"? And how do we understand the move from psychologists to urologists as the sex experts of a new era?

The answers to these questions reveal the history of how Viagra came to be. To understand the cultural paradigm shift that occurred between the 1970s and 1990s, one must take into account a changing medical landscape and the rise of social groups that together made this shift possible. As journalist Malcolm Gladwell suggests in his best-selling book, *The Tipping Point*, "Epidemics are a function of the people who transmit infectious agents, the infectious agent itself, and the environment in which the infectious agent is operating."[5] As we will see, in the 1990s, erectile dysfunction took on "epidemic" proportions due to the coordinated efforts of scientific experts and corporations.[6] Specifically, the story of the rise of erectile dysfunction and the emergence of Viagra is a fascinating tale colored by shifting blame, medical accidents, public demonstrations, Puritan intentions, profit motives, vested interests, and medical, scientific, and technological discovery.[7]

Maintaining the Twentieth-Century Penis

In their handbook on treating erectile disorders, psychologists Ray Rosen and Sandra Leiblum track the history of understanding and responding to erectile failure from ancient to twentieth-century Western societies, revealing an ongoing and global interest in maintaining a "working penis."[8] Up to the twentieth century, popular global remedies for impotence included "spanish fly," oysters, rock salt, melted fat, and rhino horn.[9] In the twentieth century, according to Rosen and Leiblum, "two major themes" emerged in the discussion of erectile disorders in the United States and Western Europe. First, psychological factors were isolated as cause and consequence of erectile disorders, as emphasized by psychoanalysts Sigmund Freud and Wilhelm Stekel in the 1920s and 1930s, as well as by behavioral therapists focusing on anxiety and distraction as causes of erectile disorders in the 1950s and 1960s. As evidence of this, impotence was listed in the first *DSM* (the American Psychiatric Association's *Diagnostic and Statistical Manual of Mental Disorders*) in 1952, and was thought to be "psychogenic," or originating in the mind or the psyche. Clinical studies of impotence, like that of Masters and Johnson in 1970, focused on physiological outcomes (e.g., stages of arousal within the body), but believed in primarily psychological causation and utilized behavioral techniques to treat sexual problems.

Social historian Lynne Luciano, author of *Looking Good: Male Body Image in Modern America*, argues that the history of sexual dysfunction had an important, often overlooked subtext. Before the 1960s, Luciano contends, women bore most of the burden for sexual dysfunction. In other words, male impotence was the "fault" of the frigid wife. In 1912, the term "frigidity" was coined by Dr. William Robinson, chief of genitourinary surgery at Bronx Hospital and author of more than a dozen books on sexual matters. According to Robinson, "women's unresponsiveness was to blame, because it didn't call out to male virility."[10] In the 1920s, Stekel declared that as many as half of all American women were frigid, especially those of higher cultural levels. While the impotent man was regarded as wanting sex but unable to perform, the frigid woman was seen as totally lacking in desire, turning her back on sex and, by extension, her husband. By the 1950s, the American Medical Association had deemed three out of four American women frigid. It took many events over the decades that followed, such as feminism and other social movements, as well as the availability of the first birth control pill in 1960, to shift the responsibility and blame for male impotency back to men and their bodies.

This transition was aided by the development and proliferation of diagnostic procedures for assessing vascular, hormonal and neurogenic factors in erectile disorders.[11] New treatments for impotence, such as the vacuum pump and penile surgeries became available in the 1970s and '80s.[12] Lynne Luciano writes that penile augmentation technology for cosmetic purposes was developed in the 1980s by Chinese surgeon Long Doachau, a specialist in the correction of microphallic penises (a rare condition where the penis is less than an inch in length). His clients soon broadened to include men voicing concern about their penis sizes. Doachau knew that one-third of the total penis length lies within the body cavity, so he cut the ligament attaching the penis to the pubic bone, pulling several inches of internal length to outside the body. This surgery was popularized in Los Angeles by Dr. Melvyn Rosenstein, who learned the technique during his NYU residency, and by his crosstown rival, Rodney Barron. In 1998, the fee for penis lengthening was thirty-five hundred dollars, widening cost the same amount, and the deluxe package was fifty-nine hundred dollars. Barron's sophisticated dermal graft augmentation cost sixty-nine hundred dollars in 1998.[13] Luciano also traces the history of the vacuum pump back to the nineteenth century, to vaudeville performer and bodybuilder Eugen Sandow, who promoted the idea that virility comes with muscularity. His vacuum device was called the peniscope.

These products emerged as public awareness and concern about impotence increased as a result of new lifelong expectations about sexual function; the increasing importance of sexuality in personal lives;

women's increased expectations of sexual gratification; and related media advertising by health providers.[14] Reflecting cultural and medical shifts in understanding, the psychiatric terminology soon changed. By the publication of *DSM III* in 1980, the term "impotence" had been removed in favor of "Male Inhibited Sexual Excitement" (MISE), but little change was evident in the use of the term. That same year Richard Spark, M.D., published a controversial article in *JAMA* entitled "Impotence Is Not All Psychogenic," signaling a turn in the way impotence was thought of.[15] While erectile disorder is listed in the current *DSM IV* (as a replacement for MISE), it is now differentiated from "Sexual Dysfunction Due to a General Medical Condition," a new category based on physiological indicators. With the new focus on organic erectile problems, treatment efforts were focused on medical therapies.

Writing in 1992, Rosen and Leiblum expressed concern that medical or surgical treatments were replacing psychological treatment for erectile problems:

> The last decade has witnessed a remarkable upsurge in the use of technological interventions for assessing and treating erectile failure . . . what is particularly noteworthy is the willingness of many clinicians to prescribe these treatments for men with psychogenic erectile failure. In the past, such medical and surgical interventions were generally reserved for men with clear-cut organic impotence. Nowadays, there is greater willingness to treat long-standing and refractory "psychogenic" dysfunction with medical or surgical means.[16]

Taking into account all newspaper articles from 1970 to 2000 mentioning erectile dysfunction, we can track the gradual shift away from alleged psychological causality.[17] Of the eighteen articles written between 1970 and 1980, one-half mention psychological factors potentially contributing to erectile dysfunction. Of the 363 articles written between 1980 and 1990, one-fourth mention psychological factors contributing to erectile dysfunction. Finally, in the more than one thousand articles written between 1990 and 2000, less than one-fifth mention psychological factors contributing to erectile dysfunction. It appears that in the last three decades, the potentially alternative viewpoints of psychologists or sex therapists have been gradually marginalized or ignored, as physiological factors gain salience.[18] It is clear that a shift in understanding sexual problems has taken place in the past thirty years, but what precipitated this?

The New Emphasis on "Hydraulics"

According to medical historian Robert Aronowitz, the medical profession's large-scale rejection of psychosomatic models for illness can be traced back to a 1933 *JAMA* article, in which medical critic Franz Alexander claimed that medicine's aversion to psycho-social factors harkened back to "the remote days of medicine as sorcery, expelling demons from the body." Alexander claimed that twentieth-century medicine was "dedicated to forgetting its dark, magical past" in favor of "emphasizing exactness and keeping out of field anything that endangers the appearance of science."[19]

In the 1950s, social theorist Talcott Parsons wanted to understand the social function and allure of medicalization. Parsons argued that medical explanations can remove responsibility and blame from the patient.[20] This "sick-role" theory can be applied to the man with sexual failure who is relieved to place blame on his physiology rather than his mind. More recently, sociologists Conrad and Schneider add that medicalization offers optimistic outcomes, such as treatments and cures associated with the prestige of the medical profession.[21]

Clinical psychologist Leonore Tiefer, author of the book *Sex Is Not a Natural Act*, suggests that physiological explanations for impotence fit with the "natural" penile functioning model that men are taught to believe—that the penis is immune when it comes to psychological problems, anxieties, and fears. Biotechnological solutions also allow men to avoid psychological treatments such as marital or sex therapy, which they may find threatening or embarrassing. The trade-off is a potentially embarrassing doctor's visit, which can also be avoided through internet consultations and pharmaceutical purchasing options.[22]

In the 1980s, professional and popular discussions of male sexuality had begun to emphasize physical causes and treatments for sexual problems over and above the earlier respected psychogenic model. Referring to her own experiences working with the Department of Urology at a New York medical center, Tiefer wrote that of the eight hundred men who had been seen since 1981 for erection problems, 90 percent believed their problem to be physical. After examination, only 45 percent of those patients were diagnosed with predominantly medically caused erectile problems. Tiefer was one of the first scholars to question biomedical assumptions, suggesting that they are based on problematic medical models as well as on expectations that normal men must always be interested in sex and that that interest leads easily and directly to erection. Tiefer links these expectations to Masters and Johnson's famous statement that "sex is a natural act," which implies that there is no "natural" reason for decline, so erectile problems must reveal (unnatural) bodily dysfunction, which can be corrected (and bodies restored to normal) with suitable treatment.[23]

Others working in the field of sexual medicine have different explanations for how this paradigm shift came about. Some point to social trends in constant flux, recent influential sex research, or the economics of health care. For example, John Bancroft, former director of the Kinsey Institute for Research on Sex, Gender, and Reproduction, cites a number of factors as crucial to the shift in thinking and practice regarding sexual "function" from psychology to biology: cycles of interest in medicine, changing priorities with increasing technological developments, the need for clinicians to make money, and the high level of involvement of pharmaceutical companies in medical-scientific research and development.[24] Others, like University of Washington psychologist Julia Heiman, explain the change by pointing out the role of researchers Masters and Johnson and the restructuring of health care and coverage in leading the way for a paradigm shift:

> [Medicalization] preceded the Viagra phenomenon. If you think of Masters and Johnson, she was a nurse and he was a medical doctor. They did not do a lot of medicalization for a medical team. They used a much more nonmedical approach. But it favored physiology. Fifteen or twenty years afterwards there's a reaction against this which moves towards the biological. For example, the story of male erection treatment is dominated by medicine. So this is back to the 1970s, when things shifted to the biological. Also, this was part of a larger movement when treatment became considered a medical act. Diagnosis is only available in the *DSM*, so if you diagnose, this is what you use. Psycho-social diagnoses can be done but they aren't usually because they don't communicate anything to one's colleagues. And there is no reimbursement for that. It's really a guild issue. Anyone

doing treatment that is diagnosis related is usually associated with medicine.[25]

Journalistic examples from Viagra media coverage exemplify the seductiveness of medical reasoning in relation to sexual problems. In 1997, two very different publications (to say the least), *JAMA* and *Playboy*, posited similar arguments that impotence is "mechanical," ignoring psychological dimensions entirely and relying exclusively on biomedical explanations.[26] It is perhaps fair to say that *JAMA* may be invested in promoting the idea that impotence is primarily biological for many reasons, including the fact that this construction is in line with *JAMA*'s regular promotion of medical-science models, as well as the medical community's interest in further developing medical subfields, such as urology. *Playboy*, on the other hand, may have other reasons. Promoting the idea that impotence is a mechanical dysfunction, easily fixed, relieves *Playboy*'s male readership of personal responsibility, blame, or guilt by portraying the condition as one in which the sufferer has no control (but happily, does have access to optimistic outcomes).[27]

In the Viagra era, impotence is no longer blamed on the mind or the wife but, more likely, on human physiology. Locating the problem in the body enables many to benefit, including the patient himself. Lynne Luciano sums up the benefits of medicalizing impotence as follows:

Transforming impotence into a medical ailment was beneficial not only to physicians but also pharma companies, penile implant manufacturers, and hospitals. Medicalized articles and advertising made information about impotence more acceptable to the mass media by treating it as a scientific issue. Most significantly, medicalization of impotence made men more accepting of it, both because of the centrality of the erections to their self esteem and because modern urology seemed to offer a near-magical technofix—a pill, a shot, and not a long session of psychoanalysis. Medical approaches seemed action-oriented. Doctors were doing something about impotence, not just talking about it. In addition, in the 1980s, as health care cutbacks and the proliferation of HMOs eliminated coverage for therapeutic counseling, genuine medical problems were more likely to be covered by insurance. And treating the condition as a medical problem made it more palatable to men by absolving them of blame and failure.[28]

In the 1980s, ideas were changing about who and what to blame for sexual problems. But practitioners and journalists still needed convincing that physiology prevailed over psychology. In 1983, the urologists got their proof.

Sexual Chemistry

Well before "the truth" of sexual function was discovered in scientific laboratories, it was quite literally demonstrated fifteen years before Viagra at a 1983 American Urology Association (AUA) meeting in Las Vegas. As the popular story goes, the silence on impotence was boldly broken (followed by several moments of awe-struck stillness) when Giles Brindley, a fifty-seven-year-old British physician,

> stepped from behind the lectern at a Las Vegas medical conference, dropped his pants, and showed his erect penis to hundreds of colleagues. Brindley had just presented work on injectible drugs to treat impotence and was displaying an erection he had induced by injecting his own penis. The results were quite good.[29]

Or, as one attendee who describes himself as "wondering why this smart man was giving a talk in his jogging outfit," put it in more visceral terms, "It was a big penis, and he just walked around the stage showing it off." *Playboy* reported this (and how could they not?),

> What the brave Dr. Brindley demonstrated on himself—and allowed urologists in the front rows of the auditorium to examine by hand to be sure he was not hiding an implant—was the injection of a drug directly into the smooth muscle cells in the tunnels of the penis.[30]

The impact of Brindley's demonstration was enormous, according to some. The conference demonstration was planned to spur further research and preempt skeptics who believed impotence was not a "fixable" body mechanics problem.[31] Brindley's research on impotence treatments and penile injections was suddenly unforgettable in medical circles, inspiring discussion and motivating a handful of urologists in the audience to investigate impotence and further Brindley's search for treatments. Brindley's "respectable" erection became a new masculine ideal, and the chemically induced erection "paved the way to new medical and commercial horizons."[32]

Thus, in 1983, the master's tools were turned on himself, and the doctor's body became both the test site and evidence for new scientific truths. Several media reports recounted this central event that broke Americans and urologists out of the "denial stage" and set the stage for Viagra. According to *Fortune* magazine, this event put the erection "back in the spotlight" and "triggered the stampede" to create pharmaceutical treatments for impotence.[33] This event also solidified relatively new ideas about the biological causes of impotence. Now scientifically provable and literally visible, the chemical erection cemented the paradigm shift.

John Bancroft claims that the discovery of penile injections by Brindley and others who were experimenting at the time was yet another medical accident that changed the face of medicine.[34]

> The discovery [of penile injections] was serendipitous, as most discoveries are. People think clinicians try to find a certain thing, but so much is accidental. Certainly this started a new era in understanding sexual response. Prior to the injection there was the prosthesis or the pump or psychological intervention.[35]

A decade after Brindley's demonstration, the first prescription drugs for impotence became available: alprostadil, packaged as Caverject and then MUSE; each had to be either injected or inserted into the penis as an intraurethral pellet.[36] In their debut years, the injection treatment grossed twenty-five million dollars, and the suppository grossed two hundred million dollars. Including nonpharmaceutical therapies such as vacuum pumps and surgical implants, the market for impotence treatments expanded to seven hundred million dollars in the late 1990s.[37] However, apart from any consideration of alprostadil's effectiveness, its means of delivery left much to be desired, creating a market for a simple and effective oral therapy.

Clearly, these major events set the context for Pfizer to develop an impotence treatment and hire well-known urologists and researchers to find and produce research on impotence.[38] Fifteen years after Brindley's stunning demonstration, somewhat unrelated chemical research on nitric oxide, a vasodilating molecule, won the Nobel Prize.[39] This medical research led to, among other things, the new "science of erections," as nitric oxide was found to aid in penile engorgement.[40]

In the 1980s and '90s, new impotence experts trained in urology and partnered with experts in biology, physiology, and chemistry were increasingly prominent, overshadowing "outdated" sex experts in the psychological realms. Thus, years after Brindley's shocking demonstration at the AUA, urologists dominated the field of sexual medicine. Similarly, new medical nomenclature such as the term "erectile dysfunction" was adopted in place of "outdated" and "stigmatizing" terminology like "impotence." In this context, the little blue erection pill was "discovered" and introduced by Pfizer Pharmaceuticals just as erectile dysfunction was receiving public attention as an "old" medical problem with widespread and debilitating consequences.

The Rise of the Urologists

A new group of "experts" in understanding and treating impotence soon emerged and came to dominate public discussions about sexual problems. A 1999 documentary, "Sexual Chemistry," produced by The Learning Channel (TLC), highlights this shift in ownership of sexual problems by playing down public demonstrations and accidental discoveries, and instead playing up the new partnerships between basic scientists and urologists.

The video traces the technology of sex back to the invention of "vacuum therapy" in the 1960s when a tire shop owner in Georgia invented a vacuum pump for limp penises.[41] For the most part, those living with impotence in the twentieth century had very few resources available to help them overcome the condition, and doctors had limited understandings of how the condition comes to exist. Fast-forward to the late twentieth century, during which chemists and scientists were working together prior to the discovery of Viagra to understand the anatomy of the penis and the physiology of an erection. This "sexual chemistry," the narrator suggests, exists on the "cutting edge of science" in the late twentieth century.[42] Urologists are quoted celebrating new biotechnological achievements such as Viagra, commenting, "How far we have come!"

What this documentary does not make explicit is that a shift in thinking about sexual problems reveals a shift in expert-ownership. As sexual dysfunction increasingly came under medical purview, medical researchers, including chemists, psychiatrists, and, primarily, urologists, "claimed" sexual dysfunction, replacing psychologists and sex therapists as the primary experts regarding sexual problems. In the late 1990s urologists may have been looking to bolster their client base after new technological solutions for kidney stones and benign enlargement of the prostate became available.[43]

The rise of urologists and the general increase in the medicalization of impotence coincided with technological innovation, particularly the introduction and increasing acceptance of new medical treatments, with the most widely used medical approach in the 1980s being the surgical implantation of a penile prosthesis, performed by urologists. Thus, the problem of impotence transferred from psychologists to surgeons or, more specifically, urologists, with the introduction of a straightforward "technological solution to a technical problem." With this new approach to "fixing the problem," the medical model eclipsed the psychogenic model.[44]

JAMA quotes urologists who describe the potential causes of impotence as age, cardiovascular risk factors, depression, spinal cord injuries, pelvic fracture, arteriosclerosis, and side effects of some prescription drugs.[45] Cultural or social factors are either marginalized, overshadowed, or outright ignored, as when Boston urologist Irwin Goldstein asserts that impotence is "all hydraulics."[46] Tellingly, countless articles present this medical model as "good news" because problems are now highly "correctable."[47]

By 2001, the obvious winners in the struggle to treat and understand impotence were urologists; according to Luciano, their victory was not an accident.

> In a medical field becoming overcrowded with specialists, urologists would take an altogether different view of male sexuality. As the urology profession tried to bring more treatment areas under its control, male sexual dysfunction would be declared a disease rather than a psychological disorder. Virtually overnight psychogenic conditions were downgraded to contributing factors, if they were recognized at all. Animosity quickly developed between doctors and psychologists: while urologists sneered at therapists as ineffectual handholders, the psychological community portrayed doctors as greedy usurpers.[48]

This change in "ownership" of sexual problems was confirmed in my recent conversations with urologists, who sometimes turned our discussions about Viagra into celebratory sessions heralding a new science of sex and new understandings within their discipline about the biochemistry of the penis. In these discussions, I found that practitioners juxtaposed the era of psychological treatment of impotence with the "new" advanced medical understanding of sex. But scientific knowledge and medical advances did not necessarily precipitate the shift in ownership and understanding of sexual problems. Instead, technological advances and the development of drugs, surgeries, and treatments came first, followed by science and medicine.

Drugs before Science

While Pfizer may call the Viagra discovery a case of "serendipity and science," sociologists Michael D. Cohen and his colleagues would assess this as a case of "garbage can decision process" in which "solutions [are] looking for issues to which they might be an answer."[49] In other words, in the case of Viagra, the cart came before the horse. Dr. Bending, a urologist I spoke with, told me that the science of sex and medical understandings of erectile dysfunction came after the development of drugs, highlighting a range of unanticipated or "accidental" developments that furthered scientific knowledge:

> What Viagra really taught us . . . is the physiology of an erection, which is much more complicated than we thought. We used to tell people, thirty years ago, if you're sixty-five and can't get an erection, see you in a year because there's nothing we can do. Then came along penile prostheses, injections, and now we had something to do. With the injections we understood that blood vessels could respond to a medication so that taught us about the physiology. Then this fellow comes along who wins the Nobel Prize for his work on a coronary vasodilator, and people are getting better erections. Then with nitric oxide tension in the penis you find out those with erections have higher nitric oxide tension, precursors needed to dilate blood vessels. So we learned about the biochemistry of the penis—it has been a fascinating learning experience. *The drugs have caused us to look back and figure out what the process is. It's not that we understood it and directed ther-*

apy toward it. It's as each thing happened, we began to get another piece of the puzzle of what erectile dysfunction really is. (Emphasis added)[50]

Bending insists that drugs drive science, not the other way around, as in the case of Viagra. Viagra ushered in a new and influential group of sex experts, including Nobel Prize–winning scientists, as well as physiologists and biochemists, who, Bending claims, after studying how Viagra works in the body are responsible for crucial shifts in mapping, defining, and understanding sexual function. According to Bending, urologists have embraced and "hailed" these new experts for discovering and constructing new scientific fields of study, including "sexual chemistry," sexual pharmacology, and sexual medicine. In the process, these scientists, along with urologists, have used medical charts and laboratories to expose what they allege to be "the truth" of sexual dysfunction.

Thus, the story of Viagra's discovery reveals two important trends. First, some "science" may be more accidental than not. Second, in an age of pharmaceutical dominance, it is becoming common for drugs to drive science. When a new treatment for impotence arrived unexpectedly at Pfizer, intrigued scientists "went backwards" to try to understand the science of erections. Ironically, the first to truly "discover" the effects of sildenafil were not scientists, but a group of middle-aged male clinical trial subjects with heart problems. These men were in for a pleasant surprise.

The "Happy Accident"

The story of Viagra's discovery is a powerful one—a story that Pfizer has carefully crafted for the public. In 1989 the chemical composition of sildenafil existed in Pfizer Pharmaceuticals labs and test tubes as UK-92,480, a cure for angina. In development and then in clinical tests from 1989 to 1994 in Sandwich, England, at Pfizer Pharmaceutical's research headquarters, sildenafil's success in sending blood to the hearts of trial subjects was not realized. Instead, trial subjects and clinicians discovered that sildenafil increased blood flow to the genital region, causing and sustaining erections, and noted this as a common "side-effect."[51] After a preliminary ten-day safety trial for the angina treatment in 1992, one clinician who was running the trials reported common side effects to his supervisor, Allen, at Pfizer:

> He mentioned that at 50 mg taken every 8 hours for 10 days, there were episodes of indigestion [and of] aches in patients' backs and legs. And he said, "Oh, there are also some reports of penile erections." It was not a Eureka moment, as portrayed in some popular accounts, said Allen. It was "just an observation." Obviously, a crucial one.[52]

Armed with limited information from Pfizer's public relations office, numerous reporters played up this "accidental discovery" story of a new erection drug, even years before Viagra was FDA approved.

> As so often is the case in medicine, sildenafil's effect on impotence was discovered quite by accident. Researchers . . . were testing the drug for the treatment of chest pains. Study participants said it did not do anything for their heart muscle, but did seem to add an extra zip to their sex life. Pfizer researchers quickly took a crash course in something they had never addressed scientifically. . . . As they plowed through the existing research on impotence, they realized they had a potential blockbuster on their hands.[53]

Two years later, *Time* recounted,

> Sildenafil, as it turned out, was not so good at opening coronary arteries, but happy test subjects did notice increased blood flow to their penises, a side effect brought to Pfizer's attention when the test subjects were reluctant to turn over their leftover pills.[54]

Playboy's 1997 product announcement framed the story slightly differently:

> Researchers at Pfizer's labs were intrigued when a drug they were testing to combat Angina . . . failed at that task and turned out to improve blood flow to the penis instead. [Trial] subjects kept reporting that, screw their hearts, they had started having all of these marvelous erections. Pfizer began tests to turn the drug into an erection pill.[55]

Overall, the most common Viagra origin story[56] in the mainstream media prior to Viagra's public debut in 1998 recounts the "accidental" discovery of a drug that created and sustained erections and produced intense demand among dumbfounded yet delighted trial subjects.[57] The story generally goes on to suggest that such demand and subsequent public curiosity fueled Pfizer Pharmaceutical's effort to develop and market an impotence drug they later named Viagra.[58]

Such "unanticipated consequence" stories carry public cachet, but only in certain circles. Social scientists Latour and Woolgar argue that scientific accounts are fundamentally about the "creation of order" out of disorder.[59] In this vein, when an article in *JAMA* declared that "better understanding of the mechanisms of erection led to the development of the new oral agent sildenafil," the scientist authors of this article (many of whom worked for Pfizer) predictably tell a more staid version of this story that avoids mention of medical "accidents" and instead favors an ordered, scientific-method approach.[60]

The substitution of science over mischance is repeated by a senior vice president at Pfizer, Dr. David McGibney, in a talk delivered to the Royal Society for the Encouragement of Arts, Manufactures & Commerce in February 1999, one year after Viagra's public debut:

> A Nobel prizewinner has said: "Research is the art of seeing what others see, but thinking what others don't think." That was certainly true of one of our recent discoveries, Viagra, with our own preclinical and clinical studies, together with emerging science from academic laboratories, refocusing our therapeutic target from angina to erectile dysfunction.[61]

In Dr. McGibney's narrative, Viagra's discovery is not accidental but the result of creative thinking, research, and "refocusing." Happy clinical trial subjects are nowhere to be found. Dr. McGibney's pride in Viagra one year after its debut also hides Pfizer's initial corporate ambivalence about developing and marketing this drug. By 2001, the "happy accident" story had become popularized enough that Pfizer published and distributed a version of it to Pfizer-affiliated sexual-dysfunction specialists. But it seems that in order to maintain its reputation in the public sphere as a serious company dedicated to drug development and disease treatment, Pfizer continued to develop a corporate strategy and promotional campaign that associated Viagra with debilitating medical dysfunction or disease.[62] And this is exactly what they did, with astounding success.

Sanitizing the Sex Drug

Despite the enthusiasm around Brindley's demonstration and rave reviews from oral sildenafil trial subjects, medical professionals and pharmaceutical companies expressed general skepticism about treating impotence with a pill. By the 1990s, four major pharmaceutical companies, including Pfizer, were investigating impotence remedies while remaining uneasy about the "seedy" history of sex medications and concerned about the size of potential markets, as well as the potential for lawsuits. Popular media venues, including *Time* and *Fortune* magazines, reported on the cautious and puritanical intentions of the industry:

> It is because of its potential for abuse, and more to the point, the traditionally seedy organizations that cling to impotence remedies (witness the ads in the back of low-rent men's magazines for spurious Spanish fly, hard-on creams, and the like) that drug companies have only recently turned their attention to sexual dysfunction. This would account for the tone adopted by Pfizer chairman and CEO William Steere even as he figuratively licks his chops over the potential market in "aging baby boomers." He is careful to point out that "quality of life drugs are gene-based just like those for serious medical conditions. In areas like impotence, aging skin, baldness, and obesity, the science is just as profound as if you were working in cancer, asthma, or anti-infectives." In other words, Viagra is sober stuff and not at all akin to Sy Sperling's Hair Club for Men.[63]

> The impotence curing business has always been one of medicine's shadiest niches. Hundreds of bizarre remedies, from boar gall to tiger-penis soup, have won believers over the ages—desperate males are easily fooled by placebo effects, which can temporarily ameliorate mild impotence. A century ago men even mail-ordered electrified jockstraps in hopes of jump-starting their inoperative parts. Drug companies with sober public images to maintain tended to view impotence remedies, like aphrodisiacs, as taboo.[64]

Pfizer's decision "to break a taboo and intervene into sex with pharmaceuticals required showing the drug cures a physical condition."[65] Thus, from the beginning Viagra was coupled with erectile dysfunction, and Pfizer worked hard to sell both. The "Sexual Chemistry" documentary reveals how Pfizer-funded researchers worked with University of California at Los Angeles (UCLA) pharmacologists during an "exciting time of emerging data" (in the period after Brindley's demonstration) to understand the natural functioning of an erection. A successful erection, Pfizer scientists deemed, requires arousal, brain messages to the penis, release of nitric oxide, expanded blood vessels, and increased blood flow to the penis. After visual demonstrations of countless scientific models, Pfizer-funded urologists commented that oral sildenafil only enhances (the above) "naturally occurring mechanisms" to produce an erection in impotent men. In other words, to break the sexuality taboo, Pfizer offered "sexual chemistry" only to those with debilitating conditions, creating a legitimate, sanitized medical campaign.

In the interest of gaining legitimacy and cutting out "seedy associations," Pfizer was making it very clear that their business was to enhance natural biological processes and to treat serious medical conditions. Pfizer representatives and researchers are quoted in countless media venues warning that oral sildenafil is not a sex pill, nor an aphrodisiac. Further, the Pfizer employee handbook soberly advises employees to "redirect humor by pointing out the seriousness of the subject matter—to remind people that erectile dysfunction is a serious medical condition that affects the lives of millions of men and their partners."[66]

Despite all of Pfizer's efforts, its medical project was still under suspicion in some medical circles, and sexuality crept into discourse about Viagra. As oral treatments for impotence, like sildenafil, loomed on the medical horizon, the American Urology Association, most likely concerned with ethics and legal matters, issued an official caution stating that oral impotence drugs were not a "viable alternative for patients with organic erectile dysfunction, and will not work for everyone."[67] Furthermore, prior to Viagra's release, cautious medical practitioners (who were not affiliated with Pfizer) were quoted by the mainstream media expressing concerns that an anti-impotence pill could be subject to widespread abuse or casual recreational use, potentially leading to overdosing, psychological addiction, and/or permanent impotence:

U.S. doctors say that men who don't have potency problems are using the drug to enhance their sexual performance. Although there is no evidence that Viagra increases sex drive or staying power . . . Dr. Arthur Barn, a urologist at Johns Hopkins Medical Center in Baltimore expects men will experiment with the drug to see if it will give them super erections or an increased amount of erections over a limited period. (*Maclean's*)[68]

A trio of new drugs promises to help men suffering from impotence, a condition that affects millions of Americans. But some doctors fear the pills will be abused by men seeking instant virility. (*Insight on the News*).[69]

Doctors are concerned that an anti-impotence pill could be subject to widespread abuse. Reports indicate that some Hollywood bedroom athletes have already tapped into an underground market for an injectible erection drug. The danger is that otherwise healthy men will take sildenafil to bolster their sexual performance and then become psychologically addicted, unable to achieve an orgasm without it. (*Time*)[70]

Such media coverage momentarily interrupted Pfizer's sanitized campaign for Viagra and erectile dysfunction. Concerns about the drug being associated with enhancement and recreational use threatened the legitimacy Pfizer was trying to achieve. The potential for a drug to be improperly used or abused is a common concern among drug companies, according to Dr. John Bancroft, but particularly so in the case of Viagra. Pfizer hired Dr. Bancroft, a specialist in clinical studies and drug research, to consult on this potential problem and provide the necessary reassurance. When I spoke with him, he said,

They are terrified of being sued by someone because he took their drug and went out and raped somebody or sexually assaulted them. I know that companies like Pfizer and [Eli] Lilly are concerned about ethical aspects of this sort. Also the idea of a drug getting a sort of street value, being marketed on the street. . . . More often than not it's a matter of reassuring them. On the other hand, it does not make them immune from litigation. They know people will try it on, and if they can blame a drug, they will. [Pharmaceutical companies] are twitchy about it.[71]

With ethical and legal issues as potential threats to Viagra's profitability and Pfizer's reputation, Pfizer seemed to work harder to market its product to "safe" populations, primarily those males who were heterosexual, married, and aged forty and above. Pfizer convened ethics panels, and even sent a delegation to the Vatican to find out how the Roman Catholic Church would respond to the pill. The Vatican gave its blessing on the basis of Viagra's contribution to improving family relations.[72]

Once Viagra was expedited for approval by the FDA and launched in 1998, profit goals, scientific rhetoric, and exaggerated statistics drowned out cautious voices and industry taboos.[73] This was largely a result of the work of a handful of Pfizer investigators and consultants who claimed, adapted, and expanded the medical category "ED" and, armed with scientific rhetoric and medical legitimacy, became visible spokespeople for the product and the medical problem. These spokespeople, with the help of journalists, constructed a sexually dysfunctional populace—a market primed and ready for Viagra.

"Branding" Erectile Dysfunction

By the 1990s, several people and events had set the stage for Viagra. A paradigm shift had taken place in scientific understandings of sexuality, which now located the source of sexual problems in the body, not the mind, the society, or the relationship. Brindley paved the way for the chemical treatment of erections. Urologists were now recognized as the new sex experts, with some poised to become paid consultants to the pharmaceutical industry. A drug for treating impotence was accidentally discovered. Now Pfizer needed a marketing plan that would sanitize and sell sildenafil.

Before starting clinical trials, Pfizer had to solve the problem of how to construct a market for their product and build up public anticipation and practitioner interest. According to philosopher Carl Elliott, author of *Better Than Well*, the industry has learned that the key to selling psychiatric drugs is to sell the illnesses they treat. Doctors treat "patients" and must be convinced that the problem being addressed is a medical disorder. In other words, from a doctor's perspective, Paxil must treat social phobia rather than relieve shyness, and Ritalin must treat attention-deficit disorder rather than improve concentration. The technology in question must treat the proper illness, or else there is no reason why doctors should be obliged to provide it.[74]

One writer in the trade journal *Pharmaceutical Executive* compliments Pfizer on successfully claiming and "branding" ED. To do so, Pfizer had to make sure that from the beginning Viagra and its corresponding medical disorder, ED, were clearly understood and inseparable in the public imagination.

> How many people knew ten years ago that there would be such a term as "erectile dysfunction"? That's brilliant branding. And it's not just about branding the drug; it's branding the condition, and by inference, a branding of the patient. . . . What kind of patient does a blockbuster create? We're creating patient populations just as we're creating medicines, to make sure that products become blockbusters.[75]

The project of "branding" ED and teaching doctors and the public at large about erectile dysfunction went largely to one Pfizer consultant, Irwin Goldstein. Goldstein is a slender man with graying hair who wears conservative suits and eyeglasses. He is also a Boston University urologist known for his energetic, media-friendly personality and his ground-breaking research on the relationship between impotence and bicycle riding.[76] Already established as a trail-blazing medical expert on impotence and a media darling, Goldstein was the perfect choice to be a key Viagra spokesperson, and he soon came to make convincing claims about sexual dysfunction on behalf of Pfizer.[77]

Although the diagnostic category "erectile dysfunction" existed prior to Viagra's debut, Pfizer borrowed the term and introduced it and Viagra together in 1998, thus constructing a public association between problem and treatment.[78] According to journalists Stipp and Whitaker writing for *Fortune*, over ten years *before* Bob Dole made "ED" a household term in television ads as a Viagra spokesperson, erectile dysfunction[79] was a medical category redefined by Irwin Goldstein and his team of researchers in the first federally funded study on impotence. The term "erectile dysfunction" was used in the Massachusetts Male Aging Study (MMAS), which took place from 1987 to 1989.[80] In this important study for the field of urology, impotence was assigned a new name and redefined more broadly. A new subjective and elastic category, "erectile dysfunction" replaced the older stigmatized term "impotence," thereby blurring disease and discontent.[81] Impotence, which is the inability to get an erection, was replaced by ED, which is "the inability to get and maintain an erection adequate for satisfactory sexual performance."[82]

Thus, the MMAS questionnaire characterized erectile potency not as an either/or but as if potency existed on a continuum. Subjects were asked to rate their potency on a scale of one to four: (1) not impotent, (2) minimally impotent, (3) moderately impotent, or (4) completely impotent. These responses were then assigned gradations of erectile dysfunction, ranging from "no ED" to "mild ED (usually able)" to "moderate ED (sometimes able)" to "severe ED (never able)." In other words, men who reported "unsatisfactory sexual performance" or who were "usually able to penetrate partner" were included in the "mild ED" category. Given these flexible definitions, of 1,290 men surveyed, aged forty to seventy, 52 percent fell somewhere in the "mild, moderate, or complete erectile dysfunction" categories. This statistic—that half of men over forty experience ED—is now cited regularly by Pfizer Pharmaceuticals. Thus, by measuring erectile dysfunction both physiologically and subjectively, Pfizer created a "wider range of troubles" to address.[83]

Incidentally, little of this may appear to matter during the typical doctor-patient visit, which is usually constrained by time and mutual hesitance to discuss sexual matters. Doctors are thus dependent upon subjective measures of ED, preferring to take a patient's word for it than to engage in tests of erectile functioning during office visits. Only one practitioner I spoke with (whose clientele is primarily men claiming ED) consistently asks his patients to test their erectile functioning with in-office visual pornography or take-home nighttime rigiscan devices. Others described a series of questions they ask to determine whether the problem might be caused by psychological or relational factors. Finally, some prescribed Viagra without question to patients who requested it.

But "diagnostic expansion," or the expansion of medical boundaries and medical categories, may be what is sending record numbers of men to their doctors and spurring record-breaking profits for Pfizer.[84] The big picture of diagnostic augmentation, embedded within a corporate context of market expansion, is that more people are prescribing, selling, taking, and profiting from prescription drugs than ever before. Philosopher and bioethicist Carl Elliot explains,

Drug companies are not simply making up diseases out of thin air, and psychiatrists are not being gulled into diagnosing well people as sick. No one doubts that some people genuinely suffer from, say, depression . . . or that the right medications make these disorders better. But surrounding the core of many of these disorders is a wide zone of ambiguity that can be chiseled out and expanded. The bigger the diagnostic category, the more patients who fit within its boundaries, the more psychoactive drugs will be prescribed.[85]

According to journalist David Friedman, enlarging ED markets to include all men dissatisfied with their sex lives can be a confusing and potentially dangerous move:

Surveyors created a "mild ED" category . . . for men who have erections, but worry that they're not getting quite as hard, or lasting as long, as they used to. (And how many men over 40, even those who have a regular sex partner, don't worry about that?) It's only when you count these men that the number of "impotent" men reaches 30 million. Dr. James Barada of Albany, NY, a member of the American Urological Association's Treatment Guidelines Committee, is one of a small but growing number of urologists concerned about this "inflation" of the patient pool. "There's a difference between erectile dysfunction, which is a real disease," Barada said, "and erectile dysphoria, which is a vague sense of dissatisfaction. I worry the line is getting blurred."[86]

With the change in definition and nomenclature, initial impotence numbers tripled.[87] Pfizer promotional materials for 2000 confusingly pronounce erectile dysfunction a "common condition that's commonly undertreated."[88] In 2001, Pfizer's official website, www.Viagra.com, used the MMAS statistics to claim, "Erectile dysfunction (ED) affects over 30 million men *to some degree* in the United States" (emphasis added). Apparently, erectile dysfunction, while appearing to be a precise, objective measure, is flexible and subjective enough to include almost any male with sexual insecurities, dissatisfaction, concerns, or intermittent erectile "failures."[89]

In 1994, Irwin Goldstein and others published a report on the prevalence of impotence in the *Journal of Urology* with statistical conclusions "as startling as Brindley's lectern stunt" a decade earlier. The number of American males "impaired" by sexual dysfunction was now estimated at thirty million, creating a huge potential market for oral sildenafil.[90] Goldstein's ED figures are now cited consistently in Pfizer's promotional campaigns, medical and media reports, and NIH and government-sponsored research.[91] Such scientific empiricism cloaks any evidence of subjectivity as well as prevents the assignment of blame or responsibility to men.[92] Such figures are also used to urge men to seek treatment from their doctors, who, as Conrad and Potter point out, also stand to profit from this medical "diagnostic expansion."

The year 1994 was also the year that prominent sociologists and sex researchers Edward Laumann and John Gagnon published general statistics on sexual dissatisfaction from their large-scale national study, *National Health and Social Life Survey*. Laumann and Gagnon found that between 30 and 50 percent of men and women complain of sexual dissatisfaction in America. This was the type of data Pfizer needed to create legitimacy for its new drug. In 1997, Pfizer hired a multidisciplinary team of consultants, including Laumann and psychologists Ray Rosen and Julia Heiman, to "ease the transition."[93] When I asked Ed Laumann to tell me about the now-famous 43 percent statistic, he responded as follows:

> I was invited to the international academy of sex research by Ray Rosen, who was president at the time, and I was his speaker. He told me that the information from the 1994 study on sexual problems did not exist in the medical literature so let's do something about it. I said that isn't my area of expertise, so we worked on it together, and brought in a [quantitative] guy, Tony Pike, to write something for *JAMA*.[94]

At that point, terminology had shifted from "sexual dissatisfaction" to "sexual dysfunction," and the social explanations for these problems were left out entirely. In what appeared to be an attempt to capitalize on the female market for Viagra, Irwin Goldstein also used these statistics in *Urology Times* to claim that 30–50 percent of women experience "organic dysfunction."[95] Thus, by the time Viagra was to debut, Pfizer was able to selectively use research data from the two major large-scale sexuality research projects of the decade in order to demonstrate the necessary compelling statistical evidence needed to create large medical markets.

Disease Mongering and Doctor Salesmen

Journalists David Stipp and Robert Whitaker of *Fortune* reported in March 1998 that Irwin Goldstein, in his capacity as a paid consultant for Pfizer, was part of a larger project supported by Pfizer to construct and reveal the necessity for an impotence drug such as oral sildenafil. In 1997, the AUA's newsletter, *Urology Times*, had forecast that urologists saw a "new field of medicine about to explode" and featured Goldstein "as the Paul Revere of Impotence." Goldstein had already been featured in *Time* and the *Journal of Urology* suggesting that "impotence should be considered as a major health concern."[96] Goldstein popped up in media venues everywhere, from *Playboy* to ABC's *Good Morning America*, touting Viagra as "a dream practitioners in this field didn't think possible" and "the start of an exciting revolution."[97]

Today, the use of paid practitioner consultants by pharmaceutical companies is common. Yet Goldstein and Laumann are among the many who do not readily divulge affiliations with Pfizer, thus appearing to the public as unbiased experts.[98] Investigators and consultants such as Goldstein generally must sign nondisclosure agreements that block them from divulging data that might conflict with the company's reports.[99]

Pfizer's shifting of medical definitions in what looks like an attempt to create and expand markets is common in contemporary medical marketing.[100] Medical journalist Lynn Payer shares these concerns in her book *The Disease-Mongers*.

> Disease mongering—trying to convince essentially well people that they are sick, or slightly sick, or slightly sick people that they are very ill, is big business. To market drugs to the widest possible audience, pharmaceutical companies must convince people—or their physicians—that they ARE sick. . . . To tell us about a disease and then to imply that there is a high likelihood that we have it . . . by citing the fact that huge numbers of Americans do . . . is to gnaw away at our self-confidence. And that may really make us sick.[101]

> Disease mongering can include turning ordinary ailments into medical problems, seeing mild symptoms as serious, treating personal problems as medical, seeing risks as diseases, and framing prevalence estimates to maximise potential markets.[102]

With the publicity machine in gear and public anticipation high, thanks to the work of Goldstein and other Pfizer consultants, the final phase of preparing America for Viagra required quickly concluding clinical trials, earning fast FDA approval, and associating sildenafil with a name that people would remember. Viagra symbolism and imagery were particularly useful when it came to naming, one of the final stages in the making of the drug.

According to sociologist Joel Best, "naming" is crucial because it "shapes the problem" and the solution.[103] Various journalists have suggested that "Viagra" is a mixture of the words "vigor" and "Niagara"—thus constructing the little blue pill as a powerful, vital, potent, thundering entity, and thereby implying that "the problem" is vulnerability, powerlessness, and helplessness and the solution is the opposite of these states. Such symbolism appears regularly in popular media, as in the *Harper's Bazaar* suggestion, "[Viagra's] name seems meant to evoke the pounding power of Niagara Falls. . . . It's expected to thunder onto the market sometime this year."[104] And this symbolic name is no coincidence. According to Greider, it is common for pharmaceutical companies to hire outside consultants to conduct market research and screen names, because the name is central to "branding" the product.[105]

The product name and inflated statistics infused investors' hopes for the Viagra bull market. Pfizer stocks rose 75 percent in anticipation of the pill that could work on anyone. "Among the ideas that excited some analysts was the possibility that millions of men and women with no medical need for the new drugs would take them to enhance sex, vastly amplifying sales."[106] Pfizer would never officially admit that Viagra was for anyone but those with medical need, but it did profit from the widespread concern with sexual dissatisfaction it helped to create.

Selling Viagra

With its media-savvy spokespeople, constant back-stage public relations work, and excited stockholders, Pfizer had a large degree of control in the public creation of the drug and its associated diagnosis. This construction of a serious treatment for a serious medical problem became the perfect set-up for blockbuster, record-breaking sales, new female markets, and a precursor to the myriad (primarily optimistic) stories written about the drug once it became a public product.

Despite the promotional claims associating Viagra with "effective" treatment of erectile dysfunction, few have pointed out that its success does not reveal the source of the problem. In other words, sexual problems are not necessarily biological in origin just because they may have impressive physiological effects. In fact, it is unclear if Viagra, or just the idea of Viagra, is the most effective quick fix for impotence. While media reports generally took for granted that Viagra proved successful in clinical trials as a strictly medical treatment for impotence,[107] one savvy medical journalist from *Time* magazine, writing in 1996, interpreted the sildenafil clinical trial statistics differently, and picked up on the potential placebo effects of the drug.

> It is also possible that some of the benefit is psychological. In the largest study, of 351 men, almost 40% of those who took the placebo reported enhanced sexual function. Their improvement was not due to any biological action and thus must have been triggered by the men's belief that the pill they were taking would do some good.[108]

This journalist suggests that psychological dimensions, such as simply the *promise* of erectile functioning, can prove "effective" as well.[109] It should come as no surprise that reports of the high Viagra placebo effect were notably absent from product announcements, especially since Pfizer had a large degree of control over the initial information about their drug. In a related note, a Boston psychiatrist writing in *JAMA* has introduced the "nocebo" effect, citing studies that have shown adverse health effects among those with higher "dread" ratings. Thus, the more anxiety a corporation can produce, the larger its market. In other words, worrying about ED may in fact cause ED.[110]

There was plenty of public and private worrying over ED. According to historian Lynne Luciano,

> Viagra eclipsed penicillin and the birth control pill as most talked about drug of the 20th century. By the late 1990s estimates of impotence had been adjusted upward to thirty million. ED was beginning to look like a circular malady, the more it was talked about, the more of it there was.[111]

This "talk" intensified in March, when Viagra was approved by the FDA, and then in April, when Viagra became available to the public. On March 28, 1998, newspapers across the United States displayed headlines such as this one in the *New York Times*: "U.S. APPROVES SALE OF IMPOTENCE PILL; HUGE MARKET SEEN." This article, by medical reporter Gina Kolata (coauthor with Laumann and others of the popular book version of the 1994 national sex study), exposed the "secret shame" of erectile dysfunction, an "affliction" thirty million American men share, and heralded the first pill for male impotence, "natural" Viagra. According to Kolata, "Pfizer scientists discovered the erection-producing effect of the compound by accident six years ago by a stroke of dumbfounding luck and leapt to develop the drug as soon as they realized what they had." Kolata went on to quote clinical trial subjects for Viagra who had begged Pfizer to be allowed to keep their pills and had slipped some to their friends. Near the end of the article, Kolata quotes urologists who warn that Viagra is not for "normal" men. This article, typical of thousands of other Viagra product announcement articles nationwide, reflects Pfizer's "official Viagra story," complete with market optimism about Viagra, Pfizer-generated statistics and scientific rhetoric, Pfizer-affiliated "expert" spokespeople, and the suggestion that one-tenth of American males were medically abnormal. This official story has survived in many permutations since Viagra was released. Immediately, urologists' phone lines were jammed with requests for prescriptions.[112]

Since its debut, I would like to suggest, there have been four other master framings of Viagra in mainstream reporting, including what I will refer to as (1) Risky/Fatal Viagra (2) Bob Dole Viagra, (3) Romance Drug Viagra, and (4) Masculinity Pill Viagra. All but the first have been largely orchestrated by Pfizer Pharmaceuticals, revealing the success that powerful companies have in controlling mainstream accounts.

Perhaps most importantly, though, because the FDA lifted the ban on direct-to-consumer advertising just six months before Viagra was released, it was possible for Viagra to be among the first pharmaceutical products to be publicly advertised. Ironically, these advertisements tell us much more about American cultural norms and ideals than about the drug itself. In the words of Carl Elliott,

> Advertising is no longer just a means of selling goods: it is also an instrument for the transmission of values. Like television and the movies, it teaches us how to dress, furnish our homes, eat well, and be cool. It also tells us what kind of people deserve respect and which

deserve ridicule, what romantic love looks like and how to find it, how
to lead a successful life, and how to be a failure.[113]

Pfizer's Viagra ads reveal cultural investments in masculinity, heterosexual sex and romance, youthfulness, whiteness, and much more.

First, the "Risky/Fatal Viagra" phase was a scare period lasting off
and on for roughly six months, beginning a month or two after Viagra's
debut, when heart-related death rates linked to Viagra appeared to be
growing quickly.[114] Americans were concerned about Viagra's safety
early on, as we tend to be with many high-profile drugs when they are
first approved, revealing a cultural ambivalence about medications.
This is the only period where Pfizer's optimistic message may have
been overshadowed by fear and concern. In November 1998, after the
FDA had received notice of 230 cases of deaths associated with Viagra
use, the FDA required Pfizer to issue warnings about Viagra's use in
"patients with existing cardiovascular disease" or those taking nitrates.[115] The Viagra death scare appeared to last for over six months,
until enough medical reports refuted these stories, insisting that the
numbers of Viagra-related deaths were no different from general mortality rates in certain age groups. But this claim, backed by Pfizer and
the FDA, still remains controversial.[116] And even in the year 2000, *JAMA*
was running articles entitled "Some Men Who Take Viagra Die—
Why?"[117]

Most people associate the "Bob Dole Era" with the debut of the
drug. In actuality, Pfizer's first print and television ads for Viagra did
not appear until nine months after the debut, in early 1999, featuring
presidential candidate Bob Dole selling ED. In these ads, Dole is pictured formally and patriotically dressed in a blue suit, red tie, and white
shirt, sitting on a couch in an elegant setting, urging men to speak to
their doctors about ED, or erectile dysfunction, in relationship to
prostate cancer, and perhaps with a nod towards his war injury. He uses
words like "courage" and "worthwhile" but never the word "Viagra,"
only "erectile dysfunction." "Pfizer" appears in the bottom right-hand
corner of the screen, in case this association is unclear.[118]

According to Bob Dole's urologist, Dole was invited to be a Pfizer
spokesperson when he mentioned using the product in a 1998 interview with Larry King broadcast on CNN. It turns out that Dole was
one of Pfizer's happy clinical trial subjects. His urologist told me, "He
was the target generation Viagra was being marketed to, and Bob Dole

It is no surprise that people generally think of Viagra as an aphrodisiac given ad campaigns such as this one, touting a pharmaceutical product as the "official sponsor" of Valentine's Day. Published in *Parade,* February 13, 2000.

was interested in being a spokesperson about diseases, prostate cancer in this case. It wasn't uncommon for him to talk about his own health in an open forum. For him, this was commonplace."[119] Pfizer appeared to cut through any "seedy" associations with their drug by choosing a war veteran and presidential candidate to endorse, and sanitize, their drug.[120] Ironically, at some point Pfizer realized that this "target generation," specifically those post–prostate cancer, had among the lowest likelihood of Viagra success, and quickly created a new ad campaign.[121]

"Romance Drug Viagra" was a marketing campaign launched by Pfizer close to a year after Viagra's debut with the tag line, "Let the Dance Begin." These print and television ads associated Viagra with romance between heterosexual, mostly white couples in their forties, fifties, and sixties, pictured embracing and dancing. During this period,

Ads like this one target those men who fall into the "mild ED" category, or those with "occasional problems." Note that this man is considerably younger than Bob Dole, the first Viagra spokesman. This ad exemplifies how diagnostic expansion, or creating a "wide zone of ambiguity" around a diagnosis, can work hand in hand with increasing market share for Pfizer pharmaceuticals. Published in *Newsweek*, May 29, 2000.

Pfizer ran ads with hearts, roses, cupids, and a slogan that read, "Viagra, an official sponsor of Valentines Day," thus playing up the "romance" promise of the drug. At the same time, Pfizer spokespeople warned that Viagra was not an aphrodisiac.

Most recently, "Masculinity Pill Viagra" is associated with several of Pfizer's recent ad campaigns focused on individual males in their thirties, forties, and above, testifying to erectile dysfunction. These men were depicted either alone, looking earnestly into the camera, or as "masculine" men performing "masculine" activities, such as professional athletes likening sexual functioning to consistent batting practice or racecar drivers smashing through barriers marked "erectile difficulties."[122] These campaigns advised viewers to "Love Life Again," "Step Up to the Plate," and "Ask Your Doctor." Perhaps the most popular recent Viagra ad depicts a confident, smiling African-American man walking through his workplace, encountering perplexed coworkers commenting to him that he looks different somehow, but not knowing why. At the end of the ad, we learn that this man has "asked his doctor."

In general, Pfizer targets as their Viagra demographic primarily white heterosexual males around forty years of age with a desire to be "young again." Pfizer's commonly cited statistic, one that appears throughout their promotional materials, states that half of men over forty have ED. Men, who generally visit their doctors much less frequently than their female counterparts, seem to be changing their ways since Viagra has achieved so much publicity. Investments into impotence treatments of all types continue to soar globally as more and more men admit to their erectile dysfunction and flock to urologists, male clinics, and internet sites seeking treatment.

As one can see, in its five years of advertising Viagra, Pfizer has moved from promoting the treatment of primarily a "severe" and debilitating ED (à la Bob Dole) to promising medical enhancement for men who have "mild" problems or desire improved penile functioning. At the same time, Pfizer is promoting American values like romance, courage, power, and rugged individualism. No longer promoting the message "not for 'normal' men," Pfizer has expanded its markets to include men of most ages, races, and backgrounds (excluding minors and gay males, although it is used by these groups as well) who see a need for erectile improvement. This was confirmed in an interview I conducted with Brad, a veteran sixty-year-old Pfizer sales representative:

> Frankly I think Viagra—*the real use of Viagra—is not in cases of absolute medical need* where guys either have got severe diabetes or blood pressure, have had a radical prostetectomy, or spinal cord injury. . . . That's what it's intended to be used for but I think the real use of Viagra is, say, for the guy who is probably forty-plus to age sixty-five that just isn't what he used to be and assuming he has a willing and interested partner, I think Viagra is a real enhancer to, uh, I hate the word "performance" but . . . It will make it like he was when he was twenty. If he's still a functioning guy—his nerves are still intact down there—and takes Viagra, it's gonna make him . . . He's forgotten what a really good erection is.[123]

Manufacturing Need

As this chapter has shown, the story of Viagra is not just about the manufacture of a little blue pill. It is also about manufacturing "needs," so that every man in America could see himself as a potential Viagra consumer. If nothing else, Pfizer advertisements and expert claims might cause a man to question whether he is young enough, sexual enough, or man enough. While this may seem exaggerated, it is the case that currently most, if not all, American insurance providers pay for Viagra prescriptions, granting legitimacy and value to Viagra and erectile dysfunction, as well as to efforts to normalize male potency and confidence levels, *and* making it possible for all insured men to simply "ask their doctor."[124] It is not accidental that most insurance companies cover Viagra. Kaiser Permanente, the nation's largest HMO, aroused a furor by initially declaring that it would not pay for Viagra, but then backed off. Oxford Health Plans, a Connecticut-based HMO, refused to cover Viagra and became the first insurer to be sued by an irate client. Even the Pentagon agreed to cover the drug once it was estimated that Viagra could eat up one-fifth of the entire pharmaceutical budget of the Veterans Affairs Department, roughly the cost of forty-five Tomahawk Cruise missiles.[125] It is important to note that while insurers tend to cover Viagra, most limit the prescription to six pills a month, with "doctor-diagnosed" erectile dysfunction. Many commentators have pointed out that when the most powerful members of our society or those who control our economy make demands, they are answered. Meanwhile, women's prescriptions such as birth control are still not covered by most insurance plans. Insurance coverage of Viagra and not birth control has spurred a "contraceptive equity movement" nationwide, in which fifteen states have passed contraceptive equity laws that require insurers to cover birth control.

Erectile difficulties are real. But so are the fears that men have about such difficulties, as well as cultural ideals conflating potency, manhood, and individualism. Taken together, those men suffering from erectile problems, those fearful of developing impotence, and those interested in ensuring potency provide Pfizer with a sizeable market for its product. Herein lies the problem for anyone concerned about the construction of normal masculinity and the sexual body. Pfizer and its networks are uniquely positioned to send an important message to men about illness, sexuality, and masculinity—and many will listen. But, the message they have chosen to send is disappointing, for it is the most profitable message they can send: illness in epidemic proportions. The target audience is individual men with aging bodies. And the goal is to get men to their doctors. While this marketing move makes sense, it is oversimplified and highly problematic. Male insecurity may reach epidemic proportions, but the number of men with severe ED is much smaller. By targeting individual men and their dysfunctional bodies, Pfizer obscures the impact that "dysfunctional" social norms or relationships can have on men's insecurities and bodies. Sending men to doctors may be a good thing, but shouldn't they talk with others—such as partners and friends? Pfizer's overemphasis on individuals obscures the sociocultural, medical, relationship-based, and age-related factors that contribute to the concerns and difficulties of men, and it therefore results in mass reinforcement of silence and social insecurity.

The rise of ED is due to the successful proliferation of the Viagra message as well as the Viagra messenger. The Viagra era heralds the rise of a new type of medical expert, the affiliated expert. A urologist spokesperson featured on the local evening news or in a national newspaper talking about Viagra may appear neutral and unbiased to the public at large, but this is generally not the case. Even one's personal physician may have a vested interest in the success of a product such as Viagra, after being offered perks associated with sales quotas or attending a Pfizer-funded Viagra information session.

The Pfizer-affiliated experts and spokespersons quoted in this chapter have imagined Viagra and its ideal consumer in particular ways. In the next chapter I draw on interviews with Viagra consumers to get at the "other side" of Viagra: the way consumers make sense of Viagra in relation to their lives, bodies, and relationships with medical professionals. As scholars point to "masculinity in crisis," Viagra appears to be a medical and pharmaceutical attempt to restore, cement, and "fix" masculine confidence, power, and potency. But how does this play out in men's daily lives, in doctors' offices and bedrooms? My interviews reveal new relationships between consumers and medical professionals. Doctors become pharmaceutical gatekeepers (with sample packs waiting for consumers) in a direct-to-consumer advertising environment. Doctors and consumers also create their own meanings around Viagra use and the accomplishment of masculinity at the turn of the century.

Cartoon by Tom Tomorrow. Reproduced by permission.

3

Fixing the Broken Male Machine

THE QUEST FOR MANHOOD—the effort to achieve, demonstrate, and prove masculinity—is rooted deep in American history, starting at least with the nineteenth century's self-made man.[1] But in the early twenty-first century, when gender equity is believed to be increasingly achievable and men are no longer the sole family breadwinners, male power and control are no longer assured. Scholars specializing in masculinity studies have had much to say about male confusion in the roughly thirty years preceding Viagra. Attempts to understand and locate "masculinity in crisis" are varied and incomplete, but crucial to an understanding of the success of the Viagra phenomenon.[2]

Beginning in the 1970s, movements to liberate men and/or "recover" different forms of take-charge masculinity have resulted in numerous male rebellions.[3] Such recovery movements came in response to record numbers of women entering the workplace and rising to prominence in the public sphere. As a result, men's traditional sources of validation were newly challenged. With work, politics, and family no longer viable arenas for proving masculinity, new sites for recovering male power and control have emerged in the past several decades, including Christian revival meetings,[4] the gym, exclusionary men's clubs, and wilderness retreats. At these sites, various male liberation leaders have suggested that proving or recovering one's manhood could be achieved through self-control, exclusion, and/or escape.[5] Mostly, masculinity movements have been about reclaiming something that has been lost. The majority are profit-based and predicated on a version of masculinity that, at the core, asserts and reclaims male dominance.

Today, a new and profitable masculine recovery movement is being generated with the aid of a pharmaceutical drug, and the male body is reemerging as a site for confidence and control. We have seen a similar phenomenon with over-the-counter male steroid use popularized in the late twentieth century. Now, millions of men turn to Viagra to reclaim something they lost. As opposed to the masculinity movements mentioned previously, this one is a silent movement, forged by individuals who may be vaguely aware of other men pursuing "recovery" of potency, confidence, and "life" at the same time. But for most of the participants, the recovery process is too personal and too stigmatizing to discuss.

The silence, privacy, and relative invisibility of this movement proved difficult for a sociologist wanting to talk with Viagra consumers. Many times I asked myself, Where do those who are wanting to recover their potency "hang out," besides in doctors' offices? This question was difficult to answer and left me feeling sympathy for the men who wanted an answer to the same question. Where did men turn who wanted to talk with other men about their experiences with ED or Viagra? In the end, the communities I found that are built around the experience of erectile dysfunction and recovery were support groups and internet chat rooms. The majority of men featured in this chapter were members of male support groups or ED-themed internet chat rooms when they agreed to talk with me. What emerges is a discussion of bodies in need of "fixing."

Male Bodies in Need of Fixing

In the late twentieth century, masculinities scholars began to write about the connections between manhood and men's bodies. Australian social scientist R. W. Connell wrote, "True masculinity is almost always thought to proceed from men's bodies."[6] Sander Gilman's work revealed how "aesthetic surgeries" such as penile implants can help in the achievement of masculinity. And sociologist Michael Kimmel suggested that the realms of health and fitness have replaced the workplace in the late twentieth century as the next major testing ground for masculinity, where body work inevitably becomes a "relentless test."[7] But few masculinity scholars have taken a critical perspective on current theories of the body as a machine or as a surface imprinted with social symbolism.[8] Likewise, limited scholarship on male sexual bodies suggests that sexuality, particularly heterosexuality, is a proving ground for masculinity.[9]

Only recently have researchers, particularly feminist social scientists, begun to expand their inquiries to include the medicalization of male bodies.[10] Since Viagra's release, a small number of women social scientists have written about the ways in which this product promises to reinforce "phallocentrism" or, in my words, "erect the patriarchy."[11] In other words, some are concerned that a product like Viagra may hinder ongoing efforts for gender equality. Others are concerned about the new commodification of masculinity and the related proliferation of mass insecurity around manhood.[12] Additionally, medical sociologists Mamo and Fishman have written about Viagra's potential for liberatory or disciplinary effects.[13] In contrast, most male scholars who study masculinity have yet to fully take up the question of the new medicalized male body or, more specifically, the Viagra body.[14]

How have men themselves responded to this newfound medical attention? In the following pages, medical professionals and patients use the language of "trouble" and "repair" as they grapple with "deficient" body parts, the concept of manhood, and medical diagnoses. In the process, they expose as constructs that which we take for granted; they imagine their bodies as machines, and they use Viagra as a tool for fixing their broken masculinity. And finally, they discover that Viagra not only solves problems but sometimes produces them as well.[15]

A Problematic Package

Several years after Viagra's debut, I had a fascinating conversation with a doctor and his long-time patient about sexual dysfunction. Upon hearing about my research, a man I will call Gray had volunteered to help by bringing me to talk to the only expert he knew on Viagra, his doctor.[16] Dr. Bern, an internist in private practice in his seventies, and Gray, a retired business owner in his eighties, had a fifty-year history together.[17] As we sat in Dr. Bern's office in Los Angeles, California, discussing my research project, both men tried to convince me that masculinity was intimately tied to penile functioning.

> DR. BERN: You see, sexual dysfunction in males is peculiar. I'm sure if someone is a paraplegic and can't walk he would feel psychologically deprived. But beyond the great obvious lack—people who don't see or hear as well, they don't feel like they have lost their manhood, you see. I must tell you, and I'm not a psychiatrist, but I think it is far more prevalent in males than it would be

in females. The fact that if women don't have sexual gratification
. . . It isn't that they don't miss it, but they don't have the psychological burden that males seem to have. Maybe it's a throwback to
the time when the caveman went and dragged a woman out on his
shoulder.

ML: So sexuality is integral to male identity?

GRAY: Absolutely! [My wife and I] talked about it for a long time—
well, a couple of weeks before the [prostate] operation itself. We
talked about it's possible we may not be able to have sex because
the apparatuses they had out didn't necessarily work. So you could
go for the rest of your life without having sex. And [the doctor] is
so right. You feel part of your manhood is gone.[18]

Doctor Bern uses an evolutionary example to construct contemporary male sexuality as overt, desirous, assertive, and central to masculinity, in contrast to femininity, which is passive and nonsexual. Manhood is seen as the ability to have sexual control of and desire for
women. Most importantly, though, Dr. Bern and Gray agreed that the
trouble associated with erectile dysfunction involves the psychological
burden of the loss of manhood. Most of my male interview subjects,
both consumers and practitioners, were in agreement on this point. If
the penis is in trouble, so is the man.

You probably wouldn't understand it—it's a big part of manhood.
Ever since you're a little boy growing up that's a part of your masculinity. And whether it's right or wrong, and however you deal with
it—that's, well, I'm dealing with it and I seem to be okay. If a man gets
an erection, or the boys in the shower compare each other, that's your
masculinity. A lot of men don't like to admit it. (Phil, fifty-four years
old, white, heterosexual, insurance broker)[19]

[Viagra] makes my penis larger, length and widthwise, and that's in-
herent to the macho thing of men. With impotence, I felt like part of my
manhood has been lost. (Byron, seventy years old, white, heterosexual, unknown occupation)[20]

After many of these conversations, I began to see that for men like
Byron, Phil, and Gray, gender and sexuality may be difficult to separate
out. Masculinity requires sexuality, and vice versa.[21] In contrast, femi-

ninity has traditionally been constructed in opposition to masculinity and, thus, sexuality.[22] What these men were telling me was that sexuality, or "erectile health," is compulsory for men, integral to achieving and maintaining manhood. (Implicit here is the requirement that heterosexual desire is compulsory for men.) Or as Australian cultural critic Annie Potts would put it, in a phallus-centered world, "Every man must pump up for phallocracy."[23]

While many men may not discuss their masculinity problems openly with a doctor, the comments above and Viagra's recent blockbuster success are representative of a new global concern for the "broken," or impotent, male. Some social scientists have argued that gender is "accomplished" in daily life through our interactions with others. In other words, we perform and interactively "do" masculinity or femininity through our appearance, body language, tone of voice, etc. Following this logic, the "accomplishment" of masculinity is situated, to some extent, in erectile achievement.[24] Fixing the "male machine" and ensuring erectile functioning, for the patients quoted above and countless others, is a way to ensure masculinity. Just as some social scientists have argued that cosmetic surgery is institutional support for women to successfully accomplish and "do" femininity,[25] Viagra can be seen as a biotechnological tool used to ensure masculinity by fixing the broken male machine.

The Poorly Functioning Male Machine

As Donna Haraway first argued in her ground-breaking essay the "Cyborg Manifesto," we are all "cyborgs." A cyborg is a hybrid creature composed of both organism and machine who populates a world ambiguously natural and crafted.[26] Think of Arnold Schwarzenegger in *The Terminator*, for example. Today, most medical language about the body reflects the overlap between humans and machines. Medical texts regularly describe bodies using mechanical terminology such as "functioning" and "maintenance." In her research into twentieth-century understandings of health and the body, anthropologist Emily Martin found that the human body is commonly compared to a disciplined machine. Like a machine, the body is made up of parts that can break down.[27] Similarly, Elizabeth Grosz argued that in a postmodern world, the body is treated as a machinic structure in which components can be adjusted, altered, removed, and replaced.[28] Illness, then, refers to a broken body part. Fixing this part ensures the functioning of the machine. The metaphor of the body as a smoothly functioning machine is central to the way Viagra has been presented. In this chapter, you will see how doctors and patients use mechanical metaphors to make sense of body and gender trouble, or "broken" masculinity.

Such industrial metaphors are used regularly by Viagra spokesperson Irwin Goldstein, who is known for describing erectile functioning as "all hydraulics" and suggesting that dysfunction requires rebuilding the male machine. Following this metaphor, common treatment protocols for erectile dysfunction center on treating the penis, the broken part, separately from the body, the machine. In the new science of sex, penile dysfunction can be measured in a variety of ways: degree of penile tumescence (rigidity), penetrability (ability to penetrate the partner), sustainability of erection, and satisfaction with performance. These measures are figured into Pfizer-distributed "sexual health" scales and questionnaires. While they may not always do so, doctors are encouraged by Pfizer sales representatives to use these resources and to center their sexual health discussions with patients around erectile performance, asking patients to rate their erections in terms of penetrability, hardness, maintenance, and satisfaction levels.

For Pfizer, the focus is on treating the dysfunctional penis. Emphasis is on "optimal" or "maximal" performance—rigidity and sustainability of the erection—which means that anything less than such performance constitutes erectile dysfunction. We see this in Pfizer marketing, when "Alfred," a Viagra consumer and member of the Pfizer speakers bureau, a traveling marketing team, shared how he promotes Viagra:

> Men ask me, "What's it like? What's it like?" These are men who are in their 50s and 60s and I always look at them and ask, "Is your erection now as good as it was?" They look at me and say no. And I just smile at them.[29]

Likewise, in the world of science, Goldstein has written that "submaximal rigidity or submaximal capability to sustain the erection" is another way of understanding erectile dysfunction.[30] In other words, "maximal" erectile rigidity and longevity are normal and expected.

This understanding of the penis as dysfunctional and fixable (even perfectible) is exemplified in the following statements by two white men in their fifties; Dr. Curt, a urologist in a medical clinic, and Chuck, a heterosexual architect.

> What I do is say [to patients complaining of erectile dysfunction], "Tell me about the erections. When you were twenty years old let's say they were a ten, rock hard. Where would they be now on a scale from one to ten?" So I give them some objectible [sic] evidence that they can give me. They'll say, "Oh, now it's a two." A lot of guys say it's now a seven or eight. I say, "Can you still perform with a seven or eight?" They say, "Yeah, but its not as good as it was." (Dr. Curt, urologist in medical clinic)[31]

> I'd say as far as functioning sexually, I'm probably at 70 percent. I just can't get hard enough to penetrate. Everything works but the erection. If I were to rate my erectile functioning prior to surgery, with now, I'd say it's at 75 percent. It will never be back to 100 percent, I know that. So I'm somewhat satisfied. And the doctors always tell me that this is a long process, and that I need to be patient about getting back to functioning. So I'm in a wait-and-see mode. (Chuck, fifty-three years old, white, heterosexual architect)[32]

Many patients who are currently looking for treatment for erectile dysfunction inhabit the in-between, "mild ED" arena (in terms of performance rankings from one to ten) and appear to be concerned with restoring their "machine" to a "normal" level of functioning. Despite Chuck's focus on "getting back to functioning," sexual standards have changed, I believe in part as a response to Viagra, and now "normal" is often not enough.[33]

It is important to point out that while many of these discussions are focused on the penis, they may also reflect expectations about normal manhood and aging. As we have learned, to be normal sexually means being normal in terms of gender, and vice versa. Also implicit in these pursuits of "normality" is a sense of denial and rejection of bodily change and perhaps aging. Thus, Chuck may be just as focused on "getting back to" manhood and youth as he is on "getting back to" normal sexual functioning.

Trouble with Normal

In some cases, Viagra is used by heterosexual and homosexual men who feel that normal penile functioning is not good enough, and extra-normal functioning is now the goal. While these men claim they do not "need" Viagra, they are more satisfied with their performance when they do use it.[34] In the quotations below, Viagra consumers Will and Stanford imply that the pre-Viagra penis is slow, unpredictable, and uncertain, and, thus, problematic.

> [I was] totally surprised in my ability to stay erect without effort and the ability to repeatedly snap to attention. Amazing effect. Sorta magical in a way. (Will, fifty-three years old, white, homosexual, program coordinator)[35]

> I noticed that if I get titillated [after using Viagra], then the penis springs to attention. Not atypically. But more facile. It's easier. I don't know if it takes less time. It's more convincing. It's not like maybe I'll get hard and maybe I won't. It's like "Okay, here I am!" (Stanford, sixty-five years old, white, heterosexual, counselor)[36]

For Will and Stanford, the Viagra body may be preferable to the natural body because it is consistent and predictable. While rigidity is the goal, part of optimal penile performance is to appear flexible; thus, the Viagra body is, in part, a flexible body.[37] According to cultural anthropologist Emily Martin, flexibility is a trait cherished and cultivated in all fields, including health.[38] In *Flexible Bodies*, Martin shows how the healthiest bodies in the postmodern era are disciplined machines that also exhibit current cultural ideals such as flexibility, fitness, and elasticity. Viagra can be used as a tool to achieve this ideal elastic body—a body that is always "on call."

Interestingly, the Viagra body is both flexible and controlled, in contrast to the cultural stereotype of men as virile and "out of control." Whereas women have historically been called upon to regulate and control male (mostly teenage) hypersexuality, men are now able to regulate, as well as empower, their bodies with the help of a pill. For Stu, the "on-call" Viagra penis will consistently respond when it is needed, whereas the "natural" body is unpredictable, and therefore unreliable.

Erections are a lot more temperamental than people are willing to admit. But we have this image of masculinity and expectations of male sexuality as being virile and always ready to go and be the conqueror. And I think that this pill allows people to finally live out that myth (laughs). That was one of the things I had to learn early on is that I had irrational expectations of sexuality. And that men don't have big erections every time they want to, usually, and that to believe that one did was to set oneself up for disappointment. (Stu, thirty-six years old, white, homosexual, student)[39]

As Stu points out, Viagra exposes the flawed "natural" body and enables a man to achieve mythic, powerful, and controlled masculinity. By appearing "natural," the Viagra body can easily replace the problematic body in order to avoid the inevitable disappointment. In this way, the Viagra body exists somewhere between artificial and natural, and even beyond to super-natural levels.

For many, the promise of Viagra is the fact that it can deliver "optimal" results, pushing the consumer beyond his own conceptions of "normal" functioning. In this way, Viagra comes to be seen as a miracle cure because it not only "fixes" the problem but also makes it "better." Below, Viagra is described as an enhancement drug by practitioners across medical specialties, as well as consumers like Will.[40]

It's pretty amazing if you can take a pill and get a better erection. Or even an erection . . . [Viagra is] the first type of medication like this, and for it to work, I mean, is it a wonder drug? Well maybe some of the antibiotics maybe, or diabetes drugs—those are wonder drugs. But in the sexual area, you could say in terms of sexual activity and all of that, yeah, it's a wonderdrug. (Dr. Tobin, urologist in private practice)[41]

With Viagra we say it's for a medical condition, not for just anyone. However, I know a fellow who was fine who took a Viagra to get himself extra-normal. (Rosemary Basson, psychiatrist in hospital)[42]

The entire world relies on drugs simply because they work, or solve—or help—physical conditions. Why is Viagra any different if it is able to extend—excuse the pun—the full and most zestful part of being human? (Will, fifty-three years old, white, homosexual, program coordinator)[43]

As the voices above reveal, doctors and patients tend to collaborate in imagining Viagra as a magic bullet that can "extend" the realm of "normal" and push people to the next level: extranormality, or super-humanness. By pushing the boundaries of erectile function, perform-ance, and sexuality, Viagra sets new standards and, ironically, marks countless male bodies as in need of repair. Consequently, millions of men are now convinced that their sexual and masculine performance can be improved with Viagra.

Viagra to the Rescue?

Viagra can also come to the rescue for men who feel that they are not quite masculine enough. While culture, the media, the economy, or re-lationships can be a source of "male crisis," such factors are complicated to fix. However, when the problem is located solely in the individual body and treated as a physiological dysfunction, the repair can seem easier. Even clinical psychologists, who acknowledge that the trouble can be psychological, social, or relational, may join medical practition-ers in seeing Viagra as a tool for regaining body function and repairing confidence and masculinity. Viagra, as a recent biotechnological inno-vation and medical treatment, represents progress on the path towards health and freedom.

Some consumers take Viagra hoping to restore or supplement not only "natural" physiological function but also "normal" masculinity and heterosexuality.[44] Others choose not to use Viagra, claiming that Vi-agra is more problem than solution in that it can produce an artificial and uncontrollable body. This section will reveal how patients and doc-tors grapple with medical solutions, the promise of Viagra, and the ne-cessity of repairing broken male bodies and masculinities.

In an era of advancing sexual medicine, patients and doctors now collaborate in their judgments about successful medical solutions.[45] Both may agree that Viagra will enhance or fix gender, sexuality, and maybe even health and aging. As we have learned in the years that Vi-agra has been available, countless men use the language of erectile dys-function and Viagra repair to make sense of their lives. Medicine is cel-ebrated as the solution to their problems.

Other doctors and consumers construct their own, sometimes counterhegemonic or contrary meanings about medicine and sexual dysfunction. This may mean reframing what is problematic and in need of treatment or redefining popular conceptions of what is "normal" and "natural." Below, I illustrate how the growing relationship between sexuality and medicine becomes accepted, and how the repair of broken sexual bodies becomes associated with quick and efficient medical solutions, to the point where such solutions are taken for granted by all involved. In the process, ideologies about what is natural versus artificial, functional versus dysfunctional, and excessive versus deficient are used to make sense of the troubled and fixable body.

Medicalization, or the increased treatment of previously nonmedical problems with medicines, is generally viewed as an inevitable feature of our contemporary lives. Medical professionals like Drs. Pellis, Heiman, and Redding do not question what they see as the forward march of medical science. Instead, these practitioners tend to embrace this push towards new knowledge, solutions, and healthier bodies as beneficial, inevitable, and unstoppable.

> It started a long time ago. Sexuality is a mind/body connection. Even Freud said it; one day there will be medical solutions to sexual problems. So he foresaw it as inevitable. (Dr. Pellis, psychiatrist in medical clinic)[46]

> Medicine has infused our lives. Sometimes it is hard to see where it stops and you begin. (Julia Heiman, psychologist in university clinic)[47]

> It's true—science is getting to that point. [Doctors are] better able to help the body in ways it can't help itself. We don't know what else the medications do—just what they do do. But as with guns or anything, it is a tool, and the more medications that come out, the less the coincidence of stigma around mental health seems to occur. (Dr. Redding, psychotherapist in private practice)[48]

As science enables doctors to help "when bodies can't help themselves," medical solutions are increasingly normalized and accepted, and their professions are legitimated. Even among mental health practitioners such as Dr. Redding, quoted above, medications can be seen as "tools" to help professionals do their jobs and cut through the stigma of mental health work.

Then again, for some medical professionals who don't write prescriptions or who work outside of the current medical system, medicalization is a force to be reckoned with. Drs. Blackwood, Bern, and Patt find themselves becoming defensive as they witness their previously accepted ideas about health and treatment slowly become outmoded.

Everything is medicalized, and HMOs vote in favor of medication over therapy. I think it's a travesty. I find it very disturbing. (Dr. Blackwood, psychologist in private practice)[49]

I happen to be a therapeutic nihilist. I'm a firm believer that the less medicine you take for anything, the better off you are. That doesn't mean I won't use medication. But I don't run and jump in areas. (Dr. Bern, internist in private practice)[50]

With the Viagra, my caution is, it fixes a problem that I'm not sure is really a problem. (Dr. Patt, psychologist in nonprofit clinic)[51]

These doctors take issue with a health care system and a culture that creates and validates expanding medicine. In a situation where "everything is medicalized," Drs. Bern and Patt advocate "caution" and go against the grain as "therapeutic nihilist[s]." Such contrary voices appear deviant in a world that generally embraces medical science as unquestioned progress, and even as the path towards health and freedom.[52]

More often than not, medical professionals and journalists couch the discovery and availability of Viagra in the language of scientific progress. After a barrage of Pfizer promotion, media attention, "scientific" reporting on the high prevalence of erectile dysfunction, and the clear popularity of Viagra after its debut in 1998, the medical professionals I interviewed are generally convinced that ED is a "major public health concern" and that Viagra is a "magic bullet" treatment.[53] Employing discourses of scientific advancement, most medical practitioners construct Viagra as a vast improvement over previous treatments for erectile dysfunction, which are now constructed as risky, painful, expensive, time consuming, and complicated. Viagra's success comes in part from this construction as the biotechnological answer to erectile dysfunction that promises the most freedom, simplicity, and expedience, due to its convenient pill form.

In many ways [Viagra] is expedient. The other kinds of techniques that we have which are workable are much more time consuming and economically more difficult. Most everybody, I would say, opts for the most efficient, economical, and expedient way of solving their problem. So if doing it with a pill can help, most everybody prefers to do that. It would be the rare individual or couple who says I'm not interested in being helped simply and easily by taking a pill. (Dr. Golding, psychiatrist in private practice)[54]

It has really helped a lot of people. I've seen some great successes. And it's certainly much easier to do than the other alternatives—penile injections, prostheses, all of these vacuum devices. The alternatives are all more complicated than simply popping a pill. (Dr. Loud, urologist in private practice)[55]

Viagra is really great because it is just a pill and as long as it works it's great. And you don't have to stick needles in, or use cumbersome equipment. . . . Instead of going to see a counselor and spending a lot of money and time on a problem that may not necessarily get better with psychotherapy—this way you take a pill and get better. (Dr. Cummings, urologist in medical clinic)[56]

For Drs. Golding, Loud, and Cummings, simply "popping a pill" is constructed as quick, easy, and painless—not nearly as threatening as the other options: chemicals delivered through needles, equipment hooked up to the body, or months of counseling. This sentiment is shared with consumers like Thom and Scott, who have tried other available options for treating sexual dysfunction, such as pumps and psychological counseling.

[The vacuum pump] is difficult from a standpoint . . . It's all the apparatuses, the preparation, and even with the constriction ring which is basically like a tourniquet, I still could not hold a firm enough erection for penetration. So it just didn't work for that effect. It's really tough because it takes all the spontaneity out of it. (Thom, fifty-three years old, white, heterosexual, engineer)[57]

Viagra is so popular in my belief because it cuts out the "middle man" as it were . . . all the psycho-sexual counseling that one would have to go through in order to get to the root of the problem. I know what my problem is without some psycho babbler telling me! It's lack of confidence in the size of my penis! (Scott, thirty-seven years old, Welsh, heterosexual, manager)[58]

Thom and Scott are among the millions of men who like Viagra for its spontaneity and ease. Medical solutions have been so successful that sometimes devices and pharmaceuticals appear to be the only options for treatment. Ricardo, a sixty-one-year-old Mexican-American consumer of Viagra, says he's tried every type of treatment and considered every gadget available, seemingly unaware that alternatives to prescription treatments exist (e.g., therapy):[59] "I've tried everything. There's a gadget for everything. . . . Don't forget, years ago we didn't have any of this. I'm really okay—I finally ended up with a pump that works. I tell everybody, 'Man, I'm back!'"[60] Ironically, with recent "advances" in medical technology, the production of seemingly straightforward and accessible treatments, the availability of medication online, and direct-to-consumer advertising, consumers are finally free to cut out the "middle man"—the therapist, doctor, or health-care practitioner—and just get what they need, quickly and easily. In fact, with the push towards health-care efficiency and insurers' reticence to cover counseling, I have been told that referrals to therapists to treat the psychological dimensions of ED have decreased substantially.[61]

Medicine continues its forward march, impacting bodies and lives in such a way as to blur the line between what is real and what is man made. This tension between "the natural" and "the artificial" is a common theme in my conversations with others about Viagra. Pfizer's most crucial selling point (after constructing a widespread need for Viagra) involves convincing consumers that Viagra not only is the easiest treatment to use but also is as close to "natural" as one can get. A 1999 Pfizer ad reads, "Achieve erections the natural way—in response to sexual stimulation." Not only is a pill simple and efficient, but Viagra enables the body to work normally and "naturally." Following Pfizer's lead, medical professionals construct Viagra as restorative, moving men smoothly and easily from dysfunction to "normal functioning."[62]

These are distraught, angry, guilty people. . . . We're just trying to restore them to normal. Or just get them to some functioning—to relieve personal distress. (Irwin Goldstein, urologist in sexual dysfunction clinic)[63]

One's sex life should not be dependent on external substances. But I do advocate drugs in cases of deficiency. (Dr. Lee, psychiatrist in university medical clinic)[64]

Generally, there's a need for this stuff. Many medications inhibit sexual functioning. And people with diabetes tend to need it. Viagra seems to work quite naturally. And it's selling like crazy. (Long, chain-store pharmacist)[65]

According to those quoted above, Viagra can be understood as a medical treatment for dysfunction, which can restore and relieve distressed and deficient people and bodies. Like these medical professionals, I felt for the men I spoke with, many of whom had admitted their concerns only to their doctors (amazingly not even to their partners) and to me.[66] These men wondered if they were "normal" but suffered in silence because of the shame they associated with their bodies, and because of the lack of close friendship networks to turn to for support.[67] For these men, admitting to impotence (even to themselves) was like conceding that they were no longer young or masculine in a culture that conflates these identities with sexuality and sexual health. Thus, the project of restoring "normal functioning" cannot be divorced from the achievement of "normal masculinity." In this way, both patients and doctors construct Viagra not only as a treatment for erectile dysfunction but also as a pill that restores masculinity.

Viagra: A Dose of Masculinity

"Erectile performance," or achievement of an erection with the potential to penetrate and ejaculate, is central to the "accomplishment" of heterosexual masculinity, according to medical definitions of erectile functioning. By defining terms in this way, medicine is actively shaping what is permissible and ideal in terms of gender roles.[68] Male roles and expectations are clearly laid out in Pfizer's 2000 definition of erectile dysfunction; in a brochure designed for doctors ED is described as "the consistent inability of a man to achieve and/or maintain an erection sufficient for satisfactory sexual performance." We are left to assume that successful masculine performance requires a specific and success-ful penile performance, involving consistency, achievement, and satis-faction. Is this really the case?

In my conversations with male consumers, I asked if Viagra could be seen as a masculinity pill of sorts. Most affirmed this idea, reiterating the link among erections, potency, and masculinity. Below, it is appar-ent that white, heterosexual, male consumers ranging from twenty-seven to seventy-five years of age have literally bought into the idea of a masculinity pill.

> ML: Is Viagra a masculinity pill?
> FRED: (He laughs.) I can't argue with that. Without it you aren't much of anything.
> ML: What do you mean?
> FRED: If you have an impotency problem to any degree, you look for something to help it with, or you abstain completely. If they feel like this is a masculinity problem, I guess they are right. (Fred, seventy-five years old, white, heterosexual, retired Marine)[69]

> Oh yes. [Viagra] appeals to the male ego. A drug for potency makes you bigger and longer lasting. And this is important to males. As far as the guys in the [post–prostate surgery] group, there are men in their seventies, maybe even eighties, who are still interested in performance and sex and having a normal lifestyle. I thought that after seventy, I might start to lose interest in sex. But maybe not. These men are gen-uinely concerned with getting back to normal sex lives. (Chuck, fifty-three years old, white, heterosexual, architect)[70]

> Viagra to me is a miracle pill! It does boost confidence as well as other things! I suppose it can be called a masculinity pill, for without an erec-tion, I believe that my masculinity is somewhat diminished! (Scott, thirty-seven years old, Welsh, heterosexual, manager)[71]

> Well, yeah, it's a pill that may make a man closer to what the ideal man is supposed to be—young and virile. (Dave, twenty-seven years old, white, heterosexual, student)[72]

According to these men, Viagra can be seen as a treatment for lost, "diminished," troubled, or incomplete masculinity. As Fred mentioned above, impotence reveals that a man is "not much of anything." Over and over in my interviews, in the face of erectile difficulty or even deficiency, male consumers cast themselves as incomplete, or "half a man." Taking a dose of Viagra allows men to be "whole" again. Below, Phil and Don, who have recently undergone prostate surgery, lament how "incomplete" they feel.

> You just want to be whole. You just want to be like you were before. It's like when somebody has a leg amputated. They get a prosthesis. They can now walk. They can't run, but now they can walk like they used to. (Phil, fifty-four years old, white, heterosexual, insurance broker)[73]

> Prostate cancer patients [like me] run the gamut of radiation, seed implants, surgical removal, and the thought of becoming impotent is overwhelming. They say, "Why me?—I've been strong as a bull all my life, god's gift to women, now I'm made a eunuch." (Don, sixty-seven years old, white, heterosexual, retired fire captain)[74]

Marvin, who attributes his erectile dysfunction to diabetes, echoes Phil and Don in feeling like "less than half a man":

> Are physical relations still important? Damn right they are. That is so firmly imprinted on the consciousness of males like me that one feels less than half a man without it. I cannot understand those men who show no interest. Very important! (Marvin, sixty-four years old, white, heterosexual, unknown occupation)[75]

Again, masculinity is constructed as necessarily connected to sexual desire and interest, thus conflating sexuality and gender. It is worthwhile to note that Marvin's comments, just like Pfizer's Viagra campaign, assume that heterosexual activity is compulsory for men. "Men who show no interest [in sex]" are rendered invisible in light of Viagra. Men who show interest but can't engage in intercourse, those rendered "incomplete," such as Phil, Don, and Marvin, are the focus of the campaign.

However, even for "complete" men, Viagra appears to offer an "extra boost" of masculinity. In the quotations below, both patients and practitioners describe how men use Viagra to enhance their masculinity—to construct themselves as studs and supermen. Interestingly, these medical professionals acknowledge the fact that patients may not be "sexually dysfunctional" before taking Viagra but may just be curious about having a "better" erection.

> Some men, like [my] older clients, used [Viagra] just for that extra hardness. They could always get an erection, but [they would say] "I'm sixty-five and it just don't work like it used to." So they might be a little softer. So they'd use it just to harden things up. So they just felt like studs. (Dr. Pemel, sexual health practitioner in private practice)[76]

> It's the superman complex. It's that "faster, shinier, bigger" sort of thing. Men feel they've gotta do/have this: the new TV, the car, and the latest products. You know by the numbers that not all the guys getting [Viagra] have erectile dysfunction. (Wilshore, pharmacist)[77]

> I am not a macho type at all, but Viagra certainly has made me feel more masculine and sexy at sixty! (Pal, sixty years old, white, heterosexual, retired court administrator)[78]

Practitioners also work to perpetuate the relationship between "complete" manhood and "normal" erectile function. Erectile health equals healthy and complete masculinity to many consumers and practitioners. A man who is dysfunctional may be constructed as castrated, lacking a penis, and/or lacking manhood. For example, conference programs for the 1999 conference on "The Pharmacologic Management of Erectile Dysfunction"—underwritten by several pharmaceutical companies with Pfizer as the largest donor—showed on the outside page a profile of a man cut in half who becomes whole on the inside page where "objectives for treatment" were listed.

Notice how Pemel, a sexual health practitioner, constructs a body as "dick-less" if erectile potential does not appear to exist. The way she understands it, the achievement of masculinity requires a functioning penis. Interestingly, the last two practitioners use the terms "performance" and "function" interchangeably to refer to the "normal" role of the erect penis. In other words, male performance and erectile performance appear to be one and the same.

> Some men would cry because they felt . . . A man without a dick in this society is just like, you know, he doesn't have a place. It's really horrible. [Viagra] was really, really life changing for them. (Dr. Pemel, sexual health practitioner in private practice)[79]

> It's about being able to perform sexually. Unless you can perform sexually and get an erection, a lot of men don't feel complete. Now I don't think that you can ask somebody who performs normally and ask them about that; you have to find out from people who can't perform, and then ask them. Men who perform normally don't think about it. It's there, it happens, it works, and that's a part of me. You don't think about it. (Dr. Curt, urologist in medical clinic)[80]

> [Viagra] reestablishes their ability to assert their masculinity. If an erection is a measure of masculinity, if it is—I'm not sure—then it reestablishes one of the parameters of masculinity. Men need to have, and women, all have to have a certain amount of self-esteem in order to do things, to perform well in society. You need a certain amount of self-esteem. When men lose [erectile functioning], they lose some of their self-esteem. In fact, I see this all the time when men can't get erections and I prove to them that they can [by prescribing Viagra], they come in here with a different look about them. They have a different way of carrying themselves, a little more self-esteem because they've been able to prove their masculinity—I don't know, I've never thought about that, but at least if they wanted to do something they can now do it and not be scared anymore. (Dr. Bending, urologist in medical clinic)[81]

For Drs. Bending and Curt, erectile health, self-esteem, and masculine self-identity are all linked. When erectile functioning decreases, confidence and sense of masculinity tend to disappear as well, and the body reveals this loss in its posture. Below, Bob, a black heterosexual barber in his sixties, and Pemel, a white forty-something sexual health practitioner, shared with me how the image of a "shrinking" man conveys the way erectile dysfunction can visibly take its toll.[82] As I flipped through Bob's booklet, "Keys to Great Sex for Men over Fifty," I showed him the first page, which reads in large letters, "YOUR PENIS SHRINKS 19.8% AS YOU GET OLDER," part of an ad for testosterone treatment. I asked if he believed this.

> Yes, that's what prompted me [to buy the treatment]. Oh yeah, you wake up in the morning and you know something is different. Reading this stuff makes you more aware of what is happening. After taking stuff, there is a difference, a change. (Bob, sixty-two years old, black, heterosexual, business owner)[83]

> This whole thing psychologically, men being impotent, it's just devastating. It just affects so much. Testosterone levels. The ability to produce muscle in our bodies. I mean, men just shrink when they just don't have a strong erection. So it's interesting. Not that they become waifs, but . . . in the cases I've seen once they start to have more erections, they are more interested, hormonally things are flowing, testosterone is being produced more, and they are kind of feeling bigger and bulkier and more manly in many ways. (Dr. Pemel, sexual health practitioner in private practice)[84]

Here, the norm for males is to be big and bulky, not shrinking and diminutive. This theme of loss came up frequently in conversations with practitioners and consumers, although expressed and constructed in various ways. Many times loss of erectile function is seen as a death. Social scientist Annie Potts, in a critical commentary on "The Hard-On," reminds us that the experience of "the fallen flesh"—or the limp penis causing the body to appear desexed, soft (feminine), and powerless—is a common male horror story because it feminizes the body, rendering the person unidentifiable as a man.[85] Below, we can see how Ricardo enacts this horror story as he worries about the seeming death of his sexual personhood and sexual life, as viewed by his relatives.

> I hate for people to think that I can't do this. They think about it. I talk to my aunt and she says, "Oh, you can't do that thing anymore." I thought, "I don't like that." And I hate for them to think it's over. Like we're married but it's over for us . . . I never realized how important it was till after I couldn't do it. You just take it for granted. It's fine, and then when you can't do it—I was very depressed. Not to the point of

killing myself, but I thought it was all over. [There is] so much stuff on the market, that I keep going back to try things. (Ricardo, sixty-one years old, Mexican-American, heterosexual, painter)[86]

Ricardo describes his feelings of desperation, loss, and depression associated with impotence. Ricardo repeats the phrase, "it was all over" several times, perhaps mourning the end of his masculinity, his virility, his sexuality, his marriage, his good reputation, or even his life. For Ricardo, the only way to envision new beginnings came from trying every new medical treatment on the market.[87]

Taking things one step further than Ricardo, Dr. Goldstein, Joel, and Marvin literally compared erectile dysfunction to death. For them, Viagra is constructed as a tool for restoring not only masculinity but also "life" itself.

Sexual dysfunction is no joke. These people have horrible lives, they may lose their relationships, and they come in a fairly desperate condition. Some say they'd rather be dead. Both men and women. And their lives are destroyed. They have nowhere to turn. They are not themselves. All of that. (Irwin Goldstein, urologist in sexual dysfunction clinic)[88]

I'm fifty-five and for some reason I just didn't seem to feel like I was alive and well like I was when I was twenty years old. And you know, I thought that shouldn't be so because that's not the way it is. I've never talked to anybody about that situation, so I told my doctor. For some reason or other I said I'd like to try something to see if I'm still alive or not. And so anyway he says, "Do you want to try this Viagra?" I say I don't like drugs or anything artificial. Maybe my time is over and that should be the end of that. But then I tried [Viagra]. (Joel, fifty-five years old, white, heterosexual, unknown occupation)[89]

Often [after taking Viagra] I awaken with this wonderful feeling . . . not enough to put to use, but enough to let me know I am alive . . . (Marvin, sixty-four years old, white, heterosexual, unknown occupation)[90]

When Joel and Ricardo agree that "their time is over" when they can no longer achieve erections, they seem to imply their own deaths. For most of these consumers, an active, erect penis symbolizes normal health, masculinity, and sexuality. A limp penis or absence of virility appears to symbolize death of the body as well as of manhood. To capture this disinterest in life that comes with erectile failure, Pfizer has chosen the tag line "Love Life Again" to sell its product.

As we have seen, for both male consumers and (usually male) practitioners, communicating about pain, loss, and concerns associated with sexual problems can be difficult, embarrassing, and heavily laden with metaphor, myth, and shame.[91] Phrases such as "it's over" and "I'm no longer alive," along with labels such as "shrinking," "eunuch," and "incomplete" reveal male discomfort with discussing sexuality and convey the degree of importance erectile functioning plays in men's sense of self, masculinity, and health. These men visit doctors with their complaints to investigate ways to fix their selves, their manhood, and their health. In the process, patients look to practitioners and those around them to provide a rationale for their troubles.

The Source of Trouble

How do consumers understand the source of trouble or loss in health, masculinity, and sexuality? How do practitioners make sense of erectile dysfunction for their patients? Besides pointing out health problems, disease systems, medications, and surgeries that appear to cause ED,[92] practitioners sometimes argue that "deficiency" and illness are also associated with aging, stress, social ideals, and memory.

> In our heads, our sense of our self as sexually normal is the way we were when we were maybe sixteen or eighteen years old. . . . What happens to us as we get older is not seen as different—it is seen as abnormal because we still tend to compare ourselves with the standard of what our performance was like when we were adolescents. (Dr. Golding, urologist in private practice)[93]

> I treat the dot-com world. Sexual dysfunction in the dot-com world is rampant with so many workaholics. This may seem off the topic, but we need to be clear about what we're leaving out. (Julia Heiman, psychologist in university clinic)[94]

Most consumers tend to agree with the medical explanation for erectile troubles, but male senior citizens Art, Fred, and Stanford add that erectile dysfunction could also be a symptom of macrolevel social patterns and pressures brought on by the media and changing gender roles.

> If a fellow comes home and she's making two hundred thousand dollars and he's making seventy-five thousand dollars, he's got a problem. He's going to have an emotional problem in many cases. Now that you have the women's lib and probably they are controlling a little more of their sexual life, that gives the guy a problem. It could. That's the way I think. I can only look at it from a man's point of view. The man was almost always the aggressor. Now if you watch movies or whatever—X-rated movies on TV—the woman is the aggressor. I don't know in how many cases that works. If there is give and take, that's okay, but if the woman becomes the aggressor, he may have a problem. It may become problematic. That's my opinion. (Art, seventy-six years old, white, heterosexual, retired)[95]

> FRED: Well, all you gotta do is watch TV—it gives you ideas.
> ML: What ideas?
> FRED: Well, boy-girl ideas.
> ML: Pressure to be sexual?
> FRED: You get a daily dose of it if you watch TV. I've never felt the need for it. For having my nose rubbed in it.
> ML: So you don't watch TV, but you think most people do and that they feel pressure to be sexual from that?
> FRED: I've watched enough of it to see that. To get a daily dose. (Fred, seventy-five years old, white, heterosexual, retired Marine)[96]

It is not men who oppress women. It is society which oppresses us both. My oppression comes in the form of not thinking of myself as a man unless I can satisfy my partner anytime, all the time. Unless I can make her come. Well, that's a trap. It's basic psychology. If I'm responsible for you doing something or feeling a certain way, of course it's not going to work. Ultimately it will break down and I'll become sick. However, I imagine most men don't see it the way I see it or aren't conscious of it. As a result, this would be a great thing to have—Viagra. It's like you don't have to be afraid. It's like a ready-made hard-on. (Stanford, sixty-five years old, white, heterosexual, counselor)[97]

Art, Fred, and Stanford point to different sociocultural factors that are generally dismissed or ignored in mainstream discussions of sexual problems.[98] For these guys, focusing solely on physiological symptoms and treatment does not solve the social pressures at the core of sexual problems. Finally, some consumers locate the source of trouble not in the mind, the body, or society, but in the treatment itself. In this case, Viagra causes more trouble than do erectile difficulties.

Repair = Trouble

Not all consumers buy into the techno-fix model. Some consumers commented that although Viagra may promise bodily repair or enhancement, it can actually cause more trouble than it's worth. In this section, consumers indicate that Viagra creates problems, not solutions. For Joel and Don, Viagra is constructed as techno-trouble, rendering the male body increasingly out of control.

I don't ever want to try [Viagra] again. The thing about it is, the side effects could be very dangerous for someone a little older than I am. Because you do end up with palpitations. Your body is just not your body. So if [your functioning is] not normal, I think it's better to just let it go at that. Or make pills that are much, much weaker. But I wouldn't recommend it for anybody. (Joel, fifty-five years old, white, heterosexual, unknown occupation)[99]

I have tried it. I went a long time and the bottom line is I don't like it. It hasn't done me any good and it had a harmful side effect—heartburn and indigestion. I'm a little fearful of it. I'm a healthy guy and I don't take any maintenance medicines of any kind. My system seems to be functioning nicely. I think I'll just leave it alone. (Don, sixty-seven years old, white, heterosexual, retired fire captain)[100]

As we saw earlier, some men see Viagra as a tool to create the ideal flexible body. For other consumers, Viagra may produce a body that is overly rigid and inflexible. For them, the Viagra effect is "unnatural" and uncontrollable, and consequently undesirable for both Dusty, a homosexual student, and Stanford, a heterosexual counselor in his sixties.

> Well, I also didn't like it because it was unnatural. Like you were hard and you stayed hard. And I also didn't like the fact that it guaranteed things would be sexual until you weren't hard. I didn't like the idea of being forced into being sexual. You can't do anything nonsexual when you are on it. So basically it guarantees that the entire period you are on it is going to be sexual. (Dusty, seventeen years old, white, homosexual, student)[101]

> The idea that I thought was hilarious at first—that erection that won't go away—is not hilarious at all. In fact it happens and sometimes endangers one's life. (Stanford, sixty-five years old, white, heterosexual, counselor)[102]

For Stanford and Dusty, Pfizer's Viagra tag line, "Love Life Again," is inappropriate. Instead of regaining an appreciation for life, these men see Viagra as dangerous or even deadly. While priapism or death can occur in rare instances of Viagra use, and even Pfizer admits that Viagra is not for everyone, neither Stanford nor Dusty experienced real bodily danger while taking Viagra. Nonetheless, both take Viagra seriously, remaining cautious and seeming to prefer the natural way to the artificial alternative.

Rather than lose control of their bodies or experience trouble through repair, some men construct alternatives to the pharmaceutical quick-fix model, accepting their bodies as they are or just "leaving it alone." Despite overwhelming evidence that Viagra is associated with the production of normal and/or mythic masculinity, men like Ollie and Joel work hard at reconstructing masculinity as separate from "erectile health." They insist that heterosexual masculinity can be achieved without the help of Viagra or consideration of erectile potential.

> Oh no, if you don't feel like a man before you take the pill, you're not a man anyways. No, you have to know where you're at. If you have a little misfunction, that's minor. But you have to be a man before you go through that. It's not a macho pill. (Joel, fifty-five years old, white, heterosexual, unknown occupation)[103]

I've talked to a lot of different men about this. Some cannot live without sex. They feel their sex makes them the man that they are. And I'm
not sure how important that is to me. I'm a man anyways. It's about
self-esteem. What do you think about yourself to begin with? (Ollie,
sixty-four years old, black, heterosexual, printer)[104]

For many, Viagra fits perfectly in a society that is known for pushing the limits of normal. Some men are critical of American culture and
Viagra's role in perpetuating the endless pursuit of the quick fix. Hancock and Miles warn of a hedonistic, money-driven, artificial world,
where there is a pill for everything. For them, Viagra exists in this world
as a crutch or band-aid solution to larger social problems.

We are willing to take the latest thing that is fast and painless. Also,
Americans seem to think happiness is their birthright. They take Viagra to become better, happier. And supermen. All that stuff about self-
worth, image, and sex life, it's what people want. . . . And maybe those
guys who think they need Viagra just need to chill out and reduce
stress in their lives. It's about lifestyle modification more than anything, I think. Maybe we are too lazy and it just takes too long. We
want something to work fast. (Hancock, sixty-nine years old, white,
heterosexual, retired teacher)[105]

I think there is a gross overuse of drugs for happiness and well-being.
Feeling depressed, get a script for a mood enhancer . . . feeling tired,
get a pill for energy . . . want to have better sex, get some blue magic.
What about the age-proven solution of removing or reducing the problems or stress factors affecting your life and then seeing if pharmacological agents are still needed? (Miles, forty-five years old, white, heterosexual, paramedic)[106]

Here, Miles and Hancock construct society as drug-infused, producing
individuals who are dependent upon pills for health and happiness.
They, along with Stu and Ollie, are critical of corporate and biotechnological attempts at constructing needs, desires, and easy markets for
products.

How do I express this? This is a . . . capitalist hegemony of our emotions. We live in a state of anomie, or at least we are told that we do,

and we're also told what to do about it. Have you seen these commercials? I have files of "The Paxil Christmas" that I cut out of a magazine. This young college-aged woman in a family Christmas portrait and it says, "You can go home this year and have a good time. Paxil." Paxil and Prozac and Zoloft—that's what it was. They ran these ads and marketed them to different age groups and they are telling us what the problem is—creating a problem—and they give us a solution. We all have anxieties and relationship issues, and they do this to make it look like the way to solve your relationship issue is to take Paxil. The way to deal with your crazy family is to take Paxil. That way you don't have to address the relationship issues, substantive issues. I have a big problem with that. (Stu, thirty-six years old, white, homosexual, student)[107]

I think everything we do nowadays is overblown. I just see that society is just driving us crazy, making us jump through hoops and do things we really don't need to do. So a drug for everything . . . I think they—or not they, but the way things are set up, is to make you want to do things. Even if you don't want to do it, you are driven if you pay attention to what's going on. I'm not that kind of person. I won't let you do me that way. You won't be able to drive me that way. I just don't believe in it. (Ollie, sixty-four years old, black, heterosexual, printer)[108]

These men are clearly critical of Viagra's potential to enforce social and gender ideals. They refuse to "buy into" mythic masculinity, and they see through the problematic language used to describe medical progress as well as so-called widespread public health crises. In this way some men do resist and reframe masculinity, biotechnology, and medical science in ways that make sense to them. Rather than construct their bodies as troubled, with Viagra as a techno-fix or magical solution, these consumers see Viagra as problematic, contributing to larger social problems. These skeptical voices, however, are easily drowned out by the overwhelming chorus of those who sing Viagra's praises.

Masculinity, Biotechnology, and Resistance

At the turn of a new century, the desire to "fix" and "erect" male sexuality and power in a male-dominated society appears to be strong. This desire is perhaps a reaction to the gains of women's liberation and sexual empowerment, and as some of the men I spoke with pointed out, we are also living in a time of self-help movements, expanding medicalization, great social change, and personal crisis. Today it is not uncommon to hear about American social problems such as "male betrayal," the "malaise among men," and the "masculinity crisis." Just as Betty Friedan warned against women "buying into" their own victimhood in the 1960s, so now it is argued that men are buying into commercially packaged manhood in many forms, including "amped-up virility" and "technologically-enhanced supermanhood."[109]

When Lewis Carroll wrote *Alice's Adventures in Wonderland* in 1865, the idea of an ingestible tonic that would answer Alice's wishes and make her "grow large" was a magical, fantastical fantasy. Today, we all inhabit this magical reality, surrounded and tempted by endless products packaged in promises of personal transformation. This is the era when the "magic bullet" for sexual energy, confidence, and masculinity comes in the form of a pill. Today, so-called lifestyle drugs of all types are available to anyone with access to the internet and a credit card. And Americans have a newly transformed relationship with biotechnology, one that goes beyond "healing" to "transforming" and "fixing" bodies with the help of reproductive technologies, hormones, implants, surgeries, and other technological innovations.

Today, enhancement technologies are not just instruments of self-improvement, or even self-transformation—they are tools for working on the soul.[110] The new player in this enhancement tale is the man who has been told he is sick. With Viagra, a highly successful masculine empowerment campaign is underway, centered around a new, late-twentieth-century tool, a magic blue pill that promises to produce and enhance male "magic wands." The doctor's tools are now turned back on the doctor himself. The male body is constructed as in need of repair, and is a new site for medical and biotechnological innovation and healing. With health and fitness as the new testing ground for masculinity, Viagra enters doctors' and patients' worlds, envisioned as cutting-edge biotechnology and used, I argue, as a cultural and material tool in the production and achievement of "true" manhood. Then again, Viagra can lead to male confidence without even being ingested. One of my informants told me that he purchased Viagra at a time of intense sexual insecurity with a partner but hasn't had a chance to use it. He is hoping that just having it around will make him a more self-confident lover. Others echoed this idea, that simply pills in the medicine cabinet was enough of an assurance.

The implications of constructing the male body as sexually potent, or as a technologically enhanced machine, can be both hurtful and helpful, as medical professionals, Viagra consumers, and their partners have discovered. Here I think of a friend's lesson about the importance of antidepressants: "You can't start a revolution if you're so depressed you can't get out of bed!" Similarly, during the course of this research, practitioners told me that their patients would not be attentive to their partners' sexual needs or desires if they were insecure or paralyzed by their own. Thus Viagra enabled them to be more confident and attentive to themselves as well as to their partners. In this way, it is important to acknowledge that prescription drug use has the potential to enable broad social change.

Nonetheless, social historian Lynne Luciano warns,

> Medicalizing impotence lures men into believing there is a standard for erections to which they must adhere. By quantifying the normal erection—it has to be just hard enough to achieve penetration and last long enough to achieve ejaculation—medicalization forces men to conform to its specifications for masculinity. The results are twofold: first, men, like women, have their sexuality and desirability linked to physical parameters; second, emotion, sexual technique, and the role of one's partner are rendered insignificant. By making the erection the man, science isn't enhancing male sexuality, but sabotaging it.[111]

Like Luciano, many social theorists have recently expressed concern with the state of manhood in America. Sexologist and practicing therapist Wendy Stock points out that to focus on male bodies as Viagra-infused, finely tuned, flexible machines perpetuates a detached, unemotional masculinity. She comments, "Although a common cultural male fantasy is to be able to function like a machine, as the sexual equivalent of the Energizer Bunny, both men and women may lose something if medical interventions allow us to function without the necessity of emotional connection. Is the ability to perform like a sexual machine desirable, individually or on a cultural scale?"[112] Similarly, feminist journalist and social commentator Susan Faludi warns of a "performance culture . . . where people are encouraged to view themselves as commodities that are marketed and fine-tuned with chemicals, whether it's Viagra or Prozac or Botox injections."[113]

Despite such warnings, sexual medicine continues to expand, as experts and marketers find ways to understand and treat a wider and wider range of sexual troubles for men and women. At a major international conference on sexual dysfunction in 2003, definitions and treatments for "rapid ejaculation" and "delayed ejaculation" were being discussed and finalized. For women, delay or absence of orgasm, arousal, or desire is cause for medical intervention. Insurers also intervene, by setting rules about who has access to sexual health treatments, and how many. Meanwhile, performance anxiety will only grow as the definition of "normal" sexuality and masculinity narrows. As sexual medicine gets more and more commonplace, what will be the ramifications for those who don't follow medical protocol? For those who have little interest in sexuality, or in medical models of sexuality? Lynne Luciano poses similar questions, with no clear answers:

> What happens to a man or woman who doesn't want to take drugs to enhance sexuality, who is content to age without the benefit of pills and potions? How far are we willing to go in our public discourse about how much sex is enough, and what constitutes good sex, and how central a role sex should play in relationships? Medical advances and healthier lifestyles offer men hope for longer and more potent sex lives than at any other time in history. But expectations are likely to continue to outpace reality. Not even Viagra can guarantee sexual success for all men, all the time. What it can guarantee is a continuing moral and ethical debate.[114]

The individual stories in this chapter add up to what I see as a larger, disturbing story about the pressures and requirements for being fully male in American society, and even worldwide. Are we doing our men a service in the Viagra era? As the doctors and patients that I interviewed and quote in this chapter reveal, Viagra can and is being used to enforce and perpetuate an ideal masculinity. In this way consumers collaborate with medical professionals and pharmaceutical companies in an attempt to understand and fix "broken" bodies. Perhaps of more interest, my data also reveal the struggle with the necessity for the Viagra-enhanced body, and what that struggle represents. As men negotiate their relationship to this product, mainstream ideas about sexuality, masculinity, and health are both reinforced and redefined in important ways. For example, some men insist that "doing" masculinity does not require sexual performance. Others are critical of a society that increasingly promotes and depends upon biotechnology for achieving health and happiness. They have their own ideas about manhood, medicalization, and biotechnology that may or may not fit with Pfizer's. In general, this chapter reveals men complicating manhood by constructing not only corporate corporealities[115] but also "various and competing masculinities" in the Viagra era.[116] As most of us do, the men I spoke with are constantly negotiating social and cultural pressures to be healthy, young, sexual, and in control.

For Pfizer, fixing the broken male machine is supposed to be a simple process with the help of Viagra. The men in this chapter suggest otherwise, pointing out that the bodily "repair" process, the man, and the culture he belongs to are all more complex than Pfizer may acknowledge.

Cartoon by Dana Summers, Tribune Media Services.
Reproduced by permission.

4

The Pill Doesn't Always Thrill

IN 1997, *Newsweek* ran a cover story introducing a new pill for impotence that was soon to be approved by the FDA.[1] Soon afterwards, letters to the editor, many penned by women, expressed concern about the arrival of this new drug. One letter read, "We don't need more virile senior male citizens thinking they are virile teenagers. We have enough of that already. What about birth control for men, that's what we really want!"[2] What in 1997 seemed like a lone critical voice was joined by many more in the years to come. Many of these letters, it turns out, were written by senior women. Six months after Viagra's debut, a letter appeared in Ann Landers's column:

Dear Ann:

We live in a senior community, where one must be at least 55 in order to be a resident. Most of us are in our 60s and have been married for 40 years or more. At a recent ladies' luncheon, your column and some letters regarding Viagra became the main subject of discussion. We decided to conduct our own poll. No names, of course. Everyone was told to mark a ballot number 1, 2, or 3, depending on which answer best described her viewpoint. We thought you might be interested in our results.

Three women marked number 1, which said: I enjoy sex. It is a mutual pleasure for me and my husband. I would welcome Viagra.

Eight women marked number 2, which said: I do not enjoy sex, but I love my husband, so I have pretended to enjoy it all of these years just to please him. I am not interested in any drug that will pep him up sexually. I'm more than willing to let nature run its course and am not interested in Viagra.

Four women marked number 3, which said: I have endured sex all of these years because my mother always told me it was my duty. Now it is his turn to respect my feelings and leave me alone.

As you can see, Ann, sex is not very popular among our group of wives. The one thing we all agreed on was that Viagra must have been invented by a man.

Signed,
Senior Señoras in Sonoma, September 21, 1998[3]

At the same time that the Senior Señoras were writing to Ann Landers, Bob Dole began appearing in television advertisements for Viagra. Because of Dole's distinguished stature, as we have seen, his story became the dominant Viagra story, ubiquitously retold by pharmaceutical spokespeople, medical experts, and journalists, in news cycle after news cycle.

But what about Dole's wife, Elizabeth? She is a distinguished public person in her own right, so why wasn't her sex life front and center? After all, we must assume that the erectile dysfunction was as much Elizabeth's problem as it was Bob's. However, as the Senior Señoras from Sonoma rightly point out in their letter to Ann Landers, Viagra was for all intents and purposes invented by men. And as Pfizer's first major ad campaign made clear, Viagra was for men and their sexual satisfaction. In other words, Elizabeth Dole's sex life was just not a part of this story.

As has already become clear, women's perspectives and opinions are largely absent when it comes to the Viagra phenomenon. Sex is still seen as male terrain, with women viewed as silent partners at best. In part, this silence is due to the equating of erectile dysfunction with heterosexual masculinity and male responsibility, an equation that leaves little room for women's experiences. But by leaving women out of the picture, we are only seeing half of the story. In preparing this study I wanted to discover how women have been affected by erectile dysfunction and Viagra. In order to find out, I talked to some of the wives and partners of senior Viagra users. These senior women had different experiences with and opinions about Viagra, though each had important, and often surprising, things to say about sexuality in the Viagra era. Their comments shed light on how elderly women view sex—and how much sex they are having—and whether they would like to have a "female Viagra" pill.[4]

Interestingly, the most significant feature of my discussions with these senior women[5] is that they seem to *use* Viagra differently than their male counterparts.[6] As you may recall, many of the men quoted earlier used metaphors of trouble and repair in order to imagine Viagra as a tool for fixing their "broken" masculinity. In contrast, these senior women discuss Viagra in terms of their own pleasure and danger, as well as their partners', and rather than confirming stereotypes about masculinity, they often question social expectations related to gender, sexuality, marriage, and health. Most importantly, the introduction of Viagra seems to have provided senior women with a rare opportunity, as well as permission, to discuss their sex lives.[7]

Pleasure and Danger

I met these senior women through two senior-citizen organizations in southern California: a singles social club and a seniors-only summer school.[8] I surveyed about eighty male and female seniors, thirty-eight of whom were women, and of that group, I had eight follow-up in-depth conversations by phone. These women—Agnus, Annette, Bette, Doris, Hilda, Nora, Pauline, and Sally—are the focus of this chapter, coupled with anonymous survey data. At the time of the interview, they ranged in age from sixty-seven to eighty-six years of age. Most were living either in Florida or southern California, approximately half were Jewish, and all were white, heterosexual, middle- or upper-middle-class American citizens. They all had differing relationships to Viagra: four had partners who tried Viagra, others had friends who used the product, and a couple only knew of Viagra through news reporting or conversations with friends. Importantly, all but Bette, who was divorced, were widows. At the time of our conversations, Bette and Doris were actively dating, while the others were not.

As opposed to the men I interviewed for chapter 2, many of the senior women reported that they had discussed Viagra in some way with their friends or loved ones. This eagerness to talk about Viagra was evident in the large-group discussions I had with the senior summer-school participants, in which the women were more than willing to share and "vent" their ideas about sex and Viagra.[9] The drug played a role in these women's lives in ways that may not have existed for the men I interviewed, many of whom identified as sexually dysfunctional and, probably out of shame, discussed Viagra in limited ways with doctors, with wives, and much, less frequently, with peers.

The women's willingness to speak openly about sex signals a marked difference from years past. In fact, the idea that senior women are desiring sex, and talking about it, may be a significant departure. Two decades ago, two books were published that changed the way most sexuality scholars understood women's sexuality: *Powers of Desire: The Politics of Sexuality*, and *Pleasure and Danger: Exploring Female Sexuality*. These volumes marked a complex historical moment in women's lives and feminist organizing, representing themes and sentiments expressed at a controversial feminist conference held at Barnard College in 1982.[10] The conference and ensuing volumes signaled a growing interest in women's sexuality, empowerment, and safety as important personal and political goals during late "second-wave" feminist organizing, solidifying for many the idea that women's experiences of sexuality can be both dangerous and empowering.

Today, aside from a narrow field of publications within sexology and gerontology, data on the sex lives of seniors, male and female, in America is limited. This lacuna may be linked, in part, to erroneous assumptions that pre-Viagra seniors were asexual.[11] Unfortunately, the assumption that sexuality declines and disappears with age has led to gaps and silences in the few landmark national sexuality studies that have been conducted. Research by Kinsey in the 1950s and Masters and Johnson in the late 1960s exemplifies such negligence, as there is little to be learned in these studies about senior sex.[12] Such assumptions about lack of sex may have even informed the latest *Sex in America* survey (1994), which included only those aged eighteen to fifty-nine. One notable exception came in 1976 with Shere Hite's *The Hite Report on Female Sexuality*, as Hite received questionnaire responses from women aged fourteen to seventy-eight. According to Hite, one of the major findings was that age is not a factor in female sexuality or, in other words, that "older women are NOT less sexual than younger women—and they are often more sexual."[13]

Thanks to Viagra and Bob Dole, seniors' active sexual lives are becoming more visible, legitimate, and accepted by American society. A 1999 article in *Time International* summed it all up in its title: "Old Goats and Their Libidos: Ever Since Bobby Dole Did That Viagra Ad, the Senior Class Has Been Acting Up."[14] But several of my interview subjects were eager to point out that seniors were sexually active prior to the Viagra era. As Agnes put it,

> These days seniors are still falling in love and feeling young and sexually active again. Is this new? Probably not. It has probably been the case for some time now, but people didn't talk about it. (Agnus, sixty-seven)[15]

Understandably, this exposure is creating some discomfort, but it also offers some welcome changes in social expectations. It is in the spirit of this newly expanded dialogue and the new visibility of the sexual senior that *Modern Maturity Magazine,* the official magazine of the American Association of Retired People, commissioned a report on the sex lives of seniors.[16] This "Exclusive Post-Viagra Survey Report" was a "study of the sexual attitudes and practices of Americans 45 and older in the first nationwide inquiry into midlife and old age." In brief, their findings revealed that "at every age, sex seems to hold greater importance for men than women. According to this survey, nearly 60% of men—but only about 35% of women—say sexual activity is important to their overall quality of life." Other important results with relevance for this study include the following: 70 percent of baby boomers and seniors with regular partners have sex at least once or twice a month; 5 percent of men seventy-five and older, and more than 35 percent of women in that age group, say they would be quite happy if they never had sex again; among women in their forties and fifties, only 9 percent are sanguine about such a prospect. Additionally, the survey found that for seniors, a major "partner gap" exists, as more men than women have partners, and over half of women above sixty are alone.[17]

This data provides a larger context within which to understand the voices of senior women highlighted in this chapter. For example, seven of the eight seniors I interviewed are widows reflecting on what *Modern Maturity* calls "the end of their sexual lives with the loss of husbands" and, I would add, with the loss of the potential for future sexual relationships. Furthermore, the fact that many senior women (35 percent) say that sex is not that important to them, as well as the fact that the same percentage claim they would be content never to have sex again, confirms the earlier sentiments of the Senior Señoras: many senior women are just not as interested in having sex as are senior men. That said, in the interviews that follow, some of the senior women directly contradict this, in fact claiming that it is the men who cannot keep up with their appetites. It is important to keep in mind that many of these women came of age during a period when women were not supposed to concern themselves with sexual gratification (and men were not supposed to be overly concerned with their wives' pleasure). Sex for this generation of women was officially for making babies. More specifically, those in their sixties confronted a very different sexual and social climate, having been born in the 1940s and coming of age in the era of birth control, for example, than those currently in their eighties, who were born in the 1920s Depression era and came of age during World War II, amid more restrictive norms and attitudes. For many of these women, seeing their daughters and granddaughters come of age at a time when birth control and Viagra use are normalized allows them to redefine, and perhaps explore, sexuality in new ways. Comments quoted below reveal much about women's sexuality as well as their sense of sexual pleasure and danger.

Women's Sexual Health and Pleasure

For the senior women I spoke with, Bob Dole's erectile dysfunction was not the only Viagra story that existed. The effects of Viagra weren't solely felt by men. Viagra also provided a rare opportunity for women to make sense of their own sexual desires, pleasures, fears, and selves, many times in relation to the Viagra man. For many of the women I spoke with, then, Viagra proved to be an entrée into understanding and discussing their own sexual health.

Bette, an upbeat sixty-nine-year-old, commented that sexual activity is crucial for overall health:

It is important, sex is. You see kitty cats and they are all fat and you know they are not having sex. Really. And it's the same with people. It is a really good calorie burner. My doctor told me to see my gynecologist about Viagra for women. I would, but my SO [significant other] says I don't need a thing. It's chemistry that turns me on, and maybe it takes me longer than when I was younger, but then again, it's all between our ears, isn't it? (Bette, sixty-nine)

For many, Viagra and sexual health are viewed in the context of aging, as in Bette's comment above, where she compares sexuality now to when she was younger. For senior women, like men, Viagra may represent the elusive pursuit of youth. One woman responded to my question, "How has Viagra changed your life?" with, "It has allowed us to enjoy sex again—makes us mentally feel younger." Here sexuality is equated with youth, in a manner reminiscent of the ways in which male consumers of the drug can construct Viagra as a fountain-of-youth pill, enabling them to feel "eighteen again." In contrast, very few of the women I spoke with longed to return to the sexuality of their teenage years. While some would just as soon forget about their sexual pasts, Bette and Pauline volunteer that their "sexual prime" was post-menopause:

With men they say the peak is at nineteen and after that they go down-hill. . . . I think forty-two was my sexual prime. Some women say that menopause is terrible, but I think it was great—not having to worry about pregnancy, just STDs. (Bette, sixty-nine)

Well, menopause made sex less risky for me, and I didn't have to put a diaphragm in every night or interrupt sex for that. The risks were much less, which made it more enjoyable. (Pauline, eighty-one)

Several senior women volunteered that they had been feeling "sexual urges" in recent years. But for Bette and Nora, this desire is mitigated by concerns with appearing "oversexed" or sexual in the context of widowhood, or by frustration with finding a willing and able sexual partner in their age group.

I was appalled that six weeks after my husband died somebody would want to kiss me or I might want to respond because I don't think truthfully that I was what I would call an oversexed woman. I had sexual urges but I never initiated lovemaking too much. And . . . what should I say? I have a friend who had to have a man. Not to sit across a table. But just had to have a man. She needed sex very desperately. It was part of her life to a large extent; without being a nymphomaniac she just needed a man. That's fine but I never had that intense urge because for me there were far more important things in a man than whether or not he could ejaculate. So it's chocolate and vanilla or strawberry and lemon. Who knows? (Nora, seventy-four)

I know that my [male] friend can't take Viagra for health reasons and he's so handsome. He wants all of the young women, and the young women want sex. I'm not trying to be horrible; I think it is frustrating as a young woman to want it and be excited and then frustrated. And vibrators are not the same as men. Right? . . . Each person is their own person. But when a woman needs a man, a vibrator just won't do. She wants companionship. And cuddling. And cuddling gets you hot and bothered sometimes. So you need a man there. (Bette, sixty-nine)

Bette implies that a relationship based on cuddling or self-pleasure with a vibrator is not enough. For her, Viagra may be necessary because sometimes "you need a man," not a surrogate. But actually finding a male partner may be difficult with a "partner gap" that leaves four out of five women seventy-five and older without partners, combined with social trends that lead older men to want to date younger women.[18]

Doris, a witty, practical, sexually active eighty-six-year-old, is similarly vocal about her sexual desires as well as her concerns about the lack of potential sexual partners in her age group. For Doris, men are not necessarily in short supply, but *healthy* male sexual partners are. In her comments below, Doris describes her desire to have a sexual relationship at her age, as opposed to the platonic arrangements she sees her friends having.

Bear in mind that I am eighty-six years old, most of my friends are contemporaries. Most felt that [Viagra] was going to be a real nuisance for the ones who were still dating men, and now would have to deal with this new sexual situation that would be part of their relationship. In many cases, they had a "nice" friendship with men that did not include sex, and as far as they were concerned wanted it to remain that way. They don't seem to be concerned of the health hazards involving sex with men who were dating other women as well as them. . . . [These women are] just not interested in sex. *I was not one of these. I am interested in sex under certain conditions.* Clean bill of health is my number one priority. Protection is right up there with number one, and I don't care if it does sound clinical . . . that's the world I live in. And I have to say that most of the men I have met have been inadequate in performance, so my conditions didn't either enhance or hinder the act. . . . I have about given up on the whole thing. . . . [It's] not worth the effort . . . at least at the moment. I am satisfied to have someone for company at movies, restaurants, concerts, short trips, etc. I find that the older I get, the less sex has to do with my happiness. And since I am financially independent, I really do not need anyone living with me; I can manage my daily life very well, and doing wifely things is not something I would care to do. If things get to be desperate, there is always a vibrator, which is ready to go, providing the batteries are new. Who could ask for more? (Doris, eighty-six, emphasis added)

Unfortunately, Doris's pursuit of pleasure has been thwarted by male partners she has had who cannot "perform," leading her to give up on finding a sexual partner and turn instead to her vibrator for pleasure.

I have gone through at least six men in the past thirteen years since my husband died. The first one talked nothing but sex, and he was certainly handsome, and thought his penis was the most glorious work of art ever created. With a lot of work, we could manage to get it to stand up for a few minutes, but when it came to actually performing, it would collapse at the thought of what it was expected to do. I have a TV in the bedroom, so we got to see a lot of late night TV before going to sleep. Number Two was full of ambition, but impotent in every sense of the word. Also alcoholic, which could explain the impotency. The third man lasted for almost three years, with no sex at all. By that time I had decided that it really wasn't my problem . . . it was theirs . . .

and a friendship was just as good as anything else, since we had other interests in common. And that's the way it has been ever since. I am no longer interested in relationships (whatever that is).

Perhaps these notes of sexual dissatisfaction constitute one reason we never heard from the likes of Elizabeth Dole and the other sexually frustrated partners of senior men. This is the side of the story that Pfizer doesn't talk about—women's desire for sex and men's inability to respond positively to these desires. These comments show the other side of impotency, that is, sexual frustration for women. Again contrary to the ideas about sex that we are used to hearing, these women appear to be the sexual initiators in these relationships.

This reality led me to wonder about the need for a "female Viagra" pill. It should be noted that by the time of these interviews, many articles in women's and mainstream magazines had reported on the search for a "female Viagra." Such articles quoted primarily baby boomer women saying, "If men have Viagra, women need something too." In this context, I asked the senior women I spoke with if they had heard of such efforts to develop a Viagra-like product for women. More than several claimed that such a product could be promising in helping women achieve sexual pleasure.

I do believe that sex is important to have an adequate quality of life. I personally miss the affection and companionship. But I would take a pill to be able to enjoy sex more because my medications may diminish sexual drive. See, life has many aspects and you don't ignore one that will give you pleasure. If I found the right person, I'd try a pill. But I'm probably all dried up and squinched together so I'd have to find a doctor to help me (laughing). (Pauline, eighty-one)

You know, my doctor said jokingly that there's a Viagra for women. And then when I said, "Where do I get it?" he got very embarrassed. I said, "How did you hear about it?" He said some women's magazine. He's a Chinese doctor. But he read about it somewhere . . . I don't know what it is, but I would consider using Viagra even though my SO [significant other] says I don't need it. I can't explain it. It would just make me a bit hotter, I think. (Bette, sixty-nine)

Both Pauline and Bette make it clear that sex is something that they would definitely enjoy and that both would be interested in taking a pill to increase their sexual satisfaction. However, in my conversation with Hilda, it was clear that her interest in such a drug is not necessarily tied to her age but is instead a response to her lifelong lack of fulfillment in her sex life.

> ML: Have you heard about women taking Viagra?
>
> H: I've heard of it. I think it's a good idea. You know, if I had a partner, I think I might have taken it. Because we had a wonderful marriage, but not a wonderful sex life. It was okay. But the ecstasy that people talk about—I have never experienced it . . . I don't think he would've liked me doing that [taking a pill]. . . . At this point in my life, I don't know if I'd chance it. I'm eighty, and I don't want to hasten my, you know. So I might think twice about it.
>
> ML: What would be your ideal drug?
>
> H: I'd want to experience what I've read about. The ecstasy.
>
> ML: Do you mean libido? Orgasm?
>
> H: Yes. I have two friends who make reference to the fact that they have had wonderful sex lives. They are both widows. And both very unusual for my generation since they've had more than one partner. One told me that she never experienced with her husband what she had with another man. So maybe some guys do it better than others. I wouldn't know—I've only had one. And this is the way I'm going to finish. (Hilda, eighty)

Hilda's comments illustrate one of the key differences between male and female desire for Viagra, or a Viagra-like drug: while men may need the drug to help them continue their sexual pleasure, women may want the drug to discover theirs for the first time. In a positive sense, then, the public discussions of Viagra clearly have enabled some women to openly discuss their sex lives, for better or worse, and to ask their own doctors for solutions. Still, these women are also aware that sexuality exists in relation to the medication they and their partners take (with a growing list of side effects that require other medications to balance them out) and that there are often trade-offs between sex and health. Particularly for Hilda, the promise of sexual fulfillment and enhancement is tempered by the risk of "chancing it," or "hastening" death, an issue that male consumers, particularly those with Viagra risk factors, must negotiate as well. Hilda and Pauline conflate sexual hopes with health risks, unable to separate the two. For them, sexuality occurs against a backdrop of continuous aging and health concerns. Additionally, this bleeding together of promise and risk discourses is relatively common, revealing women's confusions about what Viagra can offer in the realms of sexuality, health, and aging.[19] Finally, for Bette and Hilda, consumption of a Viagra-like product would take place in the context of a relationship, where husbands or boyfriends may "disapprove," which would clearly complicate and constrain their choices.

While some of the women discussed fears for their own health in relation to a Viagra-like drug, they clearly had concerns about men and Viagra. Below, Hilda, Nora, and Doris evaluate the health risks for male Viagra users in light of what they view as male desire for potency:

I would have wanted my husband to take it for his own sake. I doubt that he would have. I don't know what will happen with the Viagra. What kinds of side effects . . . Haven't people been dropping dead from it? I would have suggested it for his own self. I'm sitting here looking at his picture while we are talking. He never would have taken it, I'm sure. (Hilda, eighty)

You have to be so careful with meds because of the side effects. Especially with the Viagra, I understand that if men are on nitrates, they can't take it. Who would want a man to have a heart attack in the middle of enjoying sex? (Nora, seventy-four)

As for my thoughts about taking medication for sexual prowess, I can see that it might be a useful tool for younger people with a problem. As for older men, especially with Viagra, which has a spotty medical history at best, with heart attacks and sudden death as some of the side effects, I think it is unacceptable. My own feeling is that it is not all that safe, and if I were a man I would not take it. It was not originally invented for this use anyway . . . I think it was for hypertension or something. . . . Having said that, I also know that some men would risk anything to prove how manly they are. (Doris, eighty-six)

Like most Americans, Hilda, Nora, and Doris have been exposed to media reports warning that if taken in the wrong circumstances, Viagra can be fatal.[20] (As discussed earlier, Viagra is unsafe for men with heart conditions but is not a health risk for most men.) Despite such warnings, each woman balances potential for physical risk with potential for masculine potency, something they felt their husbands greatly desired. If Hilda's husband hadn't died, she says she would have tried talking him into taking Viagra "for his own sake," for emotional reasons, despite the fact that "people have been dropping dead." Nora and Doris find this a dangerous balancing act with ramifications for men and women. Nora is concerned about having a male partner die during lovemaking. Doris also highlights the risks for older men but concedes that "some men would risk anything to prove how manly they are."

While Viagra encourages discussions of individual health, it may also prove to be a risk to the health of senior communities. For example, there has been much recent concern about increased sexual activity among older people leading to the spread of HIV in senior communities.[21] Because of the newfound attention on sexually active seniors, as well as recently launched "preventative" efforts, I was not surprised to find seniors discussing the spread of HIV in their communities. Below is an excerpt from a large-group discussion between the women enrolled in the seniors-only summer education program (SW) and myself (ML), about Viagra and its social implications for senior communities:

ML: Do you agree that seniors are more sexually active than ever? (Some heads nod.)

SW: At a Barnes & Noble presentation, they gave out condoms to the seniors and told them to be careful.

SW: The HIV is coming from widowers who aren't ready to give up sex and so they find prostitutes. Those are the ones spreading HIV among seniors!

Above, senior male Viagra users are seen as the disease carriers and are thus blamed for rendering senior communities at risk. Interestingly, prostitutes are not to blame; instead, it is members of the senior community who are at fault. These women express concern that senior men are more sexually active than ever in the Viagra era—an assumption that, as Agnus pointed out earlier, may be based on increased discussion of sex and aging rather than actual increased behavior. In addition, sexual activity and desire is publicly equated with the widowers in the community, further reinforcing gendered stereotypes of women as asexual or sexually passive and men as (out-of-control) sexual initiators. As we've seen in earlier comments, such stereotypes do not always prove to be true.

Wifely Duty

Men's sexual desires can be threatening in the senior community as well as in the home. Two anonymous senior women suggested that the introduction of Viagra resulted in sexually rejuvenated husbands and unprepared, sometimes fearful, wives.

> I would wonder how many women are relieved that their active sex lives are over, and are petrified that their mates will take Viagra.

> It [Viagra] has rejuvenated some men—women are not prepared.

The second most common response by senior women to my survey question, "How has Viagra affected seniors' lives?" was to emphasize danger over pleasure—to express concern about Viagra as a potential risk to women's emotional health in the context of a relationship. In this section I quote women who talk about Viagra in the context of (changing) marital and sexual arrangements and obligations. Specifically, they use Viagra to critique and respond to traditional marriage scripts and ideas about marital duty.

Two months after Viagra's debut, Jane Brody, writing for the *New York Times*, reported on "Facing Viagra's Emotional Ripples," describing the way Viagra has contributed to exposing marital conflicts that otherwise might have remained buried.[22] This article was written in response to an article published earlier that month in the *New York Times* entitled, "Some Couples May Find Viagra a Home Wrecker." This piece emphasized the risk Viagra represents for the health of the married couple, including "devastating side-effects on relationships" such as new sexual pressures sometimes leading to divorce and extramarital affairs. Whether Viagra represents hope or danger, the existence of such a product, and the increased sexual pressures that follow its use, raise new concerns for women regarding marital obligation and sexual duty. Below, Bette discusses Viagra in the context of what she sees as a woman's obligation to please her man.

> My SO [significant other], he uses Viagra, and you know, we are not sex maniacs, but we do enjoy this. And he's such a nice person. I'd never tell him no. Sometimes you have to give a little, when you know what they want. But once or twice he's seen blue lights, and that is a little bit of a problem. But I think it really does help for the man. It must make him feel so great to be able to hold an erection. And you know the woman has something to do with it too . . . I'm learning so much about men now. Sex was so taboo when we were younger. But now I'm learning so much. I talk about it all the time. Talk to my SO. See, life is about sharing and socializing. It's not necessarily about sex or not. But you do have to put in a little bit of effort in terms of what men want to do. (Bette, sixty-nine)

Similarly, Annette points out that women will "go along with it" in the context of a good relationship; otherwise, they may wonder why they should bother. Several years after Viagra's debut, some women are now finally communicating their disinterest in sex.

> A: For men, it's a put-down if they can't have an erection. Women can simulate it and if they are happy with their man, they'll go with it even when it's not the height of enjoyment. They'll do it to make their husbands or lovers happy. You know, as the jokes wore off you were able to have a more serious discussion related to Viagra. So you're getting to feelings now which [women] didn't dare express before. I don't have this type of conversation amongst men, unfortunately. But I do discuss this with women. Now they are looking at it more realistically than when it came out. They were ashamed. Too many years of being ashamed if they weren't a

willing hot sex partner. But—now it is coming out that they could
live without it.

ML: You mean sex is not a priority?

A: Not in the older age group. (Annette, eighty-one)

How far does one have to go to make a husband happy in the Viagra
era? Concerns about "pleasing one's man" have surfaced, not only in
interview transcripts but also, more visibly, in advice columns.

Confusion about a woman's sexual duty to her husband in the Viagra era led at least three women to write to Ann Landers for advice
in 1998. In each of these letters, these sixty-something female authors
express concern about their husbands using Viagra, stating that they
are "tired" and uninterested in sex. Despite their strong stances on not
wanting their husbands to take Viagra, these women are hesitant to
bring their concerns to their husbands as doing so is contrary to what
they have been taught about marital obligation. These two women
suggest that they have "earned a rest," and then ask for Ann's comments.[23]

Dear Ann: I am 62 years old and the mother of six grown children,
and I was thrilled when my 64 year old husband began to slow down
(if you catch my drift) about two years ago. I never was crazy about
sex, but being from the old school, I listened to my mother. She said
a woman should never refuse her husband because if he isn't taken
care of at home, he will look elsewhere. . . . So now what happens? A
pill called Viagra is invented and the old goat is back in the saddle
again. I do love my husband, Ann, but I believe I have earned a rest.
Besides, these pills cost $10 each. Last week he took four. Do you
have any advice on this subject? I would like to hear it, and I'll bet
thousands of other women would too. (Nameless in Ohio, June 14,
1998)

Dear Ann: My husband (age 68) got all excited when he read about
that Viagra pill. He has been dead as a doornail for five years. His doctor said it would be OK for him to take the pill, but not to expect mir-
acles. Well, so far nothing has changed regarding his "condition" but
he is wearing me out trying to prove that he is a frisky young colt
again. Please tell those smart-aleck scientists and those big drug companies to work on a cure for cancer instead and quit ruining the lives

of millions of women who have earned a rest. Thank you. (No Name in Abilene, Kansas, June 14, 1998)

Finally, a very similar letter appeared in Ann Landers's column the following month from a sixty-four-year-old woman who reports that when her husband's sex drive began to diminish two years ago, she was relieved. She continues,

> Now comes this "wonder drug" called Viagra, and my husband has informed me that he has talked it over with his doctor who knows of no reason why my husband shouldn't take it. Well, I know of a reason. I've made it clear that the minute he walks into the house with those pills, I am walking out. I bet you have received a lot of letters from women who feel like I do. (Nameless in Philadelphia, July 13, 1998)

In these letters Viagra is constructed as a "wonder drug" that turns inactive husbands into sexualized animals (an "old goat" into a "frisky young colt"), leaving their wives frustrated and "worn out." While their husbands may embrace Viagra's promise, these wives see only risk in buying into frivolous scientific solutions and expensive drugs. All three wives imagine that they are not alone in their hesitation about Viagra's role in their marriage. Their letters may be motivated by desire for emotional support from Ann Landers, but it is Landers's female readership that the authors seem most interested in engaging in a dialogue. Rather than hanging their heads in shame, the authors see their letters as potentially reaching thousands, and they use their personal troubles to invite other "tired" women (like them) to make themselves known, insisting that such a community exists.

Landers responded consistently to all three in a detached way, avoiding the question of marital duty. Bypassing these women's concerns and complaints, Landers responds with positive accounts regarding Viagra use and warnings about Viagra's health-related side effects.

> Dear Nameless in Ohio: I have already received a ton of mail about Viagra. Most of the readers are calling it a "godsend" while about one-fourth of those writing say they wish their husbands had never heard of the drug. . . . The pill is enjoying widespread acceptance but this

miracle drug may have some [health-related side effects], so, my friends, beware.

Dear Abilene: You told 'em but don't be surprised if nobody listens. While you may or may not be thrilled with your husband's renewed interest in sex, let me assure you that a great many women are grateful for Viagra and have written to say so.

Dear Philadelphia: I have heard from a great many women about Viagra, and although some feel as you do, most say it is wonderful. . . . It all boils down to how a woman feels about her man. If she loves him and wants him to enjoy the ultimate in marital bliss, she will be happy that there is now a drug that can help him recapture the sexual energy of his younger years. But beware, there is a downside. My medical consultants say Viagra could be risky for men who are taking medication for high blood pressure or heart problems. It may possibly be linked to the recent deaths of several men who took Viagra along with their nitroglycerin. My advice is to consult your doctor.

By avoiding the marital concerns raised by a minority of her letter writers, Landers focuses on the Viagra-as-miracle and medical-danger stories supported by the mainstream media. In the process, she reinforces the idea of duty associated with marital love. In the final letter to Philadelphia, Landers espouses her own beliefs on marital duty, upholding the idea that love for a husband requires helping *him* enjoy the ultimate in marital bliss. Landers seems most interested in helping these Viagra wives attain happiness or relief through pleasing their husbands. The "downside" here is not the erasure of women's sexual desires but the health-related risks for the man.

Despite Landers's traditional views on marital love and obligation, and the thousands of letters that seem to agree with these views and the promise of Viagra, an almost equal number of letters written to advice columnists in general reveal a letter-writing movement made up of Viagra wives opposed to Viagra and what it represents—women collectively rethinking marriage, male potency, and traditional gender roles in the Viagra era. In September of 1998 *Dear Abby,* another major national advice column, posted this letter from a female baby boomer, which ends in a call for honest data on how women are feeling about sexual duty.

> Dear Abby: My husband is of the opinion that if a woman doesn't enjoy sex right up to the grave, there must be something wrong with her. At age 50, after 30 years of marriage, I would like to forget sex altogether. Believe me, I've paid my dues. Where is it written that a woman should be ready and willing to perform every time her man beckons? I suspect that many women just go through the motions because they want to do something for the men they love. I can't believe I'm the only woman who feels this way. Please poll your readers, Abby. If they are honest, I think you will find that I am right. (Tired in Lincoln, NE, September 1998)

> Dear Tired:
> I invited women to send me an anonymous postcard stating whether they agreed or disagreed with Tired. Here were the results:
> Agreed 114,005
> Disagreed 113,601

The responses *Dear Abby* reports reveal how salient the issue of duty must be for women in the Viagra era. In stark contrast to Viagra-related pleasure as modeled in Pfizer promotional materials (revealing happy heterosexual couples dancing and touching), hundreds of thousands of women are writing in to their local papers to talk back to products like Viagra—which can exacerbate various social pressures to be sexual—insisting that they are "tired," they have "earned a rest," and they have "done their duty."

Saying no to marital obligation has many possible outcomes. For some, it means ending a marriage. For others, it means negotiation:

> I know some women stop sleeping in the same bed with their husbands. But obviously there was no longer a desire or a need. These women, if they ever encountered a husband who suddenly woke up and said, "Here I am and I can do this," they find that they don't want to. It's everybody's right to say "yes I do" or "no I don't." If they feel strongly about the relationship, they'd probably hang in there. (Sally, seventy-five)

And in extreme cases, forced sexual obligation may lead to murder, as explained by the editor of *Ladies Home Journal* in a comment on public television's talk show *To the Contrary* (2002). According to this magazine editor, some Viagra wives "aren't so thrilled" with their husbands' newfound potency, pointing to the case of the "New York woman who shot her husband after he used Viagra and forced her to play along."

Sexualized Masculinity

While women may disagree about whether Viagra represents for them sexual pleasure or danger, most agree that Viagra cannot be disentangled from masculinity. In interviews and anonymous surveys, women commonly discuss Viagra in regard to men wanting to achieve confidence, youth, vibrancy, and normalcy. Below, anonymous female respondents to my survey comment on the promise of Viagra for the "old guys."

> Viagra restores feelings of normalcy and confidence, I think—
> Bob Dole claims he has benefited from it.
> It gave the old guys a chance for their last hurrah.

In contrast to these empathetic voices, some senior women have been openly resistant to the efforts that scientists and pharmaceutical companies have made to promote male virility, as revealed in the letter to the editor highlighted at the beginning of this chapter. Whether women draw on humor, empathy, or anger, most agree that Viagra, from the very beginning, was about promoting a kind of sexualized (youthful) masculinity. Widows Pauline and Doris and divorcée Bette all laughed as they recalled when and what they first heard about Viagra. For them, Viagra creates a perfect caricature of sexually out-of-control men.

> ML: What did you hear about Viagra?
> P: That it makes you want to have sex if you are older. As a matter
>   of fact, there was even a sitcom, *Mad about You*, where he had
>   taken a Viagra and he was running around trying to connect

with her. The idea is, it makes you have the urges and the erection and it lasts supposedly longer or certainly more frequent. And that was what I heard. I think that *Mad about You* probably helped to popularize it even more. That was a great program. (Pauline, eighty-one)

Oh, it was back in 1998. Wasn't it Bob Dole that was using it? Going up and down in the tulip pastures! With the little blue pill. And my friends were the first people I knew who used it. Funny, we used to joke, twenty years ago, one of my friends would say, "I'll come out with you unless something comes up." And that wasn't about Viagra—it was about chemistry then! (Bette, sixty-nine)

The first time I heard about Viagra, it did not have a name. . . . We have a female talk show host in Florida who I listened to on the car radio practically daily, since she was on from one to three o'clock and ordinarily I would be going shopping or doing my volunteer work, and about three years ago, she started talking about this new drug that could be taken any time by men, and would give them arousal and erection. I almost went off the road into a tree when I had this mental image of all those men leaving work at five o'clock, taking their pill, and having an erection on the way home, timing it to be most effective. Just thinking of all those cars with men and their penises pointing north even now gives me a chuckle. (Doris, eighty-six)

By mixing advertising and television images with humor and stereotypes, Bette, Pauline, and Doris, all sexually active seniors, associate Viagra with a particular performance of sexualized masculinity that paints a picture of masses of men led by their erect penises, or as sexualized Bob Doles. Such associations fit nicely with common, yet potentially damaging, cultural expectations about sexually unrestrained men.

At times during our conversations, Viagra humor turned serious when senior women discussed their male peers empathetically as vulnerable victims who need Viagra, or mockingly as desperate, ego-driven individuals who think they need Viagra. Below, Agnus, Pauline, and Bette try to imagine what it feels like for a man to suffer from impotence. Agnus says her friend uses Viagra to feel "complete" again:

He told me, "You can't understand how it makes a man feel." When he can't perform he said it makes him feel like not a whole man. Once he started using the Viagra . . . he feels like a whole man again. (Agnus, sixty-seven)

Pauline compares the loss of penile functioning for men to loss of a breast for women, a comparison that several of my male interview subjects made as well.

I had a breast lump when I was fifty-five years of age. And I was hysterical because I didn't know what that lump was and I said if I get my breast removed, you won't love me anymore. I think that woman have a very keen sense of breast importance to their bodies. And I think that the breast is very important emotionally to a woman. . . . The same thing is true when a man has prostate surgery and so frequently men become impotent. . . . I think that the male feels that that organ's function is very important to his machoism, or whatever you want to call it. That is why Viagra has become so important to the male mentality. (Pauline, eighty-one)

And Bette sees manhood as continually tested by history, with impotence as yet another test of male success.

When you think and read about U.S. history—what these men have gone through. Korean War, Vietnam, or World War II, they have had these experiences and have sustained injuries too. I guess when they are at the height of passion they don't want to worry about failing. That's what it's about, as I see it. But it is kinda sad too. What do they call that where they can't control their bladder? I met a guy at a dance who peed in his pants. It really is sad—so few men around and the ones who are around, they may have these problems. So what do you do? You really can only have conversations or kiss. But the women who want the passion—that's hard to find. (Bette, sixty-nine)

While some women empathize with men and their need for Viagra, other women construct male Viagra consumers as ego-driven, desperate, and penis centered. In this way Nora, Annette, and Doris use Viagra as an opportunity to mock masculinity.

The jokes [my girlfriends tell are] usually are of the men-bashing variety, like the one about the man on Viagra who died and they had trouble putting the lid down on the coffin . . . and most of them said they would contribute to a pharmaceutical research company that would find an antidote to Viagra. (Doris, eighty-six)

Men feel so much of their manhood is involved in sex. And if they can't perform they just are devastated. They can't hide it like a woman can fake an orgasm. So that's my thinking. . . . [But] some of the lengths that a man would go to maintain an erection is amazing. Like that pump thing. I don't know how anyone could have a pleasurable encounter by pumping it up. For me that would be a terrible turn-off. But it is very important for a man. (Nora, seventy-four)

A: It's a very ego-building thing to have an erection when you aren't able to have one. The dating men think that if they can produce an erection, the women will think he's great stuff—more macho. You know. It's an ego thing with men.
ML: You mean it is about confidence, masculinity, youth . . . ?
A: Well, that's all part of ego. They want to show off that they are young enough. (Annette, eighty-one)

Among the older population, impotency is very real, and since men judge their success in life by the activity of their penises, you can see how they would drink hemlock if it gave them an orgasm. (Doris, eighty-six)

Together, these senior women explain Viagra's popularity among men by focusing on the importance of masculinity. For Leonora, Annette, and Doris, Viagra exposes men as needing to be "macho," wanting to "show off," and going to "great lengths" to produce and maintain erections. While each woman projects different motives for men using Viagra, most agree that Viagra's success is due to male vulnerability and insecurity and the perceived role of sexuality in proving one's masculinity. This characterization certainly matches up with the earlier comments made by the male users of Viagra. In this sense, one can see why Pfizer would repeatedly choose to sponsor male sporting events like car races or baseball games.

Sex and Culture

While most seem to agree that Viagra produces and reinforces sexual-ized masculinities, some of the women I spoke with located Viagra and sexualized men under a larger umbrella representing potentially dan-gerous, large-scale cultural changes that affect everyone. Like some of the men highlighted in chapter 2, some senior women see Viagra as rep-resentative of a quick-fix pill culture. However, unlike the males I spoke with, the senior women conflate this culture with heightened emphasis on sexuality and the sexual fix. In this way, senior women associate the increasingly sexualized culture they live in with an overemphasis on masculine ideals. As a result, sex is used to demonstrate physicality and efficiency rather than romance and feelings.

> Let me tell you my objection to Viagra. Number one, the whole sex act has become more physical than emotional. All of that preparation an hour in advance, it makes sex not grow out of a loving feeling. It be-comes planned and purely physical. And I just don't like that. The whole idea of sex has become so physical. Such gymnastics involved! And while I'm not opposed to experimentation and variety—not at all—it's become only that. The love is missing. The affection! (Annette, eighty-one)

> When I was growing up, sex wasn't something you admitted you en-joyed. There's a lot of change in the generations. As to what was talked about, known. Today it is almost too open. Today they don't leave any-thing to the imagination. Some of it is charming when it isn't all re-vealed. (Nora, seventy-four)

Annette and Nora both construct stories about how American cul-tural norms and sex roles are changing in dangerous ways in the Viagra era. For them, Viagra is the instigator of, or the scapegoat for, changing sexual norms. Nora links this cultural change to a generational shift in sexual discourse, which is "too open" today, leaving no sexual mys-tique. Concurrently, Viagra is to blame for an increasingly sexualized culture that promotes promiscuity:

> I don't look down on sex outside of marriage. I just think sex is too commonplace today. It would be very hard to be celibate today. It is

thrown at people from every which way. And it is idealized on the TV and in movies as perfect and acceptable. And it's just not that way in real life. I'm glad I'm not raising kids right now. They have sex younger and younger and they don't know what they are doing. (Leonora, seventy-four)

The culture is teaching younger women that a violent physical sex act is part of them. And if they feel that is what they want, they will look to the pill to give it to them. And maybe it will, I don't know. But for older people, if they don't have a loving relationship, of which sex is an outgrowth, I don't think they are interested in the pill. . . . It satisfies a man to have an erection and perform. It doesn't satisfy a woman because all of that other stuff—the loving stuff—is missing. (Annette, eighty-one)

Viagra itself is not the only factor to blame in a culture dangerously focused on the sexual fix. Below, Nora mentions women's movements as central in the increasing masculinization of sexuality in society, leading women to act too much like men and ignore romance, intimacy, and emotions:

Today a lot of the romance and closeness has been eliminated from our culture because of women's liberation. Not that women shouldn't be [as] entitled to enjoy sex as a man, but it's different. There is too much promiscuousness. I don't think you have to sleep with somebody every time you go out on a date. I think we've lost some respect for the sanctity. I don't say people shouldn't live together, I'm not a prude, but I just think that sleeping around has become sort of commonplace. It is bad emotionally for women, especially. It has changed men's view of women. And I also think it's a danger as far as pregnancy and contracting sexually transmitted diseases. There it is in a nutshell. (Nora, seventy-four)

A move towards masculine sexual ideals is also implied by Agnus:

What is important to me is being in love. I wouldn't be with someone just for the sex. This is a woman's point of view. That love and affection are more important than sex. A man would say the opposite. That sex is most important. (Agnus, sixty-seven)

Together Agnus, Annette, and Nora blame Viagra for promoting new, problematic cultural expectations and pressures related to sexuality. They construct women's sexuality as emotional, mysterious, and romantic, as opposed to a male sexuality that is nonemotional and physical. With Viagra, and larger social forces such as women's liberation, these senior women claim that masculine sexuality has set new and dangerous standards for women and society.

Despite the cultural shift towards masculine ideals and sexual pressures, Sally, Annette, Doris, and Hilda agree with the men quoted in chapter 2 who suggest that Viagra is representative of a problematic quick-fix pill culture, where a drug exists as a solution to every problem or as an enhancement to every lifestyle. What these women contribute to the conversation is a sense of being caught in a pill culture that both promotes and benefits from people's limited tolerance for personal discomfort, as well as excludes people who cannot afford these solutions.

> My feeling is that if Robert Redford wants to come get me, and needs Viagra—what an evil thought—I would get some for him. But on a serious note, no, I do not believe in the pill being the answer to sexual problems. Today we have pills for everything . . . It seems to be a cultural thing now. (Doris, eighty-six)

> My age group and younger—they are taking so many pills it's incredible. In the first place, they cost a fortune. All the new pills cost more than most people can afford. They invest more in pills than they would in a lifestyle that will make them happier. We're too much a pill culture. (Annette, eighty-one)

> The only thing that bothers me about this when I hear about all of these wonderful opportunities is the price. I think the price is going to leave even the middle classes behind. The insurance companies may not want to pay for some of these high-priced wonders. But I do think that the rich will have a greater advantage in all of these things. (Sally, seventy-five)

> People's tolerance levels are really low. If it hurts, go get a pill. I'm not like that. I figure you should fight it. Like here at the pool, I tell peo-

ple with arthritis to go in the pool, because water is good for it. But they'd rather take a pill. I wouldn't. It's too easy to take a pill. Even a diet pill. They'd rather take a diet pill than go to a gym. (Hilda, eighty)

In general Doris, Annette, Sally, Hilda, and others are using Viagra to construct and critique changing cultural norms and values. Problems associated with the Viagra era include harmful sexual norms and expectations, prohibitively expensive prescriptions, a quick-fix ethic, and an underemphasis on romance and emotions. In this way, senior women storytellers suggest, Viagra offers more harm than good for women, particularly when it comes to sexuality and relationships.

What Do Women Want?

In the rush to praise and hype Viagra, most of us tend to forget about, or simplify, the "other side" of the Viagra story. But women have much to say about Viagra, and their voices are worth listening to. Much like the male voices quoted in chapter 2, women quoted in this chapter reveal complex sexual identities, desires, and fears. This "messy" side of sex and sexuality, for both men and women, is repeatedly obscured, simplified, or ignored by scientists, journalists, and marketers. The women whose voices are heard in this chapter want us to question cultural expectations, as well as to question a cultural phenomenon that ends up reinforcing ideas about sexuality conflated with manhood and male desires.

This book began with the men who first "discovered," promoted, and used Viagra. At the opposite end of the sexual spectrum, it is assumed, are the senior women whose sexual lives are largely avoided or unacknowledged in discussions about Viagra. But are these women really that different from the men behind Viagra's popularity? As they suggest, all of us exist in the same culture, share similar values, and actively reinforce or renounce sexual norms and expectations. These women remind us that just as everyone is a product of this culture, all of us have complex and conflicting ideas and feelings about sexuality in the Viagra era. Women are caught up in the social realities of our time—including medicalization, oppression on the basis of gender and sexuality, and increased commercialization—perhaps even to a larger degree than men. In addition, whether taking a pill or talking about our desires, all of us are sexual agents, actively defining sexuality in our own lives.

For all of these reasons, women's responses to the Viagra phenomenon should *matter* to those who prescribe, market, and comment on Viagra and like products; to those who use products like Viagra; and to those who write about the meanings associated with Viagra in people's everyday lives. After all, for male consumers, doctors, and marketers, the "success" of Viagra is bound up in their wives' and partners' responses to the pill. By the same token, easing, or at least acknowledging, women's concerns regarding Viagra may lead to great strides in everything from marriages to marketing. Interestingly, five years after Viagra's debut, recent drug competitors appear to be starting to take seriously the role of wives and partners as integral to drug success. But this is the case only because recent studies show that Viagra and similar products are not as successful as they could be.

Talking to these women really opened my eyes. I knew that women had responses to the Viagra phenomenon, but I never imagined how rich, varied, and self-aware these responses might be, particularly from a group of women largely without sexual partners. Just like the men, these women wanted to know if they were normal for having desires, fears, and doubts related to sexuality, marriage, and health. But unlike the men, these women didn't have much to lose. Not having current sexual partners seemed to free them up to be able to reflect on their sexual lives, and even to make plans for the future.

What I have found the most shocking during the course of this research were the comments I heard regularly from doctors, comedians, and even Viagra users in midlife saying that the thought of their parents or their patients having sex disgusted them. Culturally, we have much further to go to ensure that *all* human beings, and women in particular, are recognized as sexual beings with desires and fears. At the same time, we should be very careful not to see an inactive sex life as a sign of dying, or vice versa.

In this chapter we have explored how senior women struggle to make sense of gender, sexuality, and health in their daily lives, a process that remains private and unexplored in public discourse. Another type of sense making that occurs behind the scenes involves the activities of experts, critics, and marketers engaged in their own mean-ing-making processes. In the next chapter, medical experts and mar-keters turn to the "broken" female body and find that the repair process is not so simple, especially when it is unclear what, exactly, is broken.

Reprinted by permission from *Newsweek*. © 2000 Newsweek, Inc.
All rights reserved.

5
The Search for the Female Viagra

IN EARLY 2001, OPRAH WINFREY hosted two popular shows on the topic "Why Women Aren't in the Mood." These shows featured the attractive Berman sisters, Jennifer and Laura, a urologist and a psychologist from Irwin Goldstein's Boston University research group and new codirectors of a sexual dysfunction clinic in southern California.[1] Here's how Oprah opened the show:

> This is big, big, *big* stuff. When we first talked about this silent epidemic nine months ago, the response was overwhelming. We got thousands of letters from so many of you who have lost your desire for sex and realized, by watching the show, that you are not alone. Today we're going to tell you about some ground-breaking treatments that are finally providing some answers for the millions of women suffering in silence. We will take you inside a cutting-edge medical center in Los Angeles, where with the help of elaborate testing, women, *women,* are finally getting some solutions to their sexual problems.[2]

The show featured a twenty-something African-American woman complaining of "lack of desire for her husband." The Berman sisters walked this woman through an extensive medical and psychological examination at their Los Angeles clinic, and diagnosed her with a form of FSD, or female sexual dysfunction.[3]

Oprah was not the first to pick up on this story. Immediately after Viagra's "blockbuster" debut, many wondered if the little blue pill would work for women. Journalists and comedians reported that middle-aged wives of Viagra users were now asking, "Where is my magic pill?" Countless newspapers and magazines ran stories introducing Viagra for men, followed with the question, "Will it work for women too?"[4] Amid this curiosity, hundreds of women nationwide volunteered for Viagra clinical trials. *JAMA* shockingly reported, "sexual dysfunction is more prevalent in women (43%) than in men (31%)."[5] Many pharmaceutical companies, including Pfizer, rushed to cash in on the female market, setting up new research and clinical trials.

Years before Oprah's show, we had entered into what I call phase two of the Viagra phenomenon, or the rise of the female corollary to ED, FSD. With Viagra's blockbuster debut, the idea of finding a way to treat the "other half" of the sexually dysfunctional, and presumably heterosexual, couple, got underway with a bang and is continuing to this day. Sexual medicine clinics, such as the one the Berman sisters run in Los Angeles, are welcoming sexually dissatisfied female patients in droves. Numerous creams, devices, and lotions are in the pipeline awaiting FDA approval.[6] Avlimil, which is marketed as a "libido pill" and an alternative to hormone replacement therapy, is a fast-selling over-the-counter daily supplement for FSD that can be used for the mildest of conditions, including "a slight decrease in desire." Popular women's magazines like *Cosmopolitan* and *Vogue* feature stories on FSD.

In many ways, the rise of FSD is similar to that of ED.[7] FSD can be understood as a social phenomenon that continues to be defined, used, and critiqued by a host of experts who have stakes in this medical category, including basic scientists,[8] gynecologists, urologists, psychologists, marketers, and feminists. The key similarity is that FSD is a *medical* diagnosis, signaling that both the problem and the treatment must be focused on the woman's body. FSD, like ED, is a case of what I would call "diagnostic expansion," whereby an older diagnosis, frigidity, gets broadened to include a wider spectrum of sexual problems and concerns. However, unlike the case of ED, defining and treating sexual problems in women is proving to be slow paced, complicated, and controversial.

In this chapter, my underlying questions are as follows. Will women truly benefit from the search for the female Viagra? Will they benefit from their inclusion in sexual science, and the increased popular and medical attention paid to women's sexual arousal, desire, orgasm, and pain? How could they not, right? The answers are not as simple and perhaps not as optimistic as they first may seem. As many scholars have shown, women have historically been man-handled, quite literally, by Western medicine. History shows that women's bodies, seen as deviant and abnormal by men in power, have long been subjects of medical surveillance and control.[9] "Hysteria," "nymphomania," and "frigidity" were widely used in the modern era to label primarily middle- and upper-class women as "sick." Women have often been used as medical guinea pigs, test subjects for early harmful and even fatal medical treatments such as abortions, birth control pills, fertility drugs (thalidomide), breast cancer treatments (tamoxifen), and hormone replacement. Women (and men) of color have been and continue to be medical test subjects, many times without their knowledge and at great risk to their health.[10] Today, every aspect of a woman's life cycle has been medicalized—from birth to menstruation to childbirth to menopause to death—revealing a growing dependence on medicine that some say is risky and excessive.[11] On the other hand, some would argue that such medical solutions have empowered and enabled women in important ways, for example, in the areas of reproductive control, pain relief, and depression management. Given women's complex historical relationship to medicine, this chapter explores how medical experts have very recently attempted to make sense of women's sexual problems in the Viagra era.

The Rise of FSD

The Boston Forum is a perfect site for tracking the rise of FSD.[12] The 1999 Boston Forum meeting was the first large-scale FSD-themed conference of its kind,[13] organized by urologist and ED researcher Irwin Goldstein.[14] By the time of Viagra's debut, Dr. Goldstein was also a major figure in the classification and commercialization of FSD, having researched and written widely about new medical categories of sexual dysfunction for both men and women. Around the time when Pfizer's Viagra was approved by the FDA and released to the public, Goldstein and other Pfizer-funded physicians penned a variety of scientific articles and granted a large number of interviews claiming that 30–50 percent of men and women in America have "organic sexual dysfunction." By 1999, Goldstein had published so widely in medical and urological journals such as the *Urology Times*, the *New England Journal of Medicine*, and *JAMA*[15] that he was anointed "FSD expert" by countless mainstream publications, including *Time*, *Playboy*, and *Fortune*.[16]

In 1999 Goldstein began convening a so-called multidisciplinary group of about five hundred practitioners, clinicians, scientists, and pharmaceutical representatives who congregate in Boston annually, near the site of Boston University's medical school and sexual dysfunction clinics, to learn and share "the latest" in FSD. These meetings are the most influential scientific conferences concerning the overall understanding of FSD and have had a great deal of sway over how the scientific and medical community has come to regard women's sexual problems. I attended these four-day Boston meetings for three consecutive years, from 1999 to 2001, eager to understand how women's sexuality and sexual problems were being understood by the "experts."[17] In many ways, what happened at these meetings explains why the search for the female Viagra is still mired in confusion.

While I refer to the meetings as the Boston Forums, it is important to point out that the name has changed slightly every year. What hasn't changed over the years is the subtitle of these gatherings, which is highlighted on the annual conference program: "New Perspectives in the Management of Female Sexual Dysfunction." This subtitle reveals the "management," or treatment-oriented objectives of the meeting, which may or may not require some basic understanding of "sexual function."[18] As Goldstein told me, after the introduction of Viagra, "We work backwards, we expect a treatment for things." This emphasis on treatment-based science is made even more obvious if one acknowledges the role of the pharmaceutical industry in subsidizing the meetings as well as the research. As I will argue, their "pharmaceutical agenda"—that is, their need to find drug treatments for problems—inevitably fuels the construction of women's sexual issues as medical problems.

The Players

Understanding how these meetings operate requires recognizing the four overlapping groups of "players" that make the Boston Forum what it is. The four groups include "experts" on FSD, marketers, critics, and journalists.[19] Importantly, the "experts," or so-called Boston Forum grandmasters, are the primary FSD visionaries. They attend various medical meetings, publish in the medical journals, and are the "experts" appearing in or being quoted by the popular media. As in the case of ED, however, many of them have close ties to the pharmaceutical industry as consultants, investigators, and/or stockholders. Because of the recent influx of funding, some have even been able to make a career out of sexual medicine, as is the case with the members of Goldstein's Boston University group. For these experts, "grandmastering" and publishing are the activities that characterize their knowledge production and enable them to reach large audiences.

Marketers are those affiliated with the pharmaceutical industry. Because the Boston Forums are pharmaceutical-industry-sponsored events, companies such as Pfizer, Eli Lilly, Shering-Plough, Solvay Pharmaceuticals, and others provide the funding for the meetings (in the form of educational grants). Most are eager to support research in this area and promote their products at this venue, both in the display area and at the podium, where one can find numerous presentations by industry-affiliated researchers. Thus there is a crucial overlap between the "experts" and the marketers. Since grandmasters are not required to disclose their relationships with pharmaceutical companies during conference presentations, the industry presence and the overlap between marketers and experts is rather covert.[20] For example, I was not aware of this overlap until at one point in the 1999 conference, when an FDA presenter asked who in the audience was NOT an "industry person" and about half of the people in the room kept their hands down—a clear sign that participation in the meeting was linked to industry goals. This close relationship between science and corporate interests raises important questions regarding the nature of and motivation for the scientific claims of FSD.

Critics—specifically a feminist group of health advocates, academics, and therapists called "The Working Group on Women's Sexual Problems"—were also in attendance at the meeting, using the annual Boston conference as a site to voice concerns about the ongoing medicalization of women's bodies, the privatization of medicine, and the oversimplification of medical models. This group of critics is actively challenging the conventional scientific wisdom circulating at these meetings. "The Working Group" is also reminding participants and experts of what feminists have written about for decades—that women's sexuality is as much about politics as it is about biology. They disperse leaflets, speak in smaller venues, and hold press conferences in an attempt to challenge the biological model of sexuality that most participants seem to take for granted. And though I am calling them "critics," they may also be "experts" in their own disciplines.[21] Their leader, clinical psychologist Leonore Tiefer, is both an insider and an outsider at medical meetings, or both a noted "expert" in psychology and a "critic" of medical and pharmaceutical industries. Tiefer has been one of the few clinicians to actively express serious concerns at the Boston Forum about the social implications of the medicalization of sexuality for women and men, medical science, and society at large. As you will see, at times during the Boston meetings, the chasm between the experts and the critics is wide, and at other times, concerned experts may literally become critics, revealing another fascinating overlap.

Finally, the annual Boston meeting attracts significant media attention as journalists from the *Boston Globe,* the *Chicago Tribune, Sixty Minutes,* and other regional and national outlets attend. Journalists depend on the above players to report on conference activities, and they also create their own framings of FSD. Typically, in an attempt to get "both sides of the story," the media may incorporate both medical claims, like those of Irwin Goldstein and his Boston research group, and feminist counterclaims, like those of Leonore Tiefer and her Working Group, thus cementing "the sides" and the stakes of each group of players.

Taking into account the activities of crucial FSD players, this chapter analyzes how women's sexual problems came to be understood in the three years after Viagra's debut. Formal presentations and displays at annual Boston meetings reflect experts and marketers trying to make sense of such problems, as do the more informal activities of the critics. In this chapter, I draw on several years of interviews, observations, and journalistic reports to chart the search for the female Viagra. Five years into this search, I argue, the most enduring understandings of women's sexual problems have been medical, as opposed to, say, psychological, even in the face of evidence to the contrary.

The Pharmaceutical Agenda

In an effort to understand the rise of FSD and sexual medicine, I asked the conference "grandmasters," featured paid speakers, how the Boston Forum came about. What emerged was a very limited collective memory focused primarily on the blockbuster product, Viagra. Like erectile dysfunction, female sexual dysfunction came of age at a time of increasing medicalization, deregulation, and empowerment of the pharmaceutical industry, as well as growing scientific and mass media attention to sexual dissatisfaction in the last half of the twentieth century.

Such social, economic, and political context may be implied but rarely is it explicitly stated in grandmaster accounts of the history of sexual medicine. When grandmasters discuss FSD in a historical context, either in interviews or in their presentations, two approaches may be taken. Grandmaster sex therapists and psychologists invoke the history of sexology, highlighting the sex research undertaken by Sigmund Freud (1920s), Alfred Kinsey (1950s), Masters and Johnson (1970s), and, more recently, Laumann, Gagnon, and Michaels (1994). Additionally, they also point to the ongoing search for aphrodisiacs as a precursor to sexual medicine. Conversely, grandmaster urologists or basic scientists tend to invoke recent research into the physiological causes of ED as a precursor to understanding FSD.

Very few sexual dysfunction experts talk about FSD as related to historical understandings of women's sexuality. For example, the first woman Boston Forum president and grandmaster, psychiatrist Sandra Leiblum acknowledged in 1999 that the diagnosis FSD originates in older psychiatric notions of "frigidity." While the FSD diagnosis is "imperfect," Sandra Leiblum said, it improves upon older "unhelpful" classifications by avoiding oversimplification and embracing the many dimensions (relational, psychological, and physiological) of women's sexual problems.

> The old practice of identifying the sexually unresponsive woman as frigid was not only pejorative and insulting, but unhelpful in identifying the particular aspect of her behavior that was problematical. Was she lacking in sexual interest or desire generally or did she simply not like her present partner? Did she fail to become aroused or conversely, did she readily lubricate but fail to achieve orgasm? . . . Lumping all of these problems under the rubric of frigidity did little to serve either the woman or the professional attempting to help her. Frigidity has been abandoned as a psychiatric diagnosis, although some would argue that what has taken its place, hypoactive sexual desire and/or female sexual arousal disorder, does not represent a vast improvement! Nonetheless, over the last twenty years there has been a genuine effort in psychiatry to operationalize, and describe in overt behavioral terms, dysfunctional behavior.[22]

In her three years at the Boston Forum, Leiblum has been one of only two grandmasters (Bancroft was the other), to my knowledge, to publicly acknowledge the evolving history of women's sexuality as related to medicine and male-dominated society. The majority of physicians, clinicians, and researchers appear unaware of this history, pointing solely to recent history, or Viagra's blockbuster success from 1998 on, as the primary impetus for research into female sexual dysfunction and interest in a "female Viagra." In other words, this is clearly another case of the solution existing before the problem. Experts were ready to acknowledge, or revisit, women's sexual problems once a solution (at least for men) appeared to be available. In her presidential address in 2001, Leiblum emphasized Viagra as the motivating factor in the rise of FSD, as did many others in my interviews.

> Who knows this date? March 29, 1998. What happened on that day? That was when we all celebrated and benefited from the first FDA recognition of an oral therapy for male sexual dysfunction.... Now we are in a decade of the medicalization of sex, with many different approaches.[23]

Likewise, Viagra was invoked in my interviews with grandmasters Julia Heiman and Irwin Goldstein as a "cultural event" that changed the face of sexual medicine, literally "driving" the field in new pharmacological directions.

> All of this [FSD-related research] is absolutely the product of Viagra. Viagra was a cultural event in itself. It was an effective drug, a new type of treatment, a psychophysiology treatment, and a blockbuster product—and the fact that it was a blockbuster drug is driving the field. Viagra metamorphosized things. Research on sexual dysfunction now has a clinical emphasis. But the new ingredient is the pharmaceutical agenda. All we can do now is try to steer the discourse.[24]

Talk of Viagra's success compelled some women to visit sexual dysfunction clinics, such as Goldstein's, and demand Viagra for themselves.

> Women come with an expectation that they'll get Viagra. Since the 1998 second sexual revolution, there was a new expectation formed

that if John could get something, I want something too. But we hardly ever give out Viagra to women.[25]

Many medical professionals agree that "the search for the female Viagra" prompted pharmaceutical companies to support research and annual meetings like the Boston Forum.[26] Initially, Viagra's success brought on what Goldstein calls a "second sexual revolution" as well as enormous funding into a research area that was "virtually unexplored" in physiology, medicine, and pharmacology. This wave of scientific inquiry into women's sexual problems and treatments for these problems created lucrative career options and cause for celebration among primarily women researchers, clinicians, and practitioners. For example, sisters Laura and Jennifer Berman champion the cause of FSD and claim to have played a role in the recent recognition and treatment of it. As Berman and Berman point out in their 2001 book, *For Women Only*,[27]

> Our book grew out of this exploding new field, and we are privileged to have played a part. Female sexual dysfunction is at last on the table as a recognized and often treatable disorder, which affects the general health and quality of life of millions of women around the world. What you read here is based directly on our work when we were co-directors of the Women's Sexual Health Clinic at Boston University Medical Center. Thanks to the help of our mentor and role model, Dr. Irwin Goldstein, the pioneer and leader in the field of male erectile dysfunction, this clinic was an enormous success.[28]

Thus, excitement among the medical and psychological community that women's sexual problems were finally being taken seriously by science, along with the enormous financial boon related to the first oral treatment for male sexual problems, intensified corporate interest in and funding for women's sexual problems. The "exploding new field" of sexual medicine was largely funded and constructed by pharmaceutical companies who had medical diagnoses and pharmacologic management in mind, a factor that constrains research and treatment options. According to psychiatrist Julia Heiman, "At the moment, on every level, the kind of research more likely to be funded is the physiological research."[29] This influx of industry funding, what psychiatrist John Bancroft below calls "the Viagra effect," can be dangerous for both consumers and corporations:

> There is a wave of massive funding now, but [the pharmaceutical industry's] fingers will get burned badly on FSD, so they will move on. The Viagra effect will continue until it is clear what wreckage is done.[30]

As Heiman infers above, a "pharmaceutical agenda" can have a momentum of its own, controlling research for some time and possibly resulting in mistakes ("wreckage"). For Heiman, "steering the discourse" is all that experts can do in this context of massive funding and vested interests. Bancroft and Heiman represent the minority of FSD claims makers in their inference that private funding could be problematic. Leonore Tiefer takes this critical perspective one step further. Tiefer, in a talk at the 1999 FSD conference titled "The Selling of FSD," was one of the only conference speakers in three years of Boston conferences to address the issue of pharmaceutical funding and interests head-on during a meeting symposium. Tiefer asked her colleagues whether this meeting was simply "window dressing for commercial interests whose only goal is profit, or careerism uninformed by a larger vision of women's predicaments." To avoid the "privatization of FSD," Tiefer called on her colleagues to

> be alert to the insidious dangers of commercialization of your research. Sex sells. If you didn't know this before Viagra, you know it now. But, we are not in the retail business. Try to keep the new society (the Boston Forum) out of the pockets of the pharmaceutical industry. Remember what your mother taught you—there is no free lunch.[31]

Despite this plea, the majority of grandmasters assert that without industry funding, conferences and research on women's sexual problems would not exist, thus setting up a codependency between medicine and corporate interests. Grandmasters Sandra Leiblum and Rosemary Basson spoke with me about science's growing dependency on industry funding.

> Oh—we need the money. The field would be stagnant without it. Otherwise we'd be sitting around drinking tea at some university.[32]

> The problem is there's no money. . . . The universities have no money. So . . . the only time the pharmaceutical companies tell you what to do

is when it is their study—and you are their investigator. And if you don't like the protocol, you should say no.[33]

Not surprisingly, many of the initial research grants from the pharmaceutical industry went towards finding a Viagra-type treatment for female sexual dysfunction. FSD was originally assumed to manifest exactly like ED, as essentially a problem with vasocongestion, or arousal. Urologist Jennifer Berman, a member of Goldstein's Pfizer-funded Boston University team and one of the clinical researchers studying Viagra in women, was quoted in numerous mainstream publications claiming that the tissues in the penis and clitoris look and act similarly.[34] This assumption, that the male and female body are essentially similar, and thus that their sexual function and dysfunction may be analogous, fueled a pharmaceutical agenda beginning in 1998 when companies such as Pfizer Pharmaceuticals began to pump millions of dollars into research. The "Viagra for women" expectation became the primary and dominant medical frame for understanding FSD outcomes immediately after Viagra's debut.

Expert-Ownership

Perhaps the most fascinating occurrence at the Boston Forum, at least to me, is the ongoing competition among sexuality experts to understand and, as social-problems theorist Joseph Gusfield would say, to "own" women's sexual problems. Each year, definitions of women's sexual problems are up for debate. Thus, the stakes are high, especially when one is backed by a powerful corporation vying for control of the market in women's sexual problems.

As we saw in chapter 2, experts subsidized by pharmacological corporations are called "affiliated experts." Which female sexual dysfunction experts are "affiliated" is difficult to determine because, as noted above, disclosure is not always obvious during presentations at the Boston Forum. In 2000, disclosure statements that came with the conference program revealed that affiliated experts come from many disciplines, especially urology, basic science, and psychiatry, and all employ the scientific method to locate women's sexual problems in the body, as medical problems worth treating. Overall, about half (53 percent) of those giving a presentation disclosed a research or consulting relationship with one or more drug companies. More importantly, 88 percent of those giving high-profile, lengthy grandmaster presentations disclosed such links.[35] The most visible and vocal affiliated expert at the Boston Forum meetings is Irwin Goldstein.

In contrast, the group I will call "critical experts" do not accept pharmaceutical funding and actively promote counterclaims at the Boston Forum. In other words, while these professionals acknowledge women's sexual problems, they place the blame for these problems outside of the body, in social and cultural arenas. They make up a tiny minority of FSD experts at the Boston Forum, and, as noted before, their most vocal proponent is Leonore Tiefer.

In between these two extremes are the "semi-affiliated experts" who receive limited pharmaceutical funding (usually acting as temporary consultants rather than investigators) and actively promote sympathetic counterclaims at the Boston Forum. In other words, they express concern with medical definitions or measures but still embrace medical models. They are the minority of FSD experts, primarily those trained in psychology or sex therapy. Finally, I call those who are not associated with pharmaceutical funding or counterclaims the "neutral experts." Generally, these experts occupy less marketable research areas, such as the area of sexual pain disorders, or are government-affiliated researchers. In this chapter I am most interested in the first three groups of experts, whose positioning in relation to medical and pharmacological arenas affects the form and content of the claims they will make.

One urologist made reference to these expert groups and their competing models for understanding women's sexual problems in his description of the "scene" at the Boston conference:

> I'm not really into the scene. I just have fun watching. . . . I mean, there are such disparate groups there. You have the psychologists, the psychiatrists, the sex therapists, and the gynecologists, and then the urologists. The urologists are the most scientific—they see a clinical problem that they want to fix. As urologists, we embrace the scientific method. But the others, I can't figure out what they are doing there. I just can't figure it out. They don't embrace the scientific method at all, and they are there singing "Kumbayah" and holding hands. It is just fascinating. I mean, I see it as a problem, FSD, like chest pain. It is a medical problem.[36]

This quotation highlights three things: the dominant role that urologists play as claims makers at the Boston Forum, the chasm between urological and psychological approaches to constructing claims, and the struggle over defining women's sexual problems as medical or nonmedical.

In thinking about the dominant diagnoses of women's sexual problems in the Viagra era, I believe that we can identify six competing diagnoses that circulate at the Boston Forum meetings. Four are medical, two are nonmedical, and each diagnosis is associated with a particular grouping of experts and a location inside or outside of the body. Medical research has located "the problem" primarily within the female body generally, but the specific physiological site of the problem varies, from the genitals to the brain to hormone levels. These are the master frames for understanding women's sexual problems at FSD conferences, many of which were shaped by affiliated experts who used ED and Viagra as the model for understanding and treating women's sexual problems. In contrast, there are two popular alternatives to the medical framing of sexual problems that situate such problems within relational and sociocultural contexts. In each case, "experts" have engaged in activities and used rhetoric that attempt to construct, locate, define, measure, and fix the problem they claim exists. Affiliated experts' constructions of women's sexual problems have been the most enduring, primarily because they are backed by pharmaceutical funding and interests, a crucial variable in the construction of persuasive ideas. By focusing on these competing frames, we can chart how "the problem" has moved around and outside the female body in the years since Viagra's debut.

The Body Is the Problem

Much of the initial medical understanding of women's sexual problems was acquired behind closed doors six months after Viagra's debut in 1998, and was later published in the *Journal of Urology*.[37] The report details the first scientific meeting on female sexual dysfunction, a pharmaceutical-industry-funded, invitation-only "consensus" gathering involving an "international and multidisciplinary" group of nineteen "experts in FSD," many of whom later were paid to speak at the Boston Forum as conference grandmasters or were cited by conference speakers for their "ground-breaking" work. The meeting was convened by the American Foundation for Urologic Disease, and thus it included affiliated urologists central to phase one of the Viagra phenomenon who generally assumed erectile dysfunction to be the model for sexual dysfunction. The rest of the participants included basic scientists, gynecologists, psychologists, psychiatrists, one FDA medical officer, and one clinical development consultant. Notably, all but one participant, the FDA officer, officially acknowledged a financial interest in and/or a relationship with "affiliated research centers," otherwise known as pharmaceutical companies.[38] The meeting itself was subsidized by eight of these companies, as well as by researcher funding.

The report published in the *Journal of Urology* describes a group of "experts selected from 5 countries" who reportedly met to discuss "shortcomings and problems associated with previous classifications" and to reach consensus on a "well defined, broadly accepted diagnostic framework and classification for FSD."[39] In this meeting, participants "evaluated and refined" existing definitions and classifications of FSD from the *DSM-IV* and the *ICD-10* (*International Statistical Classification of Diseases and Related Health Problems*). Existing classifications for FSD were accepted by the experts (as they were with ED in 1998) "to maintain continuity in research and clinical practice," but previously psychiatric domains were expanded to include *organic* causes of the four existing categories of FSD: sexual desire disorder, arousal disorder, orgasmic disorder, and pain disorder. "Disorder" terminology, found in mental health classificatory systems, was changed to "dysfunction," signaling organic, or physiological causation. Additionally, a new subjective "personal distress" criterion was added to these classifications, enabling a woman to subjectively assess her own dysfunction in any or all of these four areas.[40]

In their report, nineteen medical experts concluded that FSD is "a multi-causal and multi-dimensional problem combining biological, psychological, and interpersonal determinants." Citing the *National Health and Social Life Survey*, they stated that FSD "is age-related, progressive, and highly prevalent, affecting up to 40% of women in the United States."[41] Despite the acknowledgment that FSD may be caused by multiple factors, the consensus group recommended a list of "FSD research needs and priorities" that emphasized medical research, including epidemiological research on prevalence, predictors, and outcomes of FSD. The recommendations made in this private gathering set the stage for future clinical research focused on measuring the physiology and endocrinology of female sexual function. The report, written and distributed in 1998, and published two years later, reads as follows:

> [We recommend] . . . anatomical studies on the multiple organs involved; research on biological mechanisms of sexual arousal and orgasm in women, including neurophysiology and the role of steroid hormones in women; research on aging and menopause; and urgent investigation into the development of reproducible measurement devices and instruments for evaluating physiological parameters of female sexual response in a clinical setting.[42]

Specifically, in 1998 clinical trials into vasoactive agents and steroidal therapies were "strongly encouraged," along with trials of "psychosexual therapy alone or in combination with pharmacological treatment." Three years later, as I argue below, FSD clinical trials and research are concentrated around these pharmacological solutions: vasoactive agents (for blood circulation to the genitals) and steroidal therapies (for hormone "replacement").

In conclusion, the 1998 "consensus" meeting was crucial to the initial understanding of FSD, as it asserted that certain conditions exist related to arousal, desire, orgasm, and pain, marking these conditions as problems worth fixing, and clearly guiding the future of FSD research and inquiry by laying out a strict framework for classifying, treating, and understanding FSD. This multidisciplinary group of experts reached consensus on the medicalization of women's sexual problems and set the stage for funding and research into the organicity of FSD, while marginalizing past psychological therapies for women's sexual problems.[43] Reminiscent of the way in which ED was reframed as a medical condition suitable for treatment, the "consensus" report pushed FSD beyond the *DSM* (or beyond psychological factors). At the same time, by including in the definition of FSD any woman experiencing distress or dissatisfaction in relation to sexuality, the report retained enough of the subjective dimension to expand potential FSD markets infinitely.

The "consensus" conference provided the growing field of sexual medicine with common terminology, definitions, and goals in regard to women's sexual problems. In 1998, the "consensus" group, with the okay from a handful of pharmaceutical companies searching for the "female Viagra," officially waved the flag to begin the race to locate and treat FSD, even though the race had already begun. As in the case of Viagra, FSD researchers had actually begun their inquiries into female organic dysfunction at the beginning of the Masters and Johnson sexual response cycle, the arousal stage.

Blood Flow Is the Problem

In the early days of Viagra, when looking towards women's "problems" with sexuality, most assumed that there was an arousal problem similar to ED, called "female sexual arousal dysfunction" (FSAD). Assuming that men's and women's bodies were alike, some assumed that that since ED was a dysfunction related to poor blood circulation to the penis and, consequently, limited vasocongestion of the tissue, maybe FSAD was similar in women. Research teams such as Goldstein's Boston University group focused their efforts on understanding vaginal blood flow, dilation, and lubrication in rats, rabbits, and women, with Pfizer's and other firms' financial support. Thus the first Boston conference dedicated to "the management of female sexual dysfunction" consisted largely of reports by the world's experts on the effect of vasoactive drugs (sildenafil) in managing arousal (blood flow and vasocongestion). Terms like "vaginal compliance," "genital response," and even "turbo-charged rat vagina" characterized the 1999 meeting.[44] Pharmaceutical companies such as NexMed (also a sponsor of the Boston Forum conferences) claimed in their promotional literature given out at the conference that FSAD was a true cash cow, with a market potentially larger than that of ED.

> The FSAD treatment market is projected to become a multi-billion dollar business. Projections estimate that it will quickly become comparable in size to the ED market—and may very well exceed that figure. Currently there is no pharmaceutical product approved for the treatment of FSAD. . . . NexMed's Femprox may offer the potential to become a ground-breaking treatment for FSAD.[45]

At the 1999 Boston meeting, FSAD figured prominently as the central problem, and (primarily) Pfizer-funded researchers proudly unveiled technology that claimed to objectively measure female sexual arousal (read: blood flow), such as vaginal probes, magnetic resonance imaging, duplex doppler ultrasonograms, and temperature-specific vibrating tools to be applied directly to the clitoris. When attached to a computer, these measures would produce data on arousal based on blood pulse in the vagina, heat levels, lubrication levels, and other indicators. Two years later such technologies, particularly the vaginal probe, were being used widely in clinical trials.

Despite ongoing collection of "objective" data in numerous clinical trials using such measures, scientific consensus on an official gold standard for measurement of arousal has not yet been reached. Today, more precise measuring tools are under development with pharmaceutical support. Levin, a retired university scientist who studied vaginal physiology for forty-one years "when nobody cared," is suddenly in demand and at work developing an electrode-based measuring tool with help from Pfizer. His physiology department has merged with medical science, he reports, revealing new funding sources and current directions in science. When asked about testing this technology, Levin replied, "My wife has had so many probes in her—she has been very helpful over the years."[46]

Another component of the first two conferences on managing FSD was the marketing of a new technology for treating or managing FSAD—a treatment nearing FDA approval at the time of the first conference. EROS-CTD, a "clitoral therapy device" made by the Urometrics Corporation, applied vacuum pressure to the clitoris to enhance blood flow, and thus arousal. This product was approved by the FDA in January 2000 and is available by prescription at a cost of around three hundred dollars. Notably, the Berman sisters were early paid spokespeople for Urometrics. At several Boston conferences, they stood at the display table testing the suction device on curious attendees' palms. Later, they demonstrated the EROS-CTD device on the *Oprah* show, and received giggles of delight from audience members and Oprah herself. It was not coincidental that one of the first "apparatuses" for treating erectile problems in the twentieth century, and still a popular one, was also a vacuum pump that promised penile engorgement by using vacuum pressure to create blood flow into the penis.

At the same time as the 1999 Boston conference, Pfizer had ongoing clinical tests underway across the country assessing the effect of sildenafil on women. Public curiosity about "the blue diamond" for women was so strong that some female reporters tried Viagra and wrote about

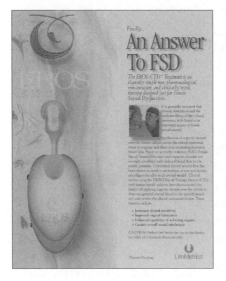
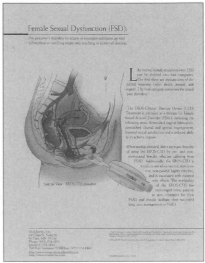

This vacuum suction device is currently the only FDA-approved technology for treating Female Sexual Dysfunction. The Eros-CTD device, like Viagra, aims to treat women's sexual problems by enabling blood flow. Promotional material distributed at the Boston Forum, 2000.

it.[47] *Cosmopolitan's* August 1998 edition featured a story titled, "Viagra—The Female Orgasm Pill?" in which a reporter tries Viagra and reports on her "intense V-gasm"—and subsequent headache and dizziness.[48] Others reported increased sensitivity, but nothing miraculous.[49] In clinical trials, "advances" in science and technology claimed to induce and measure arousal. Women volunteers were asked to watch an erotic video, wearing special 3-D glasses, and to "self-stimulate" in the lab, using a vibrator. "Objective" arousal levels were measured by a photoplethysmograph, a metal probe inserted into the vagina to test vaginal pulse amplitude. Trial subjects were also asked to complete subjective questionnaires that asked questions about their arousal levels (lubrication) before and after the video and stimulation.

Mixed reports and inconclusive Viagra clinical trials on women led many scientists to deduce that women's sexual functioning may be different from that of men. Nonetheless, even with failed clinical studies, research into the physiology of arousal (with a focus on blood flow) may still be the most well-funded area of inquiry into women's sexual problems, with new treatments currently undergoing trials. Today, Viagra is prescribed for women, off label. "Off-label" prescriptions are uses of FDA-approved drugs for purposes other than those approved by the agency. This allows doctors to experiment with medications to create a treatment more in tune with their personal preferences. Popular television shows pick up on this Viagra-for-women theme and glamorize the idea of women taking Viagra, as well as a new female sexual aggression and insatiability.[50] In one episode of *Sex in the City* the character Samantha, played by Kim Cattrall, takes Viagra (along with her lover) and embodies these masculine characteristics. Incidentally, Cattrall has recently written a book in which she extols the virtues of Viagra use for women who are interested in multiple orgasms. All of this has led to a cultural discussion about "Samantha types," or a new generation of women who are articulate about their sexual needs.[51]

The Complicated Woman Is the Problem

One year after Viagra's launch, and months after Viagra trials for women ended, journalists, reflecting medical professionals' woes, have begun to describe women's sexual problems as "complicated" and perhaps more linked to "the mind." In early 1999, the *LA Times* ran a story entitled "Key to Female Viagra Seems a Brain Teaser," which concludes that "for women, scientists are finding, the most important organ for sexual function may be the brain." A year later, a *Newsweek* cover story entitled "Searching for a Female Viagra: Is It a Mind or Body Problem?" begins with, "In the rush to unlock the mysteries of female desire, the answers are turning out to be more complex than anyone expected." This notion of women's sexuality as complicated, complex, and difficult to treat as compared to men's easy-to-solve, "shake-and-bake" sexual problems has emerged consistently as an obstacle to research and clinical studies.[52] The "complicated woman" is often invoked as a rationale for the slow-paced research and limited treatment options for FSD.

For some, the source of the "complication" comes from the oversimplified, problematic medical models that assume similar and "ordered" sexual function in both men and women. In 1999, Leiblum publicly critiqued the "misleading" assumptions behind the current classification of FSD and argued that "genital aspects" of women's sexual response may be less important for women:

There is an artificial attempt to create parallelism between male and female sexual complaints. This works better for some complaints than others, e.g., male erectile disorder is fairly obvious to diagnose while the corresponding disorder, female arousal difficulty, is much more difficult to ascertain, not only by the woman but often by her partner as well. The diagnostic categories are organized in such a way as to suggest that sexual response unfolds in a clear-cut linear sequence of arousal, desire, and orgasm when a more circular and interactive model certainly applies. . . . In particular there is a failure to identify or recognize the emotional and interpersonal aspects of sexual exchange, aspects which tend to be more important to women typically than genital response per se.[53]

Two years later, as president of the Boston Forum, Leiblum reported on "what we have learned" in FSD research. She showed a slide of an early-twentieth-century machine with countless dials and explained, "Just like with this machine, for women we have to rotate the knobs in many ways—we don't just flip a switch." FSD researchers and clinicians had reached clear consensus on the complexity of women's sexual problems.

Viagra trials for women were the first to publicly reveal how "complicated" women's sexual problems were, and soon set off a backlash. In 1999, FDA approval of Viagra for women was still Pfizer's plan, but by the FSD meeting in October it was apparent that clinical trial results revealed an "intriguing disconnect" between "objective and subjective measures."[54] According to the vaginal probe data, sildenafil worked in women, but the women did not acknowledge any changes, producing a huge scientific and marketing quandary. When asked, most clinical subjects who experienced blood flow to the genitals claimed they did not feel increased sexual desire. Such a conflict between "subjective" and "objective," or genital and psychological, reports was not anticipated. After countless sildenafil clinical trials, women still did note report arousal, and Viagra was found to be ineffective in treating FSD.

Many researchers and practitioners did not want to accept this. Psychologist Cindy Meston commented on her own assumptions that Viagra would work on women:

CM: Especially with Viagra's success, nobody anticipated how difficult it would be in finding a comparable compound for women. We've

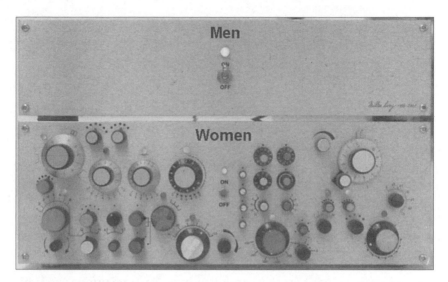

This image was used at the Boston Forum to convey how different women's sexual functioning may be from men's sexual functioning. The presenter explained, "Just like with this machine, for women we have to rotate the knobs in many ways—we don't just flip a switch." This is reminiscent of long-standing stereotypes about masculinity being simple and straightforward while femininity is mysterious.

been working backwards for three years, starting at the beginning with classifying and categorizing. . . . Three years ago we thought we'd just test Viagra on women and market it and that will be that. But we reached some obstacles.

ML: Like what?

CM: Like how do we measure things like arousal? We can measure the blood flow with particular devices, and we can be very specific that it only measures sexual response. If you show a woman an erotic film, there's a big change in blood flow. But the woman is still saying she isn't aroused, so it is desynchronous. The questionnaire and the device contradict one another. So we need more than blood flow. We need to enhance sexual well-being.

ML: What is well-being?

CM: Well, we're not sure.[55]

Meston, who worked for six different pharmaceutical companies at the time of our conversation, thought for a moment and then told me that perhaps outcomes were not clear not only because of imprecise measurement equipment but also because of the lab setting. "Maybe we need to take the women out of the lab—because there may be a lab effect—and let them do this at home. They'd keep a diary and self-report there."[56] Others expressed concern about the erotic videos women are shown in the lab, asking if this really was an effective stimulus for most subjects. Once again, what worked for men in clinical trials did not seem to work as well for women.

Dr. Basson put it this way: "We have found that women are complaining of lack of arousal, but they are [vaso]congesting just fine." In other words, while the appropriate vasocongestion of the vaginal tissues may be occurring with the use of Viagra, with vasocongestion being the measure of success for men with erection problems, female clinical subjects don't seem to know, or care. Basson summarized this "intriguing disconnect" as follows:

> For men, we found that stimulating the brain led to genital congestion, awareness of this congestion, and feedback back to the brain. For men, we found that genital feedback is a part of life, and sexual health always comes back to this. For women, who have a slightly larger brain, we found that genital congestion did not lead to a feedback cycle because women did not recognize this congestion. Women are not generally aware of what we consider measures of genital arousal: lubrication, vaginal dilation . . . Thus, we must look at women's *subjective* arousal.[57]

Such contradictions reveal a level of psychological complexity in the treatment of sexual problems that was probably ignored or less obvious in Viagra trials. As Basson points out, subjective arousal and genital arousal have been constructed as intimately linked in men. For women this may not be the case. Heiman goes further to say that by assigning solely medical or organic boundaries to sexuality, and not taking into account the mind, one cannot understand and treat the whole sexual being.

> It's not that sex can't be just a physical act, but it's rarely a decorticated act. By corticated I mean in humans there is rarely an act without a

brain involved. And without thoughts and concepts. Whether it is rape or sexually dysfunctional sex, whatever. There are some experiences you can have, like ejaculation or orgasm at night, or ejaculation with an electrical current passing though the penis. So there are exceptions to what I'm saying. But the vast majority of sexual experience is more than just the absence of a medical problem. The whole meaning of sexuality and its richness, and including its "perversity"—the ways in which it gets people into trouble and the ways in which it takes advantage of people—all of that gets left out if you just call it a medical condition. That's the struggle—and it's a struggle worth recognizing. That there is no simple solution to, and hopefully it'll keep everybody just a little humble about what they are talking about.[58]

While recent research on FSAD constructs the complicated woman as having a "desynchronous" mind and body, Heiman suggests that the two are difficult to separate out, thus presenting a complication or a "struggle" with no simple solution. Similarly, Ellen Laan, conducting Viagra clinical trials in Amsterdam, Holland, found that psychological factors can greatly influence outcomes in women. Laan consistently found that the placebo rate for women (40 percent) is much higher than for men (20 percent), implying that women's "suggestibility" plays a significant role in clinical trials and calling into question any study that does not involve a control group or show significant difference between placebo and treatment effects.

John Bancroft, the director of the Kinsey Institute, warned the audience at the 1999 Boston Forum to be cautious about jumping to conclusions about why women are harder to understand sexually, because sexual dysfunction is "harder to pin down in women." After his talk, Bancroft repeated that caution is necessary with "complicated" subjects.

> [I warned about medicalization] especially with women because they are more complicated. They are more cautious, perhaps because of a history of suppression of their sexuality. Men ask for medical help and physical solutions. Women may not.[59]

Bancroft was one of a small minority of participants at the Boston medical meetings to acknowledge these factors in the understanding, diagnosis, and treatment of FSD. Furthermore, in his second year as an

invited speaker and grandmaster, Bancroft reported on his own research on the prevalence of female sexual dissatisfaction, which con-
tradicted the 43 percent statistic from the *National Health and Sexuality
Survey*. For example, in his random-sample study, the research team
found that only 7.9 percent of women had an impaired physical response associated with distress, suggesting that the 43 percent statistic
is highly exaggerated. In this study, Bancroft and colleagues argue
against the very concept of sexual "dysfunction," as well as the treatment of men's and women's sexual problems as virtually the same.
They found that the best predictors of sexual distress were emotional
(including general well-being and emotional relationship with partner) and that physical aspects of sexuality (such as arousal, lubrication, and orgasm) were poor indicators of distress.[60] After two years of
using his grandmaster status to promote such ideas, Bancroft was not
invited to present at future meetings, in what appeared to be an effort
to quell dissident ideas and bring the discussion back to unproblema-
tized medicalization and organicity. In 2002, on the verge of retiring,
Bancroft told me that he planned to "become a feminist activist in retirement."[61]

The fact that women's sexuality has been constructed as "complicated" has forced FSD researchers to slow down and think about their
framing of the problem. This has been good news to critics of the FSD
campaign. Jean Fourcroy, an FDA medical officer, presenting at the 2001
Boston Forum meeting, pleaded with audience members to acknowledge women's sexual complexity:

> Sexual dysfunction for a woman is a complex quilted tapestry. . . .
> The act of sex includes not only her sexual self and self-image, but
> intimate relationships, family, society, and culture. The complexities
> of environment, sexual and partner history, past abusive relation-
> ships, current medical problems and hormonal status all play a
> role.[62]

Complicated female sexuality has actually been the rallying call for
feminist health advocates. As mentioned earlier, the Working Group on
Women's Sexual Problems is a feminist group actively asserting that
medical models are oversimplified. As its leader, Leonore Tiefer, pointed
out at the first Boston Forum, basic mammalian factors and "rat vagi-
nas" may not reflect the reality or totality of women's sexual problems.

The "experts" highlighted in this section speak to a breaking point in the construction of FSD. The "mind/body approach" to diagnosing women's sexual problems became important for some, as sexual dysfunction clinics made room for psychologists and sex therapists to work alongside urologists and general practitioners. This mind-and-body approach has been claimed by the Berman sisters, who promoted their "unique" approach (which includes "a battery of expensive and extensive psychological and physiological work-ups") on *Oprah* and in countless women's magazines. Similarly, Basson runs a mind/body sexual-dysfunction clinic in British Columbia, and contends that this "blended" approach is "mandatory":

> I'm an M.D. so obviously I want to understand how the body works and how we can have medications that can help the body work better and understand the negative effects of medications. But I believe in a mandatory blend of the mind and the body and we have to bear that in mind all of the time. All the time. When we are assessing and when we are treating. It really isn't either/or.[63]

As the mind/body approach becomes more accepted, clinicians are using both vaginal probes and subjective scales to test women's arousal in clinical trials. New attempts to measure arousal have resulted in some interesting results. Examples such as the widely used Female Sexual Satisfaction Scale and Female Sexual Function Index are designed to assess women's subjective responses but remain flawed, according to some critics, because they continue to focus on physiological responses that women are not aware of and do not necessarily equate with arousal. Such surveys pose questions about intensity levels related to genital wetness, warmth, pulsing, pressure, engorgement, excitement, lubrication, orgasm, satisfaction, and pain, but not about pleasure, intimacy, or context-related variables.[64] Thus, despite attempts to reclaim psychological factors as central to the problem, the most "legitimate" frame for understanding FSD remains the "organic" one, which, as we shall soon see, focuses on either the role of the brain or the role of hormones in explaining women's lack of sexual interest.

It Must Be Hormonal

The floodgates on framing FSD as a hormonal problem were opened at the final symposium of the 2000 Boston Forum. Entitled "Desire, Arousal, and Testosterone," the symposium suggested that the problems of low sexual desire or general sexual disinterest in women were due to women having low testosterone levels. Although existing clinical studies on this topic were extremely limited and problematic—"normal" testosterone levels in women were not yet defined, "objective measures" were lacking, and the concept of "androgen deficiency" was still "under development"—these cautions seemed to be eclipsed by "the take-home message" at the end of the conference. This emphasis set the stage for future meetings and forced people to leave with testosterone on their minds. In these final moments, Irwin Goldstein's wife stood at a microphone and testified about an over-the-counter supplement (DHEA) linked to testosterone production:

> It's really an amazing product—DHEA. I have been taking it for two months and it has taken away my night sweats and I feel twenty again. I am fifty and there are no side effects. This is the future of the field.[65]

Minutes later, Irwin Goldstein commented to a small group of practitioners leaving the conference,

> Isn't it amazing that it is only now in the year 2000 that we are understanding these things? For hundreds of years women have low levels of testosterone, and we're only seeing this now. So the psychological is important and all, but we've got to get women up to normal levels![66]

Despite the lack of safety and efficacy research into DHEA, Goldstein told me later that he had been actively encouraging his patients (and wife) to buy over-the-counter DHEA, "one of the amazing things on this earth," at the grocery store. He described the product as "like a female Viagra, but better."

> All I can tell you is what I tell my patients—it's like gas in a car. You can't drive unless you have gas. Testosterone is the gas. And it enables

women to achieve three dimensions of sexual functioning. What's amazing is it allows women to return to wherever they were when they were at their peak. We've seen four major changes, two of which are nonsexual. First, we find that the time to arousal increases. So the man hasn't come and gone before she even gets close. Second, we see some return of thoughts and fantasies. Then there are nonsexual effects such as great energy in the morning. They actually wake up in the mornings and feel more energy than they have ever felt before. And it even improves memory. Fifth, something that is very important to women is that DHEA improves bone density.[67]

The car metaphor used here by Goldstein is common for practitioners, marketers, and clinicians when making sense of ED and Viagra. At some conferences, Pfizer's promotional display included a Viagra sports car where conference participants could have their photo taken. References to car accessories or broken car parts have been used by consumers and practitioners to symbolize the "broken penis" and the "repair" potential of Viagra.

For Goldstein, FSD is framed not as a "broken part" but as a stalled system that lacks fuel. Testosterone, or DHEA, is constructed as one way to bring life back into the car or the immobile body, sparking a revival in energy and sexual drive, as well as improved health. Boston Forum speakers have also pointed to androgen's numerous effects in rats and monkeys, including improved libido, softer skin, and diminished hot flashes.[68] Reporting from limited human studies conducted in the past thirty years, Dr. Shabsigh claimed that testosterone replacement has been found to have "pro-sexual effects," improving on fantasies, thoughts, mood, and sexual function, and Guay characterized DHEA as "a springboard to female sexuality."[69] In sum, androgen replacement is being packaged in terms of youth (memory, energy), gender (femininity), sexual (fantasies, mood, function), and health-related ideals, much as Viagra is packaged.

By the 2001 conference, research presentations that pointed to arousal and blood flow as the central problem were complemented by a number of other presentations attempting to link lack of sexual desire in women to "deficient" hormone levels, specifically, testosterone levels. One urologist summed up this new FSD framing in his presentation, suggesting that there were now "two schools of thought in understanding FSD: the vascular, which research has shown may not be fruitful, and the hormonal, which is very tempting and should be pushed further."[70]

After shifting the focus from blood flow to hormones, some familiar sexual dysfunction experts led the hormonal replacement campaign. For example, Goldstein was "slowly moving up the body" in his organic framing of FSD.[71] Others included the Bermans, various members of their Pfizer-funded urology team, and other new grandmasters trained in endocrinology and basic science. This quickly expanding field of experts pushing for hormonal replacement argued that if arousal and desire were natural functions, something organic must be interfering with natural desire and arousal. By the 2001 Boston Forum, more and more grandmasters focused on the role of what they called female "androgen deficiency" (AD), or low levels of testosterone, as potentially the primary obstacle to female libido.[72]

By the 2001 Boston Forum conference, much of the focus was on arousal problems compounded with lack of interest, or lack of libido. FSAD and "hypoactive sexual desire" were now the two primary female sexual problems to be fixed. One pharmaceutical representative told me that her product, a hormonal supplement used for menopause, was "a libido pill for the libido problem," reflecting what she perceived to be a widespread need to bring back female sex drive. Some unveiled hormone (androgen) replacement as the new solution to this problem, on the heels of a large market for estrogen replacement in postmenopausal women.[73]

The final meeting day and symposia series at the 2001 Boston Forum seemed again designed to promote a "take-away" message for practitioners in the audience about androgen "deficiency" in women. The symposia opened with a presentation by Goldstein's mentor and the central AD claims maker, Andre Guay, Assistant Professor of Medicine and head of the Center for Sexual Function at Harvard Medical School. Asserting that sexual dysfunction was a couples issue, Guay projected onscreen a popular cartoon depicting an older man being offered Viagra by his doctor, and a woman, presumably his wife, standing behind the doctor, holding up a sign that reads, "SAY NO." This cartoon has been invoked regularly in popular media to symbolize "the female response" to Viagra, in which, according to Guay, "one-third of wives" resent the reintroduction of compulsory sex into their marriage after getting used to years of no intercourse. Guay used this example to claim that the wife in the cartoon represented a typical case of androgen deficiency, an area of science that is "underexplored" but that has "great potential" for explaining FSD. In other words, for such experts, women's desire for their husbands not to use Viagra cannot be explained in terms of relational, social, or emotional reasoning, as the columns of *Dear Abby* would have us believe, but must be explained in terms of hormonal deficiency. Later, one quotation, projected onscreen for all conference goers to see, was meant to reflect the historical presence of androgen deficiency in society, proclaiming, "The sour, shallow, sexless shrew is an imposter as a wife and her marriage is a fraud."[74]

By 2001, androgen deficiency was at the forefront of sexual dysfunction research, as controversial ideas about women's and even men's testosterone deficiencies were increasingly being presented at medical meetings around the world. With Goldstein at the helm, AD has been created as a new research arena with great potential for the understanding of sexual problems. One researcher claimed at a 2001 Sexual Medicine Symposium in Beverly Hills that if older men took testosterone, "the grumpy old man syndrome would disappear."[75]

Scientific assertions about "androgen deficiency," without conclusive research to back them up, have spawned plenty of counterclaims and cautionary warnings from concerned grandmasters, primarily women, about promoting testosterone for women. Such testosterone promotion is currently creating, in one researcher's words, "an extremely dangerous situation."[76] One of the most effective counterclaims was made in 2001 by an FDA medical officer who pleaded with scientists and practitioners at the Boston Forum to "care about their patients' safety," pushed audience members to remember medicine's long history of abusing women and asserted, "I'm over seventy, with low measures of testosterone in my blood. But I'm not bothered, and in fact, I'm sexually active."

While some practitioners are waiting patiently for clinical trials and conclusive evidence that testosterone and DHEA are safe and effective, others are actively prescribing testosterone off label and recommending over-the-counter products when complaints of "lack of interest" and related distress emerge. Is testosterone the answer?

The "Steve Problem"

Like Oprah and her audiences, most practitioners want to know, Why do women lack interest in sex? For some, the answer is not in the body but in the relationship, partner, or lack of stimulus. In her 2001 presidential address at the Boston Forum, psychiatrist Sandra Leiblum anticipated future presentations about hormone deficiency when she showed the audience a cartoon depicting one woman telling her friend, "I was on hormone replacement for two years before I realized that what I really needed was Steve replacement." Leiblum summed up this cartoon, commenting generally that "many of us know that a Steve replacement may work better than hormone replacement," which set off laughter in the room, seeming to strike a chord.

Leiblum went on to say that while "lack of desire [and] sexual response" may be considered "distressing" by medical professionals, behaviorists are finding that "women don't want to respond, even if they are capable of responding." Thus the most recent "elusive" female sexual problem is "sexual disinterest." For Leiblum, this might be called the "Steve problem," a problem that can be solved not by a pill but by sex therapy or "Steve replacement." Countering the medical and pharmacological platform, Leiblum concluded that "the perfect aphrodisiac for women cannot be bottled"; thus she represents a minority contingency of grandmasters who reject the organic construction of women's sexual problems.[77]

Following Leiblum's address, the "Steve Problem" was invoked several times. As FDA Medical Officer Jean Fourcroy said in her talk, "As my mother used to say, there's no such thing as a frigid woman, just an incompetent man. Some of us just need a new coupling perhaps."[78] Dr. Ellen Laan took these ideas one step further. Citing evidence that external factors were most influential in women's sexual problems, she insisted that "the problem" could not be located in the body. Laan disputed the assumed organic nature of female sexual dysfunctions, citing recent clinical research results that showed "no evidence for organic etiology" and "low prevalence of sexual dysfunction in women." Laan warned that exaggerated claims of organicity and FSD should be "considered in the context of the development of new medications for FSAD. . . . In order to be profitable, such a drug should be indicated for a specific disease, preferably a disease that is highly prevalent, with a

*"I was on hormone replacement for two years before I realized
that what I really needed was Steve replacement."*

This cartoon reveals women's growing cynicism about hormone replacement
therapy and medical "solutions" to what may really be relational problems.
One Boston Forum presenter used this image to make the case that women's
sexual disinterest may not be easily remedied by a pill. From Cartoon Bank.

clear somatic component." Laan's suggestion that profit goals were influencing the understanding of women's sexual problems as somatic,
rather than as social or cultural, seems on target.

Heiman also took issue with one Boston Forum speaker's assumption that FSD was a disease state, challenging the speaker on his terminology and pointing out that a medical bias tends to ignore sociocultural and interactional factors related to sexual problems. She explained
later,

> What I was objecting to was the use of the word "disease." . . . In other
> words, there may not be an illness process or disease process. . . . I
> think that a number of sexual dysfunctions are pure, and not simple,
> *sociocultural, interactional* consequences. . . . And they are not much
> more than that. That of course doesn't mean that the body isn't in-
> volved at all. It means that those phenomena are interacting with

physical phenomena to decrease desire or arousal or postpone orgasm. (emphasis added)[79]

Laan reported in her Boston Forum presentation that women's sexual problems were relational or stimulus related:

> Their [women's sexual] problems are likely to be stimulus related. Explicit erotic videos were found to induce negative affect. Arousal difficulties can therefore be explained by lack of adequate sexual stimulation that is either not available, or is avoided, because it evokes negative feelings.[80]

This focus on "stimulus" as the source of the problem (whether it be a partner, a video, or touching) has been proposed and expanded by Rosemary Basson, who in an interview suggested,

> [There may be problems] with emotional intimacy, which is so important to motivate the woman in the first place, or there may be problems with stimuli that she needs, or sexual contact isn't there, or stimuli are there but she doesn't process them as arousal because she's had past negative experiences or she's distracted—whatever.[81]

By 2001, Basson was presenting her own cyclical female response cycle, complete with complex feedback loops, at the Boston Forum as an alternative to Masters and Johnson's linear, largely physiological Human Sexual Response (HSR) model (proposed in 1966 and still largely accepted by the sexual medicine community). Basson's model, unlike Masters and Johnson's, reflects the subjective dimensions of female sexuality, revealing how women's desire is largely "responsive" or "triggered by context and stimulus." Basson contends that "sex needs to be worth wanting" for women, and thus the stimulus or trigger is constantly being appraised. When the stimulus is appraised as sexual, Basson says, genital and subjective responses will occur. But they may not match. Basson concludes that the "disconnect" found in female arousal studies proves that "genital engorgement is prompt and physiological," whereas subjective "emotions and cognitions" are complex, and could break the cycle at any point. For Basson, "poor sexual outcomes" could be related to a number of relational factors, including but not limited to a partner's lack of sexual skills, a partner's sexual dysfunction, medications conflicting with sex drive, or pain with intercourse. These factors, which may be coupled with psychological and biological factors, can break the sexual response cycle. Thus, contrary to medical models that focus on physiological outcomes, Basson claims that subjective outcomes are crucial.

Those described above are just a handful of conference speakers who lodged counterclaims from the conference podium. While they may not entirely reject the idea of organic arousal or desire problems in some women, they insist that the most important reasons for women's lack of sexual arousal exist in the world of "Steve," or other contextual problems. Unfortunately, these are not the voices that dominate either the medical or the public discussions of women's sexuality. No one wants to hear about Steve.

Medical Models Are the Problem

In contrast to the individual practitioners mentioned above who have highlighted counterclaims in their Boston Forum grandmaster presentations since 1999, the Working Group on Women's Sexual Problems has an organized campaign to reframe FSD both inside and outside of the Boston Forum. This group of feminist advocates, both practitioners and academics, formed in response to news of the first Boston Forum meeting in 1999. Their focus is on women's health, and they ask questions such as, Are women's sexual problems purely biological, or are they also social, cultural, and relational? and, Are pharmaceutical companies more concerned with profits or helping women?

The Working Group exists in contrast to other contemporary health movements focused on potentially fatal diseases, with drug and treatment development as their goals. Social scientist Steven Epstein's research on AIDS activism suggests that there has been a recent upsurge in a particular type of identity-based health activism focused on disease categories, such as prostate cancer, breast cancer, AIDS, mental illness, and Alzheimers.[82] Epstein profiles "treatment activists" as central to the push for approval of AIDS drugs earlier in the FDA development pipeline, as well as to the design and conduct of clinical trials. ACT UP was, in the 1980s and 1990s, the centerpiece of the AIDS movement and the quintessential example of an identity-politics movement constructed with medical goals. For the most part, ACT UP members were proponents of pharmaceutical treatments for AIDS, with their initial goal being "getting drugs into bodies"; later, treatment activists became less optimistic about medical solutions and pushed instead for "good science."[83] Despite this change in attitude, Epstein suggests that treatment activists have become "believers in science," wanting not to reject science but to transform it.[84] In contrast to AIDS activism, the Working Group is less interested in drug development and more interested in making visible and problematic privatized mainstream science and medicine. Additionally, unlike AIDS activists who may encourage drugs to be fast-tracked, the Working Group would prefer to slow down and interrupt FSD momentum in medical circles. (Ironically, FDA fast-tracking processes that led to Viagra's early debut were probably made possible by AIDS activists who protested the FDA's slow approval process.)

For the members of the Working Group, FSD appears to be a continuation of historical efforts to medicate and shape women's sexuality to fit the needs of concentrated male power. The Working Group is in this sense a countermovement that responds to and anticipates the "official" FSD campaign, proposing alternatives to dominant medical and pharmaceutical models. Both "campaigns" are in their infancy, learning the rules as they go along, competing for public attention, and struggling to define women's sexual problems.

The Working Group was first envisioned in 1999, in an article titled "'Female Sexual Dysfunction' Alert: A New Disorder Invented for Women," penned by Dr. Leonore Tiefer and published in a feminist newspaper.[85] In the article, Tiefer expressed her concern about an upcoming pharmaceutically funded medical conference taking place in Boston in late October, organized by "the team that brought you Viagra." In the process of medicalization, Tiefer warned, the factors that account for the lion's share of women's sexual problems (economic, social, political) will be ignored, denied, avoided, and generally said to be "not about sexuality." Tiefer invited readers to strategize about forming a "feminist welcoming committee" for the Boston Forum meetings. Fascinated by the potential grassroots response to Tiefer's call for action, I responded and boarded a plane for Boston. Before I knew it, I was both an observer and a participant in the Working Group.

In 1999, the *Boston Globe* profiled the very first Working Group "strategy session" in a feature story entitled "Doubts Heard over Sexual Dysfunction Gathering."[86] Working Group members are depicted brainstorming about ways to make women visible at this conference, including dressing up as plastic vulvas. The article highlights Leonore Tiefer as the primary Boston Forum critic, quoting her warning that "doctors are claiming to be experts on sexuality, but what is taught in medical schools is mechanical, biological stuff on the tissue and the glands." In the article, "expert" urologist Jennifer Berman responds to this concern, countering, "Since urologists have been the leading experts in sexual response difficulty in men, it's a natural transition to begin to evaluate these problems in women." Finally, a Pfizer spokeswoman is quoted as saying, "We're not defining female sexuality. We're not defining male sexuality. What we're defining is a medical condition that we have a treatment for, period."[87]

In an effort to bring attention to and legitimize their concerns, Working Group members handed out hundreds of copies of this article at the Boston Forum and other conferences in 1999. In 1999 and 2000 they also distributed to every conference participant a list of "Dangerous Outcomes" associated with promoting sexual dysfunction for men and women. The list cautioned that FSD was dangerous because it places an emphasis on sexual physiology and performance; obscures the psycho-social aspects of sexuality; gives women more reasons to feel insecure; reinforces narrow definitions of sexuality and ignores women's complex sexualities; discourages or discredits styles of sexuality that do not focus on genital arousal and orgasm; gives pharmaceutical companies impetus to invent and promote "magic bullet" treatments; slights sex education efforts; causes insurance companies to ignore counseling; and causes media, medical practitioners, and patients to continue to ignore social factors.[88]

In 2000, the Working Group moved from a "Dangerous Outcomes" list to drafting its own scientific document, an alternative (nonmedical) classification system of women's sexual problems entitled "The New View on Women's Sexual Problems." This document, currently translated into Dutch, German, and French, continues to be widely dispersed and published within "legitimate" scientific venues as an alternative to FSD classification systems.[89] While acknowledging that medical problems do exist, the "New View" takes issue with medical and psychiatric frameworks as the only avenues for understanding sexual problems.

Specifically, the "New View" points to three major problems with these classifications:

> The three most serious distortions produced by a framework that reduces sexual problems to disorders of physiological function, comparable to breathing or digestive disorders, are:
>
> A false notion of sexual equivalency between men and women . . . with over-emphasis on genital and physiological similarities, ignoring the implications of inequalities related to gender, social class, ethnicity, sexual orientation, etc. . . .
> The erasure of the relational context of sexuality . . . which often lies at the root of sexual satisfaction and problems. . . .
> The leveling of differences among women. All women are not the same and their sexual needs, satisfactions, and problems do not fit neatly into categories of desire, arousal, orgasm, or pain. . . . Differences [in values, approaches, practices, and backgrounds] cannot be smoothed over into an identical one-size-fits-all treatment [or classification schema][90]

After outlining problems with existing frameworks for understanding women's sexual problems, the "New View" outlines a new classification system reflecting the Working Group's definition of sexual problems. As opposed to most definitions circulating at the Boston Forum, this definition acknowledges medical factors as just one of the multiple factors influencing women's sexual problems:

> Sexual problems are defined as discontent or dissatisfaction with any emotional, physical, or relational aspect of sexual experience that may arise in one or more of the following interrelated aspects of women's lives: 1) socio-cultural, political, or economic factors, 2) partner or relational factors, 3) psychological factors, 4) medical factors.[91]

By 2000, both the Boston Forum and the Working Group had engaged in similar activities to become "official" or legitimate organizations in the eyes of the public.[92] The countermovement became an official organization with a name, "The Working Group on Women's Sexual Problems." It had financial sponsors, including the National Women's Health Organization and individual donors; hundreds of endorsers; a visionary leader; a core group of organizers/advocates, including the twelve authors of "The New View"; a website outlining the group's concerns and goals called FSD-Alert.org; regular bicoastal membership meetings; press releases; and a book, *A New View of Women's Sexual Problems,* published by Haworth Press.[93] In addition, in San Francisco in March 2002,the Working Group held its first shadow conference, entitled "The New 'Female Sexual Dysfunction': Promises, Prescriptions, and Profits." At this meeting 150 attendees heard critical presentations by leading health advocates on such issues as the privatization of medical research and the problems associated with direct-to-consumer advertising. These institutionalizing moves paralleled similar paths taken by the Boston Forum at almost the same time. In 2000 it was officially voted to be an organization with a name, Female Sexual Function Forum, a website, corporate (pharmaceutical) sponsors, bylaws, a board of directors, a visionary leader (president), press releases, and annual conferences.

In summary, as opposed to all of the other players at the Boston Forum, the Working Group frames FSD as problematic in itself, as it reduces complex sexualities to a narrow medical model while continuing to promote heterosexual intercourse as the sexual gold standard. While acknowledging that women's sexual problems exist, these critics insist that such "problems" are embedded in relational, cultural, psychological, and social contexts. "New View" proponents want to prevent women's sexual problems by counteracting economic, political, and sociocultural causes of these problems. They point to the double workday, high rates of domestic violence and rape, and inadequate sex education as social problems contributing to women's sexual dissatisfaction. What is problematic and dangerous for the Working Group is promoting a band-aid solution instead of looking at the big picture. If sexual satisfaction and women's empowerment is the goal, the Working Group suggests dealing with these serious social problems instead of promoting a quick fix.

A New Vision of Women's (and Men's) Sexualities

Discovery Health Channel's documentary "Sex, Pills, and Love Potions," opens with this statement: "One-seventh of all males, and one-third of all women have sexual problems. Scientists are racing to find treatments, but what *is* sexuality, and can it be bottled and sold?"[94] The documentary goes on to follow one woman's search for a female Viagra. Gabriela, a middle-aged mother of six, loses her desire for sex after her hysterectomy. We learn that she has seen many doctors who repeatedly give her prescriptions for antidepressants in response to her complaints about sexual problems. Finally, Gabriela sees specialist Jennifer Berman, who tells her sadly that important nerves had been cut during her surgery. Hope is not lost—Berman prescribes testosterone, and later Gabriela describes how she has grown a beard and has trouble sleeping but feels surges of libido. In the final minutes of the documentary, Gabriela is still searching for help with sexual desire. Out of concern for liver damage, she has stopped taking testosterone. She says that although she rarely takes aspirin, "At this point, I'm reaching for pills, anything that will make me right." Gabriela's frustrating story parallels medical experts' unsuccessful search for a magic bullet. After years of searching, both have found that there are no easy answers.

Unlike most formal medical meetings, the Boston Forum has had its share of controversy and tension, as exemplified by six competing diagnoses of women's sexual problems. At the Boston Forum, biological explanations compete with psychological, social, and cultural ones. As I write this, no one diagnosis had been packaged and promoted with a major FDA-approved pharmacological treatment, and the search for the female Viagra continues today.[95] Then again, with testosterone patches for women nearing FDA approval, concerns about a new phase of risky hormone replacement therapy abound.

FSD is still in the making, a case of a complicated problem without a solution, or an example of "diagnostic expansion" that, so far, has failed. Unlike the success of reinventing impotence as ED, attempts to reinvent frigidity as FSD and to promote a single treatment are currently stalled, and may never achieve the degree of success as ED and Viagra did. This "stalling" is largely due to the failure of sildenafil in curing women of FSD,[96] as well as to the persistence and persuasiveness of counterclaims, both inside and outside of the medical community. On the other hand, because of the success of sildenafil in producing erections in men, there appears to be very little dispute about men's sexuality being anything other than a simple issue of erect penises, which is a clear disservice to men.

Importantly, the demand for a female Viagra is not coming from the pharmaceutical companies alone. Equality, or "equal opportunity," rhetoric is used by consumers and marketers alike, as in an advertisement for the nonprescription daily pill Avlimil that claims, "After all, men have their little blue pill. . . ." One regularly finds references to a "female Viagra" in the mainstream media, on television talk shows, and even in my conversations with college students, many of whom have heard of FSD and think they might have it.

The young women students I have spoken with in their late teens and early twenties, many of whom are sexually active, wonder if they too are sexually dysfunctional if they cannot achieve orgasm or summon up desire when their boyfriend wants to have sex. For today's competitive, high-achieving students, sex is yet another arena where they experience performance anxiety, and finding solutions to their sexual problems is greatly desired. Having come of age in a pharmaceutical era, many may not think twice about desiring pills and devices to correct their problems. My fear is that, as the performance bar gets raised, taking a pill may increasingly replace conversation, interpersonal negotiation, and critical thinking about social pressures, relationship issues, and cultural expectations.

Whether or not FSD becomes a household term in the next few years, the social implications of the FSD movement are major in terms of constructing and cementing cultural understandings of sexuality and gender. Tiefer describes the struggle at the Boston Forum and in the public sphere as a competition for "a vision of women's sexuality":

> Women's sexuality is just coming into its own, for a lot of different reasons. We now have the opportunity to enjoy our bodies, our relationships, our individual development, in a way that women have never had before in the history of the world, and it breaks my heart to think about the sexual possibilities as all of a sudden being straitjacketed into a narrow model of adequate performance and sexual acts. That is not where we've been coming from. That's

why I see it as a boxing ring. It's not just us versus the pharmaceutical industry. It is a vision of women's sexuality that we're struggling over.[97]

Tiefer implies that whoever wins in the "boxing ring" has the power to create or reinforce a vision of sexuality that can be harmful, oppressive, and generally problematic in its assumptions and "normative" constructions of gender and sexuality, as has happened in the past in the case of hysteria, nymphomania, impotence, and frigidity. Seeing itself as part of a legacy of the feminist health movement of the 1970s, and the continuation of feminist scholarship concerned with the medicalization of women's bodies, the Working Group looks quite different from other reproductive-health, AIDS-related, and breast-cancer-advocate groups that have demanded drug development and have focused on organized medicine or the FDA to achieve their goals. For the Working Group, universalizing medical models can contribute to narrow sexual standards and enhanced performance anxieties.[98] The Working Group reminds us to ask who constructs and defines "the problem" as well as "the solution."

The inability to simply and easily "diagnose" women's sexual problems is one of many unanticipated consequences of the Viagra phenomenon. Today, the battle between experts hoping to understand women's sexual problems and desires rages on. In 2003, John Bancroft and his team of psychologists from the Kinsey Institute for Research in Sex completed a major study on women's sexual distress in which they argue against the very concept of sexual "dysfunction" and against the treatment of men's and women's sexual problems as virtually the same. Specifically, Bancroft and his colleagues found in their national sample of 987 white and black heterosexual women, aged twenty to sixty-five, that the best predictors of sexual distress were emotional (including general well-being and emotional relationship with partner) and that physical aspects of sexuality (such as arousal, lubrication, and orgasm) were poor indicators of distress. Interestingly, this team credits Lilly ICOS for research funding and for providing a positive example of how industry funding can be helpful without influencing analysis or reporting.[99]

With urologists at the helm of decision making and planning, masculinity continues to be imagined in medical meetings as centered solely on penile success, and thus man is conceived as the opposite of "the complicated woman." Femininity continues to be imagined as utterly mysterious and complex. Because no easy answers have yet been discovered, it is still too early to know how women's sexuality might be "fixed" in the months and years to come.

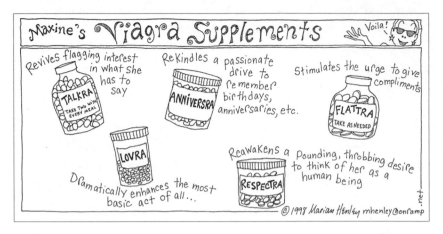

Cartoon by Marian Henley

6

A Pill for Everything?

IT WAS JULY 2003, and the Second Annual Congress on Erectile and Sexual Dysfunctions was meeting in a large conference center in Paris, of all places. Over one thousand doctors, scientists, and marketers from over thirty-five countries came to discuss the latest findings on sexual dysfunction research and treatment.[1] On the surface, the meeting was a celebration of sorts. As I walked through the conference center, I saw large, colorful pharmaceutical displays staffed by busy salespeople handing out free gifts. In the Viagra information area, I stood at a blue glass counter where I was offered my choice of blue, diamond-shaped Viagra lollipops, blue disposable cameras, and blue Viagra-themed mousepads. I signed a membership card that enabled me to use the Blue Diamond Lounge, a side room where one could check e-mail or talk with others on blue couches. In the Cialis sales area I was surrounded by large posters of attractive white heterosexual couples in their forties and by pharmaceutical representatives who busily answered questions posed by curious conference attendees while also serving up frothy cappuccinos. Behind the counter, a man on a microphone called out, "Play the Cialis quiz and win a prize!" Across the way, large, flaming torches invited passersby to the Levitra sales floor, where one could learn about "lighting the flame" faster by taking the new drug, Levitra.[2]

This carnival-like atmosphere was in celebration of three erectile dysfunction pills, each slightly different, all officially available in France and proudly displayed at the conference. Levitra and Cialis were boldly promoted as improvements upon Viagra, the industry leader, with ads for these products citing evidence that they worked faster (as early as sixteen minutes) for longer periods (from twenty-four to thirty-six hours).[3] These time factors were used to market these products in terms of improved romance and spontaneity. Each was associated with its own two-hour symposium at this conference and was introduced to large audiences by affiliated "faculty" from around the world.[4] In addition, the urologists, scientists, and psychiatrists delivered three days' worth of committee reports on the latest findings regarding men's and women's sexual dysfunctions. Lavish buffet lunches and evening wine and cheese parties flanked the daily sessions.

In one popular session, Pfizer celebrated "Five Years of Viagra"; the session featured three Pfizer-funded speakers, a pharmacologist from Canada, an American urologist, and an American psychiatrist, who addressed a packed house by posing the question, "Why is Viagra a worldwide phenomenon?" In response, the experts emphasized the widespread prevalence of erectile dysfunction, and cited Nobel Prize–winning scientific research that validates new understandings about erections. One speaker declared, "It is time to move away from body/mind dualism—we now have a clear biological disorder." The Pfizer speakers went on to congratulate the audience, a mixed group of medical specialists in sexual dysfunction, for "over twenty million patients treated, over two thousand abstracts, and one hundred million prescriptions written."

To most medical practitioners in attendance, the meeting may have been unremarkable, symbolic of the day-to-day conventions of medicine. But for a sociologist, this meeting, like all of the meetings I attended in the past five years, was fascinating for that very reason: because it revealed how medicine works in the twenty-first century. A quick glance at the Paris 2003 conference program reveals the ingredients of a conventional medical conference: experts, pharmaceutical representatives, presentations, and special events. But, upon closer inspection, these elements begin to blur, revealing intimate ties between medical professionals and marketers. Separating the two groups out becomes difficult if not impossible.

My experiences in Paris that spring were not that different from those we encounter in our everyday lives. For example, we may not all receive free Viagra mugs, but we know that we can get free sample packs if we "ask our doctors." Our doctors may not get paychecks from pharmaceutical corporations, but they get plenty of gifts, and most, if not all, of their medical information about sexual dysfunction comes from pharmaceutical corporations. While many consumers, thankfully, have not had to sit through medical symposia, most of us have seen Viagra advertising, and whether we acknowledge it or not, these ads convey powerful messages about what it means to have a good sex life, to be healthy and happy, or to be a real man or a real woman.

Five years after its debut, the impact of the blue pill on American society is now quite visible. Several products compete for the ED market, and FSD treatments are on the way. *Newsweek* magazine has introduced a new social phenomenon, "Viagra Babies."[5] Most significantly, the Viagra phenomenon has changed our understanding of sex in America and, increasingly, is changing it around the world as well. While what passes for normal is always in flux, I think it is fair to say that the way we define normal sex is different now than it was before Viagra. Normal sex now means sex on demand, sex for everyone, and sex for life. What passes for normal medicine has also changed as a result of the blockbuster profits for Pfizer Pharmaceuticals. With other drug companies increasingly in the hunt for profit-soaring drugs and treatments, the medical landscape has also changed so that more and more pills are being popped every day. Beyond these shifts in definitions, I believe that the Viagra phenomenon has also impacted our ideas about health and aging, masculinity and femininity. As I will discuss in this final chapter, the implications for this new sexual order have potentially troubling implications not just for men and masculinity but also for women, medicine, and the future of health care in America.

Normal Medicine

A professor of medicine recently commented to me, "Pretty soon, we won't even have to have sex. We'll just take a pill instead." As this remark suggests, in the Viagra era there seems to be a pill for everything, and this is considered normal. At the Paris conference, I spoke with a urologist from the University of Arizona who is currently working with dermatologists to test a drug that works on the brain not only to enhance erections but also to give you a tan and a faster metabolism.[6] A pill for everything? Just about. In the summer of 2003, Wrigley's Corporation announced that they have patented a chewing gum that enables erections. Just one stick of gum could contain a dose of the generic chemicals found in Viagra as well as peppermint flavoring, creating fresh breath while simultaneously circulating blood to the penis and providing an erection.[7] A 2003 *New York* magazine cover story entitled "Self-Medicated City: What Are You On?" discussed the way pharmaceutical pills of all types are increasingly taken as part of the normal routine of many Manhattanites. In this article, young professionals discussed the practice of "layering" drugs like antidepressants, which generally decrease sex drive, with drugs like Viagra, which enhance sexual arousal, in order to achieve the desired effect of a happy orgasm. Author Ariel Levy summed up the situation this way: "With the stigma attached to mood-improving (not to mention sex-improving) drugs all but gone, New Yorkers are becoming their own Dr. Feelgoods, self-medicating as never before."[8] While the young, wealthy, and hip may choose to layer drugs, many older Americans are increasingly prescribed a bonanza of pills to take every day. More and more often, these individuals are taking, on average, six, eight, or more prescriptions, along with over-the-counter medications, on a regular basis.[9]

The cultural emphasis on pills for happiness, well-being, and physical and mental regulation brings to mind sociologist George Ritzer's classic analysis of contemporary society as defined by "McDonaldization." For Ritzer the success of the fast-food industry has led to the current push for speed, efficiency, conformity, and quick-fix solutions. Today one could easily apply Ritzer's metaphor to on-demand, highly efficient sexuality, or the "McDonaldization" of sex, now quickly becoming the status quo.

More generally, medicine at the turn of the century clearly involves a quick-fix pill culture that normalizes prescription drugs for lifestyle and identity choices, and favors the healthy and the wealthy. Some of my informants voiced concern about this "quick-fix pill culture" that emphasizes enhancement, performance, and perfection over, say, affection, connection, and intimacy. Like Alice in Wonderland, it is difficult for most of us today not to be in awe of the many enhancement options available in our American pharmaceutical "wonderland." And in a pill-oriented culture, it is tempting to believe that if the pill works, the problem has been treated. But what if the existence of such a pill is actually causing or at least contributing to the problem? Viagra alone cannot eliminate social pressures related to sexuality, masculinity, power, and youth. Instead, I would argue that Pfizer and other pharmaceutical corporations reinforce social conventions and fuel social pressures in order to create markets for their drug. In doing so, they increasingly medicalize discontent. Ironically, though, by promoting new standards for health and well-being and by playing on insecurities, pharmaceutical companies and entrepreneurs can expand their markets infinitely.

The Viagra phenomenon raises important questions about who deserves and has access to health, medical care, and quality of life (or "high-quality erections"), and who does not. While Viagra and similar blockbuster prescription products are increasingly marketed to broader demographics, and used by diverse populations worldwide, we can assume that the majority of Viagra users are those who can afford the drug, a reality that reinforces existing race, age, and class-based hierarchies of privilege in relation to medical care and coverage. From a profit standpoint, it makes sense to treat the healthy. They live longer, so they will depend on the product for much longer than a patient who is ill. In this sense, Viagra reveals how, increasingly, medical attention, particularly in the form of pharmaceuticals, is turned to the needs and desires of the leisure class, rather than those of the poor.[10] After all, whose needs really matter to insurers and pharmaceutical corporations?[11]

On a global scale, partly because of the internet and global media, Viagra is available, legally or illegally, and sought after worldwide. In an era of direct-to-consumer advertising and globalization, our whole world is a "branded" one, and Viagra is a testament to the global marketplace, the success of U.S. cultural imperialism, and the widespread demand for confidence, youth, potency, and masculine ideals. While drug advertising is illegal in Europe, companies like Lilly ICOS get around this by sponsoring radio talk shows on men's health issues and concerts featuring Blondie's Debbie Harry and tenor Jose Carreras performing duets.[12] Step across the U.S. border into Mexico and one might see and hear vendors hawking Viagra, no prescription needed. In China and the Philippines, for example, Viagra has a bustling underground market,[13] and counterfeit Viagra pills are manufactured by the millions and sold in Hong Kong, New York, and over the internet. In Saudi Arabia, Viagra prescriptions are available only to those with proof of marriage. In many countries, Viagra "knock-off" products, such as drinks, creams, or "all-natural" pills, circulate widely. For example, a highly profitable soft drink named "Niagara" (then changed to "Nexcite" due to copyright infringement) is being manufactured in Sweden and distributed out of Little Rock, Arkansas. A popular drink containing sildenafil, the active ingredient of Viagra, was banned in Japan.[14] And a product called "Viacreme" is currently being marketed and sold largely by housewives in North America.[15] Pfizer continues to seek ways to capitalize on the global Viagra market.[16] They are currently conducting research measuring the meanings and incidence of sexual dysfunction in Asian and European nations, presumably with hopes of creating markets based on cultural need.[17]

One way to begin to comprehend the ways in which the Viagra global marketplace has altered cultural practices worldwide is to look not only at men's lives but also at the newly protected lives of endangered animal species. Perhaps the most unexpected positive ramification of the global Viagra phenomenon is the effect Viagra may be having on endangered species worldwide. For example, harp seals and rhinos may be saved because Viagra has replaced the regional aphrodisiacs supplied by these species, such as harp seal penises and rhino horns.[18] In addition, researchers at China's major urban zoos are using Viagra to help pandas mate, with the hope of increasing the general population numbers of this endangered species.[19] Viagra's numerous applications around the world testify to Pfizer's global success—a level of success that is not surprising once one realizes the amount of power and control held by companies like Pfizer.

In America normal medicine has come to mean that pharmaceutical companies now have "unprecedented levels of control" over every aspect of the medical process: education, sales, advertising, awareness, advocacy, research, and regulation.[20] Katharine Greider begins her book, *The Big Fix: How the Pharmaceutical Industry Rips Off American Consumers*, by warning readers that drug makers have become "deeply enmeshed" in the process that determines which drugs Americans use, and when, why, and how we use them. The *British Medical Journal* has taken this message one step further with their May 31, 2003, issue depicting pigs and snakes carousing together on the cover with the caption, "Time to untangle doctors from drug companies." On a related note, recent articles published in the *British Medical Journal* and the *Chicago Tribune* have accused the pharmaceutical industry of abusing their power by inventing numerous diseases and dysfunctions in the name of profits.[21]

As we have seen, a big part of the Viagra story is about the entanglement of doctors and marketers. Pharmaceutical interests are integrated into all things medical, from drug trials to scientific reporting to education and beyond. The Viagra phenomenon exemplifies the increasing privatization of medicine, or the growing interdependencies between pharmaceutical corporations and doctors. Experts and marketers are increasingly dependent upon one another, as experts need funding to get research done and marketers need expert status to achieve legitimacy and publish data. Thus, although I treat them as separate categories, one argument I make in this book is that a growing number of experts are marketers, a fact that is rarely evident to the public but that has major implications for future health research and education. This fusion of science and capitalism has left America, in Greider's eyes, "oddly impoverished in the way of unbiased, approachable information about the usefulness and cost of one drug versus another."[22] It has also left American men impoverished in their options for achieving true masculinity.

Men Performing Badly

Viagra, commonly seen as a quality-of-life drug, can also be seen as an identity drug, promising men the opportunity to "do" masculinity and better perform sexually with the help of the pill. We can see this quite literally, as Viagra is now both a boon and a requirement for men working in the porn industry, where a fast, hard, powerful, and potent penis is the name of the game.[23] Is the porn star's pressure to perform that much different from that of everyday American male?

While much has been made of Pfizer's efforts to empower men in the short term, I argue that in the long run, the Viagra phenomenon is every bit as constraining as it is "freeing" for males. Pfizer has both capitalized on and contributed to a type of "masculinity crisis" by reinforcing the pursuit of potent and powerful manhood. Who wins when sexuality is narrowed down to penile-vaginal penetration and perfect erectile functioning? That pharmaceutical companies are prescribing and promoting unattainable standards related to sex and gender is of grave concern. Such unattainable standards both propel and result from the growth of "performance medicine" and the endless promotion of performance standards in popular magazines and on television. Together, media and medicine have ushered in an era of widespread performance anxiety.[24] Some of the doctors and patients I spoke with pointed to these social pressures when discussing how Viagra can be dangerous or harmful for men both physiologically and psychologically. More recently, popular attention has turned to men's use of testosterone therapy, prescribed by doctors off label, despite potential long-term harmful effects.[25] The success of Viagra-like products and testosterone therapy has no doubt spurred on the masculinity industry. And masculinity for sale at the turn of the century threatens to match the commodification of femininity that has arguably both empowered and constrained women for centuries.

As I have shown, women encounter the Viagra phenomenon on a different playing field, as partners and as patients. Very little has been written about the experience of women partners of Viagra users. But newspaper advice columns, articles, internet postings, and my own conversations reveal many women who are skeptical of medical solutions and their social ramifications.[26] This caution may stem in part from the fact that, as patients, women have endured centuries of medical maltreatment. The 2002 findings on the dangers of hormone replacement therapy (HRT) have refueled medical cynicism among women. This history of maltreatment is even more pronounced for women of color. What this means for "phase two" of the Viagra phenomenon and the ongoing construction of female sexual dysfunction is unclear. Many women would like to see medical science pay more attention to their sexual concerns. But as I've shown here, this movement is now being fought on a medical terrain where the male body is still the universal standard, and attention to "the woman surrounding the vagina" is clearly lacking.[27]

Sex Forever

A recent *Newsweek* cover story featured "No-Sex Marriages" in which a handful of thirty-something couples admitted that they are making less time for sex in the face of extended work hours and child care.[28] This "news" should be no surprise to most Americans, but in the Viagra era, there is no excuse for a no-sex marriage and the "normal" sexual life course is now seen as a long and active one. Age, too, is no longer an excuse for older couples, with Viagra to combat the effects of aging. Of course, for Pfizer, extended lives and lifelong sex means lifelong marketing potential and lifelong sales for their product.

Increasingly, health is correlated with sexual activity. Along with its numerous advertising allusions to regaining "life," and its recent advertising message, "Pfizer for Living," Pfizer's advertising regularly implies that sexual activity for men not only is healthy but also is central to survival. According to Pfizer, there is no excuse for not being sexual or desiring sex. For example, one Pfizer promotional brochure states, "Frequency of sexual intercourse is a significant predictor of longevity in men." It continues, "Mortality risk is 50% lower in men with high orgasmic frequency than in men with low orgasmic frequency."[29] These are scientific findings excerpted from studies published in medical journals such as *Gerontologist* and *BMJ*. Pfizer appears to use these findings to add legitimacy to the cultural expectation that sexual activity is compulsory. Notably, Pfizer seems to be suggesting that sex is only healthy and normal if it is intercourse- and orgasm-centered, thus shaping and maintaining narrow ideas about heterosexual sex.

For Pfizer the major ingredient in a healthy sex life is a healthy, functional penis. But because Viagra doesn't work for everyone, men have turned to other arenas to achieve sexual health. Men's sexual health clinics have proliferated across the country, and the penile implant industry has been rejuvenated in an effort to get, seemingly by any means necessary, the perfect penis.[30] Researchers are busy working on ensuring healthy penises for centuries to come, forecasting "genetically re-engineered penises" and brain-focused sexual-dysfunction treatments for the future.[31] Urologist Hunter Wessels, at the University of Arizona, is perfecting a treatment for ED that works through the brain: "The brain is such an important sex organ. Viagra takes half an hour to work, but the brain can get an erection in 10–15 seconds. That's what we're aiming for—something spontaneous and rapidly acting." Other researchers are working on gene therapy, suggesting that the "penis is the perfect site for gene therapy because it is separate and dangling from the body, ensuring that treatments bypass the rest of the body, enabling reengineering the penile tissue or the ability to put higher chemical amounts in the penis."[32]

While sex is a requirement for good health in the Viagra era, aging is the antidote. In 2003, Pfizer launched its "Pfizer for Living" program, a personalized health-information program that promises to "give you sensible advice with real solutions." General mailings sent by the "Pfizer for Living" group assert, "Okay, so there isn't a fountain of youth. Here's a backup plan." The mailing goes on to offer "a free health info source" that takes a "young at heart" approach to health, suggesting that "youth is wasted on the young." The brochure is covered in statistics about aging. The envelope for the mailer says, "Every 8.3 seconds someone turns 50" and "50% of men and women are about half gray by age 55" and "Americans spent 1.2 billion on anti-aging products in 2001."[33] Aging is Pfizer's lifeline, literally and figuratively.

For most pharmaceutical companies, aging is where the money is. So why not play it up?

Viagra's debut marked the beginning of medical and pharmaceutical efforts to make aging into a treatable medical problem. Viagra, along with recently FDA-approved Botox, the antiwrinkle drug, signal the proliferation of anti-aging treatments soon to be available.[34] Recent estimates suggest that by 2030, one out of five Americans will be over sixty-five years of age. With the help of medicine and technology, life expectancy has increased dramatically—twenty years since 1950. By the year 2050, the United Nations estimates that global life expectancy will average seventy-six years of age.[35] Thus, as the baby boomer generation ages, this group will play a major role in defining aging for future generations.[36]

According to the *Los Angeles Times*, the development of anti-aging treatments promises billions in profits for pharmaceutical companies in the twenty-first century. There are currently 178 new compounds aimed solely at the symptoms of aging, such as impotence, reduced bone density, memory loss, and balding. "For the 76 million potential customers of the baby boom generation, who are turning 50 at the rate of one every 10 seconds, the expensive pills and prescription nostrums are the newest weapons in a war on time."[37] New products packaged in anti-aging messages will further increase cultural anxieties and redefine "normal" bodies based on new unattainable ideals. Clearly, the pharmacology of aging will be another rich and troubling research site in years to come.

Dangers of Viagra

A responsibility towards public health means acknowledging possible dangerous uses of drugs, and their consequences. In part due to its easy availability and association with sexuality, Viagra has become a recreational drug, most commonly used by young people, both gay and straight, in combination with Ecstasy—now known on the street as "Sextasy."[38] I have heard personal reports from emergency room doctors complaining about the partiers and pimps who end up crowding big-city hospital emergency rooms after creating dangerous drug combinations with Viagra. Several articles have appeared over the years in gay publications such as the *Advocate*, warning about the potentially lethal combination of Viagra with crystal meth, poppers, and Ecstacy, as well as the potential for "risky sex" and HIV transmission with such drugs. While Viagra's recreational use is a big story in the mainstream press, it is rarely acknowledged by Pfizer, presumably because Pfizer wants to protect Viagra's "sanitized" image.[39]

The threat of rising numbers of deaths linked to Viagra use did lead Pfizer to publicize several "warnings" in gay publications and on news shows, in the months following the drug's debut. Writing in the *Advocate* in late 1998, journalist John Gallagher reported that the potency pill doesn't mix well with recreational drugs and can be fatal when combined with protease inhibitors or poppers, for example. He went on to report that Pfizer did approach AIDS.org and the Gay and Lesbian Medical Association within weeks of Viagra's introduction to issue alerts about potentially serious drug interactions.[40] But perhaps Pfizer has not gone far enough. More recently in the *Advocate,* on April 29, 2003, journalist Christopher Tkaczyk reported on ongoing and, thus far, unsuccessful efforts to get Pfizer to add warning labels on the product that would address the link between Viagra use and infection rates for STDs, for example.[41]

Today there also seems to be limited acknowledgment that many prescription-only pills are distributed not through doctors but through "virtual" pharmacies and the black market. In this way, Viagra has made visible some important shifts in the organization of health care in America. Viagra was one of the first drugs to be made available on the internet; and most of us have received junk e-mails alerting us to Viagra's availability on the web. Today, a typical online pharmacy (for example, RX.com) offers "a complete online consultation in less than five minutes, and medication received within twenty-four hours." Particularly in light of the stigma attached to using and asking for Viagra, and the escalating price of medical insurance, multitudes of individuals are choosing online medical checkups and prescriptions over visits to doctors' offices.[42] For liability and general health reasons, Pfizer may be more interested in luring Viagra consumers to doctors' offices than to internet sites. In 2002, Pfizer began offering free sample "six-packs" to those who "ask their doctors." But this will not affect the millions of uninsured Americans. Interestingly, the Viagra phenomenon has demonstrated the potential role that the internet can play in future medical care and treatment. If online medical clinics and pharmacies take responsibility for growing amounts of health care in the United States, how will this affect the organization and quality of health care in the future?

Backlash

As the most profitable industry in the United States, pharmaceutical firms have an immense amount of power over the government, while government regulators have steadily seen their power decrease.[43] As Greider points out, the pharmaceutical lobby was "625 members strong in 2000 . . . bigger than Congress itself."[44] With so much money available for federal and congressional lobbying, it is no wonder that the FDA has had to continually roll back its standards.

More and more, "health" as we know it is defined by powerful corporations. I believe it is paramount that we become critical about such relationships by asking, Who gets hurt when the most profitable industry in the United States is also the institution defining and solving most public health issues? In a market-based economy, corporations must be focused on the bottom line. But should companies that determine a population's health be just as focused on profit motive as the local car dealer? Many have chimed in on this question in recent years, raising new calls for enhanced industry responsibility and regulation. Investigative journalist Philip J. Hilts concluded his 2003 study on one hundred years of FDA regulation with a sad note, saying, "Essentially . . . the logic of 'profit alone' that dominated [pharmaceutical] companies in the 19th century dominates them today. This is one reason the FDA's job is difficult, and necessary."[45] But, in a world in which the FDA's regulatory power is diminishing, the medical industry in general needs a new type of wake-up call.

Several brave editorials in the *New England Journal of Medicine* have been critical of medical conventions such as the Boston Forums, specifically on the score of industry responsibility and ethics. One such essay, entitled "Uneasy Alliance—Clinical Investigators and the Pharmaceutical Industry," describes how the transition from university-based science research has led the pharmaceutical industry to hire its own clinical investigators and run its own clinical trials to expedite the research process and save money. When running their own trials, pharmaceutical companies can and do play a crucial and dangerous role in trial design, data analysis, and publishing, as well as in the suppression of information. Other editorials—entitled "Is Academic Medicine for Sale?" and "The Pharmaceutical Industry: To Whom Is It Accountable?"—discuss similar conflicts of interest between academic medicine and pharmaceutical and biotechnology industries. Importantly, the latter editorials were written by the former editor of the *New England Journal of Medicine,* Marcia Angell, who ultimately called for enhanced corporate responsibility.

> An industry so important to public health and so heavily subsidized and protected by the government has social responsibilities that should not be totally overshadowed by its drive for profits. There needs to be a better balance between the interests of the shareholders and those of the public.[46]

Fortunately, a strong body of work has emerged in the past five years that champions regulation, warns about public health in a market-based system where profit is always the bottom line, and reveals a growing social movement developing in response to profit-centered medicine and drug-company incursion in the daily lives of Americans.[47] While I have focused on one specific group of critics in this book, I am encouraged to see other critical groups emerging, partly in response to the Viagra phenomenon. For example, a group of U.S. physicians have organized the "no free lunch" campaign to oppose pharmaceutical perks, calling for health care professionals "to *Just say no to drug reps* and their pens, pads, calendars, coffee mugs, and of course, lunch (not to mention dinners, basketball games, and ski vacations)."[48] In New Zealand, feminist scholars have organized their own Viagra research group, similar to the U.S. Working Group, headed by psychologist Annie Potts, with the intent of investigating gendered responses to the Viagra phenomenon.[49] Even network television has become critical, with ABC dedicating two of their spring 2002 evening news shows to critiquing pharmaceutical "education," doctor enticement methods, and consumer deception.[50]

The Viagra phenomenon has exposed the workings of male privilege on a global scale, making visible the power imbalances of gender in medical research, care, and coverage in America and beyond. In response to these imbalances, consumers and practitioners have used Viagra to push for equality and social change. In Japan, for example, Viagra was approved and made available to men before the birth control pill was available to women. In the United States, Viagra was covered by many health insurers, while birth control pills were not.[51] Feminist groups in both countries have rallied to expose these power injustices and push for social change. As a result, the Japanese government approved birth control pills six months after Viagra was publicly available.[52] Japan's birth control approval in late 1998 was due, in part, to the work of one women's advocacy group. Five hundred Japanese medical practitioners and activists known as the Professional Women's Coalition for Sexuality and Health paved the way for birth control approval through health education efforts and through a media information campaign, in which the group sent the results of their research to newspaper opinion pages and television and radio station producers. The group also deluged the national pharmaceutical council, the group responsible for advising the government on medication approval, with letters urging the approval of the birth control pill.[53]

Similarly, in the United States Viagra has been used as a vehicle by feminist groups lobbying for "contraceptive equity," which would require employee insurance plans to cover birth control and other contraceptive options for women if they cover Viagra.[54] In the state of New York, Senator Hilary Rodham Clinton made news when she declared the local Medicaid program "sexist" for covering Viagra but limiting poor women's access to contraceptives.[55] According to recent reports, contraceptive equity laws have passed in sixteen states.[56] Despite these (late) gains, the speedy approval of Viagra seemed to exemplify the sexual double standard in America. Feminists have pointed out that while technologies of sex have been readily available and legitimated for men, technologies of sex for women—namely, the birth control pill and the vibrator—have experienced long delays before being made available and have been enshrouded in sexual morality and obscenity debates from the beginning.[57]

Recent calls for increased government regulation of pharmaceutical companies have made some progress. The majority of medical journals and medical organizations, including those affiliated with Continuing Medical Education credits, now require their authors and presenters to disclose their affiliations with drug companies. In addition, the FDA has removed several extreme pharmaceutical advertisements that engaged in false marketing.[58] In 2002 the FDA issued a "guidance document" and a "code of conduct" for the pharmaceutical industry. This includes a request to end all "gifting" practices as a method to win over doctors.[59]

Despite these small gains, medical education continues to be largely subsidized by the pharmaceutical companies. Almost everything doctors and patients know about medication comes from pharmaceutical companies, including the patient package inserts that detail side effects and drug warnings, drug advertising in many forms, medical research distributed by pharmaceutical salespeople, and even the ubiquitous *Physician's Desk Reference,* the leading reference for physicians that is purchased by thousands of consumers per year.[60] Practitioners have mixed feelings about this increase in public medical education, especially when the majority of this information is backed by profit interests.[61] Continuing Medical Education conferences, the meetings that offer required education credits to doctors, are largely funded by pharmaceutical companies. Direct-to-consumer ads provide corporations with new opportunities to "educate" doctors and patients about the latest illnesses and treatments, and according to a 2002 Kaiser Family Foundation study, one out of eight Americans who see a drug on TV ends up buying it, many times over the internet.[62] Pharmaceutical companies produce and distribute the ever-present informational brochures available in doctors' offices. Pfizer Pharmaceuticals recently awarded large Unrestricted Educational Grants to eight major U.S. medical schools for training medical students in sex education. When one considers the wealth of the industry, it makes sense that the funding for education would come from this source. But as many have pointed out, the industry would not fund such things without the potential for profit—and, furthermore, consumers may ultimately pay these costs in the form of higher prescription prices.[63]

The Viagra phenomenon continues to be a dynamic, rich site for tracking cultural ideals, identifying social problems, and inspiring social change. While the blue diamond has exposed and shaped unattainable cultural ideals and troubling new trends, the experts, critics, marketers and distributors, and consumers highlighted in this study remind us that life is more complicated than a pharmaceutical or techno-science conspiracy. Without a consideration of human agency, the humanity behind technology is lost, and individual choices and decisions, acts of resistance, and efforts for social change are rendered invisible.[64] The stories that make up this book reflect a populace grappling with the Viagra phenomenon. As more drugs continue to be introduced for a seemingly endless list of physical and mental "problems," this struggle will only continue.

Reproduced by permission from *New York*.

Epilogue
A Hard Act to Follow

OVER FIVE YEARS AFTER VIAGRA'S APPROVAL in the United States, evidence of the Viagra phenomenon is still everywhere. Instead of lists of Viagra jokes, my e-mail inbox now contains numerous spam messages selling penile enhancements and cheap Viagra pills. The morning paper reports that bags of counterfeit Viagra pills were seized in Vancouver at its port of entry. Ads for "masculinity clinics" abound. My students point out the Viagra clock hanging on the wall of their dorm lounge. It, along with the pills passed around at several parties last weekend, came from a relative who works in the industry, they say. And if you ask young, sexually active men and women, many will say they are interested in medicine promising sexual pleasure or confidence.

Flipping television channels, you cannot miss commercials for Viagra and its two pharmaceutical competitors, Levitra and Cialis, as well as its "natural" product knock-offs. For example, in a commercial for Enzyte, the "natural male enhancement drug," "Smiling Bob," their silent spokesman, is dressed as Santa with adult women lined up to sit on his lap and make their holiday wishes known.[1] In another ad, a white man in his forties makes several unsuccessful attempts to throw a football through a hanging tire. Later, he is smiling, and we assume he was successful at something, as his wife stands by and the voiceover says, "He asked his doctor for Levitra." The Viagra ad is not much different. A man enters a party looking confident, people wonder what has changed, and the voiceover tells us that he "asked his doctor." Without the Pfizer logo in the corner of the screen, this ad could be selling anything. Interestingly, these men's lives are transformed "just by asking." Pfizer's most recent Viagra television ad features men leaping into the sky to the tune of Queen's "We Are the Champions." Since when have we seen men on television looking this joyous and self-assured?

NFL Hall of Fame player and coach Mike Ditka, renowned for his toughness, appeared in several television ads during the 2004 Super Bowl, admonishing men to "stay in the game." By sponsoring the NFL and integrating athletic models and metaphors into their marketing message, Bayer and Glaxo-SmithKline are advocating high performance standards on and off the field. Published in *Newsweek*, March 2004.

If you are a sports fan, you are the ideal candidate for "male enhancement," it seems. Try as you might, you cannot avoid the marketing blitz. Pfizer, in cahoots with major league baseball, wants you to "step up to the plate." The NFL, together with Bayer and Glaxo-SmithKline, wants you to "light the flame" and "get ready, set, go" with a new pill that promises to work almost immediately to create "3-D erections."[2] Pro golfers, together with Lilly ICOS, want you to be spontaneous and romantic with a new pill that can stay in your system for as long as thirty-six hours. And if you are watching TV in Latin America or Europe, renowned soccer star Pele will tell you that he doesn't need Viagra, but if he did, he'd take it.

For the women watching ESPN, we know that most of these ads are not speaking to us. At most, women are marginally depicted in the ads for male enhancement. In 2004, "thirty-six-hour Cialis" is the exception to this rule, after Lilly ICOS hired a women-headed ad team that has chosen to integrate spouses in its marketing of romance and spontaneity. We have yet to see a major FDA-approved product aimed at female sexual dysfunction, although a testosterone patch for women, produced by Procter and Gamble, is up for FDA approval this year. What we do see are advertisements for "natural" products borrowing from the newfound pharmaceutical legitimacy of direct-to-consumer advertising. For example, Avlimil, produced by Warner Health Care, is featured on various cable television stations, and in magazines such as *Woman's Day* and *First*, as a "gentle, once-daily tablet that can help you achieve a healthier, more satisfying sex life, without hormones or prescription drugs." In the television ads, anonymous, attractive women in their thirties and forties are featured sprawled out on couches confessing to low libido and "reclaiming their sensuality." Flip to the Discovery Health Channel, and the Berman sisters are chatting it up on their sexual-health talk show about how to have "explosive orgasms." Finally, ask your local pharmacist about the explosive increase in the past several years in off-label testosterone prescriptions for women complaining of "low libido."[3]

What is going on here? The Viagra phenomenon has only intensified our otherwise sexualized society. Sexual health and pleasure are endlessly promoted everywhere and appear to be the keys to "life" itself. Five years ago, pharmaceutical companies could not advertise directly to consumers, and men rarely spoke publicly about sexuality, much less erectile insecurity. Today, celebrity spokesmen like Mike Ditka (aka "Iron Mike"), former NFL player and coach, are paid by pharmaceutical companies to say, "I have a problem. I didn't want my life to come to an end." After hearing this repeatedly, listeners come to associate living with sex and, concurrently, lack of sex with dying. In other words, after several hours watching ESPN, one could easily find oneself believing that fast-acting 3-D erections for thirty-six hours might be just the ticket to enhance a man's overall confidence, his relationship, his sense of manhood, his athletic prowess, and life in general.

Women's-liberation and equality rhetoric appears in recent ads for Avlimil, a nonprescription daily tablet that looks a lot like birth control: "They have Viagra. Now we have Avlimil." By advertising on television, in women's magazines, and at doctors' offices, this corporation is selling an over-the-counter drug to women of all ages by borrowing on pharmaceutical legitimacy but distancing itself from recent controversy over hormonal supplements. Published in *Cosmopolitan Magazine,* February 2003.

Next thing you know, if you are a man who is insecure in any of these areas, you're "asking your doctor." And if you are a woman with a "libido problem," you want answers too.

Interestingly, the bedroom may be the place where the Viagra myth ends. To Pfizer's horror, while millions of men asked their doctor for a prescription in the past five years, only half of them have requested a refill. Many of my informants confirmed this. Harvard urologist Abraham Morgentaler, in his new book, *The Viagra Myth*, discusses how he and his patients have spent the past five years learning that a hard penis is not always the best solution to relationship or self-esteem problems.[4] With time, some are questioning whether the Viagra phenomenon is actually solving or creating more problems.

In July 2003, Brazil's version of the FDA realized that constant exposure to pharmaceutical marketing can be harmful to one's health. Concerned about health risks associated with rising numbers of men using Viagra recreationally, Brazil banned the Pele advertisement and all other ads for Viagra and similar substances. This gutsy and responsible move occurred in a country that is the second-largest

This ad demonstrates pharmaceutical "branding" and the changing sexual standards of the Viagra era. Just as Pfizer was successful in coupling Viagra with ED, Bayer and GlaxoSmithKline are attempting to couple Levitra with 3-D imagery in their advertising campaigns. As the ad text suggests, men and women are ready for the transition "from ED to 3D"—in other words, from no erection to a larger-than-life erection. Published on the back cover of the *British Medical Journal*, May 2003.

market for Viagra. Pfizer, unfazed, is taking its Pele campaign to the rest of Latin America and Europe. Bayer, GlaxoSmithKline, Lilly ICOS, Lifekey Healthcare, and Warner Healthcare are only a few steps behind.[5]

In May 2003, *Medical Marketing & Media,* a monthly health-care marketing magazine, featured an article about "The Art of Branding a Condition."[6] The article reads like a how-to on "fostering a condition and aligning it with a product." Authors point to Pfizer's successful effort to link a newly defined condition, ED, with the drug Viagra as the most well-recognized example today of "condition branding." According to the authors, "ED was an acronym suitable for mass promotion, it functioned as an easy password between doctor and patient, and had a brand personality—simple, discreet, and empowering—that aligned beautifully with that of Viagra, an elegant and effective solution to this redefined condition."

Maybe it is just me, but something seems painfully out of whack when medicine is just another marketable commodity coupled with simplified values, identities, and names. People around the world are getting used to calling Cialis by its nickname, "le weekender." And pharmaceutical marketers are getting good at sending press kits to late-night talk-show hosts and sitcom writers.[7] Judging from the research presented at recent conferences on sexual medicine, the sex-in-a-pill trend has only just begun. In the next few years new FDA-approved products will most certainly emerge, coupled with "medical conditions" such as "rapid ejaculation," orgasmic dysfunction, arousal disorders, etc.

By now, if this book has succeeded, you should be concerned about what constitutes normal sex and medicine in the Viagra era and where all of this is headed. At the same time, you should be assured that "normal" is always evolving and changing, and we all play a role in the shaping of expectations in our roles as parents, teachers, colleagues, and significant others. For me, it comes down to this: if we all spent half as much time being concerned about big pharmaceutical corporations and their intentions as we did worrying about our sex lives, this world might be a better place. In other words, what would the world look like if we all turned those beloved 3-D glasses on the pharmaceutical industry, to measure its amazing growth and power in the past few decades? Why don't we claim the "business" of sex for ourselves and "ask our doctors," our friends, and our significant others to talk openly and honestly with us about intimacy, companionship, and sex? Or rather than ask your doctor what to do, ask yourself: are you happy with the way medicine and sexuality look today? That seems like a fine place to start.

© The Washington Post Writers Group. Reprinted with permission.

Appendix: Studying "Up"

THIS APPENDIX EXPLORES the nuts and bolts involved in studying the Viagra phenomenon. What follows is the story of how this research came to be. I answer the who, what, where, when, why, and how questions of this research, address larger methodological issues, and share anecdotes about my own attempts to capture a cultural phenomenon, to study powerful groups and institutions, to situate myself as an activist scholar, and to conduct research on sexualities in general.

Every Path Leads to Viagra?

Most of us have multiple entry points when it comes to the Viagra phenomenon. For me, Bazooms and "Monicagate" were only the beginning. When Viagra emerged I was just completing a case study on one contemporary women's sexual-empowerment-based business. Viagra, in many ways, appeared to me to represent a male corollary to the movement embodied by Toy Box (a pseudonym), a San Francisco sexual-products business started in 1977 with distinct roots in prosex feminist organizing. The Toy Box mission statement and democratic work structure link feminism and profits. From the perspective of Toy Box's owners, for a woman simply to enter this store constitutes a brave and radical act: acknowledging her sexuality. If she wants to take this one step further, she can admit to her sexual desires and literally "buy into" sexual empowerment by purchasing a vibrator, book, or other sex toy. I found that what Toy Box offered was more than simply sex for sale. With products packaged in prosex feminist ideology, Toy Box was selling female sexual liberation.[1]

Viagra is about male sexual liberation, and many journalists associate Viagra with "a second sexual revolution" to convey this point. But the Viagra script was a bit different from that of Toy Box. Instead of visiting a store, brave, white, middle-aged and older male customers interested in sexual empowerment would enter their doctors' offices and pharmacies, admitting to their desires and weaknesses, and the subsequent purchase of Viagra promised male sexual gratification, power, and assurance. However, the contrasts between the two empowerment "campaigns" were striking: Viagra emerged from a pharmaceutical marketing campaign, not grassroots politics, and Viagra received so much public attention with its blockbuster success that it touched many more people than did one small business.

Thus, I came to this project with research questions initially focused on profit-based sexual-empowerment campaigns and on women's stakes in the Viagra phenomenon, both as consumers and partners of Viagra consumers. I wondered, Can consumption practices and commodities affect social change? These questions were fueled by my past research, which interrogated various contemporary forms of sexual commodification, my investment in feminist research, and a strong concern for social inequality. My own biases were evident in the framing of this study from the beginning, as they are in most research. I wondered, Is Viagra simply about erecting the penis, or does it lend itself to a broader sociological analysis of the way patriarchy is supported in cultural, economic, and political realms? I joked that this book would be entitled "Erecting the Patriarchy?" These early positions were reinforced by my feminist friends, advisors, and colleagues, who, upon hearing about my research, would consistently ask me about gender inequalities rendered visible in the Viagra era, ranging from inequities in insurance coverage to changes in heterosexual relationships. Rarely did I hear these concerns reflected by men; the few men who did acknowledge them were practitioners concerned about their patients. Thus, I was convinced early on that the Viagra story was about male privilege, but what might it say about class, age, race, and sexuality? In the process of this research I have found that reducing Viagra to male power—my original assumption—obscures the complexity of what Viagra reveals about a culture and social groups. In this case, "patriarchy" has a new public and private face—that of the ashamed, vulnerable, dysfunctional, white, middle- or upper-class, middle-aged, heterosexual American male.

Viagra Research Sites

I chose to focus my field research on two concentrated sites of coordinated activity related to the Viagra phenomenon: Boston and Los Angeles. Each is a medically sophisticated urban area with somewhat different medical scenes. Selecting these two urban areas allowed me to have access to a range of medical institutions, most of which are producing and profiting from the Viagra campaign. Boston has a large number of medical schools, research centers, and institutes dedicated to mapping, defining, and curing sexual dysfunction. The majority of my participant observation took place at the Boston Forums discussed in chapter 5.

As I was beginning my research, many people advised, "You should have no problem finding people taking Viagra in southern California." This is what one would expect in Los Angeles, home to the porn industry and a booming sexual-enhancement marketplace linked to both entertainment and medical industries. Advertisements in the *Los Angeles Times,* especially the sports section, tout a large variety of sexual-enhancement products and services, including advertisements by doctors offering Viagra consultations. Southern California "masculinity clinics" claim to solve masculine self-esteem problems with cosmetic (penile-enhancement) surgeries. A wide variety of adult stores sell everything from penis pumps to libido creams. Health- and youth-centered Los Angeles is also home to a lucrative herbal-sex-remedy industry promoting countless varieties of potency pills, including products with names like Cobra and Herbal V. Most importantly for my research, Los Angeles is a major research center for sexual medicine. In the 1970s UCLA opened one of very few human-sexuality academic institutes in the nation. In recent years, sexual-medicine clinics have found a base in the Los Angeles area (including UCLA's sexual-medicine clinic, now run by Boston University transplants, the media-savvy Berman sisters). Countless clinical trials dedicated to testing sexuality treatments take place in Los Angeles. In large metropolitan areas such as Los Angeles and Boston, Pfizer and other pharmaceutical companies frequently underwrite conferences aimed at practitioner education on the topic of erectile dysfunction. For all of these reasons, Los Angeles and Boston are crucial sites for exploring the Viagra phenomenon.

Most interviews with doctors took place at medical conferences either in Boston or in southern California, including the cities of Beverly

Hills, Santa Monica, West Hollywood, Santa Barbara, and Goleta. This region offers a high concentration of medical facilities (including some university-affiliated hospitals) and "male-enhancement" services serving diverse communities as well as a spectrum of class levels, from a very wealthy Beverly Hills clientele to lower-middle-class patients in neighboring areas.

Getting at the Phenomenon

Researching the ever-expanding Viagra phenomenon and its social implications meant casting a wide net and designing a research project that would capture the complexity and multivocality of this phenomenon. I employed qualitative methods to capture this evolving cultural phenomenon. Specifically, I used a triangulated methodological approach, including interviews, participant observation, and content analysis. Together, these methods allowed me to do a close, in-depth study of social groups invested in the Viagra phenomenon, as well as to closely track the evolution of medical, historical, and cultural phenomena over time.

First, I conducted a total of seventy semistructured conversational interviews targeting four distinct social groups invested in the Viagra phenomenon: consumers (male and female), critics, experts, and marketers (including distributors).[2] In an attempt to find additional types of interview subjects, I also collected sixty completed surveys from selected (mostly senior) populations in which I asked respondents to describe their relationship to Viagra and what the product symbolized for their lives and communities. These surveys included an invitation to be interviewed by myself, "a University of California researcher," about their answers to selected survey questions.

Second, to understand the Viagra phenomenon in more depth epistemologically and institutionally, I logged over three hundred hours of participant observation at medical sites dedicated to knowledge production and sexual commodification, including medical conferences, "men's clinics" run by urologists concerned primarily with penile enhancement, physicians' offices, sex therapy clinics, herbal-sex-remedy outlets and specialized sexuality businesses, and both "virtual" and "real" pharmacies. I paid great attention to the institutions dedicated to legitimating, defining, mapping, institutionalizing, diagnosing, and/or producing "experts" who would speak on behalf of sexual dysfunctionality and the role of Viagra. My participant observation also had an advocacy component, as I have been involved (since its inception in 1999) as a participant observer and health advocate in the Working Group on Women's Sexual Problems, which is described in chapter 5.

Third, I amassed and analyzed hundreds of mass media reports and Pfizer promotional materials centered on Viagra. I have coded and analyzed news and features reporting from a select group of nationally respected newspapers and a variety of specialty magazines aimed at fitness subcultures, medical communities, men, women, and senior citizens. Also included in my media sample are several important medically focused representations of Viagra's genesis, including two Viagra-related documentaries aired on The Learning Channel (in 1999 and 2001), television news reports on Viagra, advertisements for Viagra and similar products, and Pfizer promotional and training materials from 1999 to 2000.

Experts, Consumers, Marketers, and Critics

A basic principle of symbolic interaction is that all objects, events, and situations acquire their meanings through processes of human interpretation. The meanings attached to objects, events, and situations are not built into them. Instead they are products of our responses to them.[3] This project aims to get at Viagra meaning making as it has been undertaken by a wide range of social groups and individuals.

In an attempt to collect a diversity of perspectives on the Viagra phenomenon, I targeted four different but overlapping groups of individuals for interviews, primarily in the Los Angeles and Boston areas. As described earlier, these groups are: (1) *experts,* or a mixed group of medical professionals including practitioners and therapists, (2) *marketers and distributors,* or Pfizer representatives and pharmacists, (3) *consumers,* both male and female, and (4) *critics,* primarily feminists mobilized against the medicalization of sex. I chose these four social groups because they represent a broad range of investments (financial, work related, and emotional) in Viagra and what it represents. For many informants, Viagra is central to their daily lives—whether in the bedroom or the workplace—as individuals who use, prescribe, promote, or fill prescriptions for Viagra. Other informants remain "outside" the Viagra phenomenon, as curious or critical commentators regarding Viagra and other similar products. Despite their level of investment in Viagra, all of these people have something to say about what Viagra means for their lives, their communities, and their society.

My methods for locating interview subjects are discussed below. I chose interview methods because of the sensitivity of the subject matter and the complexity of the questions I wanted to ask.[4] For all groups except the critics, perspectives on the Viagra phenomenon were collected through taped, semistructured interviews either in person or over the phone. Due to issues of confidentiality, seven interviews with consumers had to be solicited and conducted over the internet. In contrast, the bulk of data on critics, as well as a significant amount of data on experts, was collected in the field, rather than through formal interview processes. Regarding the interview process, whether I was speaking with a consumer or practitioner, therapist or pharmacist, I started our conversations with personal information (experience with Viagra, problems with erectile dysfunction, and discussions about Viagra) and then broadened my scope to discuss macro issues related to the popularity of Viagra and the medicalization of sex. All names (with noted exceptions) have been changed to ensure privacy and confidentiality.

Experts

The experts I interviewed are medical professionals in the fields of urology, general medicine, gynecology,[5] psychiatry, psychology, and sexual health who prescribe Viagra or deal with clients who take the drug. Such professionals are uniquely positioned as crucial players in the Viagra phenomenon, for a number of reasons. The number of "scripts" practitioners write per month can determine the success of a new drug. Most doctors are offered incentives by pharmaceutical companies to sell their product, including money and trips. Also, medical professionals play a unique role in men's lives, as they are, I found, among the few people male patients will open up to about sexual problems and concerns. Finally, medical professionals, especially those who keep up with and contribute to medical research, can speak to the ways in which products like Viagra have changed the face of medicine.

By phone or by mail, I contacted a representative sample of thirty medical professionals in the southern California and Boston areas who appeared to have expertise in sexuality[6] (an equal mix of urologists and therapists listed in the phone book) to ask for an interview. After follow-up calls, twenty responded and agreed to speak with me, and several referred their colleagues as potential interview subjects. Seven professionals either did not respond or claimed to have no time or too little expertise in the area of sexual medicine. Those who did speak with me were more likely to work in private practice (and thus may have had more time) and appeared to be interested and invested, as I was, in the Viagra phenomenon. Many times doctors (especially general practitioners) would not agree to an interview, claiming they were not experts on sexuality and therefore would not be good people to speak with. I was only able to convince four that I was seeking interviews with a broad range of practitioners with varying levels of expertise. On the other hand, practitioners who were known as experts in the field of sexual dysfunction were many times too busy to speak with me.[7] Despite an initial round of letters, then phone calls, sometimes these individuals agreed to an interview only when I met them in person at medical conferences.

In the end, I conducted twenty-two interviews through a mixture of snowball and purposive sampling. In other words, interview subjects referred other potential interviewees, and I targeted particular types of interview subjects to achieve a relatively diverse pool in terms of sexual orientation, age, race, and class level/occupation. Six of the twenty-two medical professionals I spoke with are female; sixteen are male. Eight are acclaimed experts in sexual medicine, regularly publishing and delivering lectures on female sexual dysfunction. The majority of expert interviews were in-person, semistructured conversations, with phone conversations being the exception. Several of the medical professionals I spoke with worked as consultants or investigators for pharmaceutical companies like Pfizer, which fact reveals their investments in Viagra. I would guess that one-third of the practitioners I spoke with have temporarily worked for pharmaceutical companies, though this is difficult to determine since this information is rarely made publicly available.

Interviews lasted from thirty to sixty minutes,[8] depending on how much time a doctor could spare in between seeing patients. Open-ended conversational interviews began with the question, "How does Viagra fit into your practice?" The first half of the interview usually centered on clinical experience, clients, doctor-patient dialogue, discussions with friends about Viagra, and general understandings about Viagra, and the last half focused on more macro issues centered on the popularity of Viagra and on recent trends in medicine and marketing. The more time I was allotted, the more successful I was in getting doctors to step out of their limited doctor-patient script, which included a presentation of options for treating ED and a cautionary mini-lecture on Viagra side effects. The most helpful interview subjects thoughtfully addressed my "big picture" questions and concerns about profit-oriented medicine, American dependence on pills for happiness, and the medicalization of sex. I pressed for these conversations to take place in person, but several doctors with limited time insisted upon the convenience of phone conversations. Interestingly, practitioners assumed that my being a woman meant that I wanted to hear about Viagra being tested on women. Many brought this up without my asking. Only one practitioner volunteered information about personally using Viagra.

The data I collected from medical professionals took place both in doctors' offices and at medical conferences dedicated to sexual dysfunction, where I logged roughly three hundred hours observing presentations, meetings, and informal gatherings. Specifically, I attended and observed the annual four-day Boston Forums for three years starting in 1999. As a doctoral student I was able to legitimately attend such conferences, decline the medical credits, and pay a significantly reduced student rate ($100 for students versus $450 for practitioner registration and medical credits). Additionally, I attended and observed two two-day Beverly Hills "international symposia" on "The Pharmacologic Management of Erectile Dysfunction," as well as the "2nd International Consultation on Erectile and Sexual Dysfunctions" in Paris in 2003. Finally, I turned to a number of archival sources to supplement my expert interview data. I analyzed conference syllabi, complete with presentation abstracts on sexual dysfunction, from conferences I had attended in the period from 1999 to 2002. I collected and analyzed popular and medical reporting about sexual dysfunction and Viagra from 1999 to 2000. Many of these publications featured interviews with experts I had or had not interviewed.

Marketers and Distributors

The marketers and distributors are a mix of pharmacists and Pfizer representatives, or the supporting cast to the celebrity, Viagra. They can be found discussing the research that went into Viagra, the safe reputation of the product, and maybe even the fact that Viagra has sent more men to see their doctors than ever before. Both are minimally trained in medicine, but they are focused largely on pharmacology, the distribution of information and pharmaceuticals, and, thus, sales. Both groups act as intermediaries, serving the practitioner, the insurer, the pharmaceutical corporation, and the patient. In some ways, pharmacists are very similar to medical professionals, with training in medicine and a wealth of experience engaging with patients. To most in the medically trained helping professions, pharmacists and pharmaceutical reps exist on a lower rung of the ladder.

Both pharmacists and pharmaceutical reps are responsible for distributing Viagra; the pharmacist fills prescriptions and the Pfizer representative dispenses sample packs to doctors. While the emphasis for pharmacists is not on promotion and sales figures per se, they, like Pfizer reps, get to know their product quite well, including diagnoses, pricing, FDA regulations and warnings, and commonly reported side effects, and they too have a vested interest in sales figures. To be successful, pharmacists and Pfizer reps must really know their trade, their products, their clientele, and the medical community. Both groups tend to be marginal players in medical/research worlds, aware of clinical trials, perhaps, but rarely attending medical research conferences or subscribing to the academic journal of the American Medical Association, *JAMA*. Despite these commonalities, it is important to view each as a separate group with differing relationships to the Viagra phenomenon.

Pharmacists fill Viagra prescriptions and work directly with diverse communities linked to Viagra—practitioners, consumers, insurers, and Pfizer representatives. Because pharmacists are publicly accessible, in comparison to the medical practitioners, they are much easier to find, and generally more willing to talk. Because pharmacists are used to being called upon by customers for information about different products, almost every pharmacist I contacted was willing to take a break from filling prescriptions to speak with me about Viagra. In some cases I called ahead, introduced myself, and asked if there was a slow time when I could come in and conduct interviews. In other cases, I walked into a pharmacy and asked to speak to the pharmacist on the spot. Those interviews tended to be fairly short (averaging twenty minutes) but more convenient. I attempted to target a good mix of pharmacies situated in a range of communities. For example, I anticipated that a pharmacist in West Hollywood—a largely gay, young, singles community—would have different things to say about Viagra than the chain-store pharmacist on Wilshire Boulevard in Beverly Hills—a wealthy, primarily straight, older community—or the small-town pharmacist in a privately owned pharmacy. When asked about their clientele, they did turn out to have different stories.

Pharmacists (and Pfizer representatives) generally spoke about Viagra in a very detached, straightforward, scripted, clinical way—similar to the doctor-patient script, but with more discomfort in speaking about sexual practices and body parts.[9] Every pharmacist I spoke with offered to give me the FDA list of side effects related to Viagra—making sure I knew how this drug worked and what potential dangers it might be associated with. They were much more practiced at speaking about how the drug worked or how it sold (most placed Viagra in their list of the top twenty-five best-selling drugs, with antidepressants and allergy drugs in the top ten) than at sharing anecdotes about customers or thoughts about the meaning of such a drug. In most cases, because pharmacists were needed "on call" and pharmacies lack a true "backstage" region, three of the five interviews were conducted in pharmacy waiting areas, near where consultations with patients took place. The other two interviews were prescheduled and took place during the pharmacists' breaks, which allowed for a longer, more detailed and frank discussions about Viagra. In one case I conducted an interview in a corner of the pharmacy and was told that a long line of customers waiting to get prescriptions filled listened intently to our conversation about the medicalization of sex, appearing uncomfortable at times. The space constraint, the public visibility, liability issues, and their "on-call" status most likely led to pharmacists being more conservative and professional in their responses to my questions.

Pfizer representatives, otherwise known as "detail men" in previous generations, are the public faces of Pfizer, a mixed-gender cadre of attractive salespeople trained to promote a host of Pfizer drugs in a given region of the United States. Drug companies realize that doctors can determine a drug's success, and sales representatives form the crucial link between the pharmaceutical company and individual doctors' offices. Pfizer representatives aim to keep doctors updated on success stories, educated about sexual dysfunction, and stocked with information sheets, free Viagra samples, educational videos, and other Pfizer paraphernalia. The most effective reps make regular visits, befriend staff members in each doctor's office, bring food and gifts, and offer regular incentives (even trips and money) to secure and maintain practitioners' awareness of Pfizer products' benefits.[10]

I interviewed four individuals working for Pfizer's promotional machine. Kari worked in Pfizer's southern California headquarters training Pfizer reps on how to sell doctors on Pfizer products, including Viagra. The other three were assigned to "the field," making the rounds of doctors' offices. Brad was referred by a pharmacist he served, and Kellen and Chris were referred by urologists. When I spoke with Kellen, he had just recently lost his job with Pfizer as a result of downsizing related to Pfizer's merger with Warner-Lambert in 2001. All agreed to talk with me for over an hour, and while the conversations were partly sales pitches (especially in response to questions about who uses Viagra and what it does), I was surprised to hear them share critical perspectives on Viagra and the pharmaceutical industry as well.[11] Several months after I spoke with these three, only Brad continued to work for Pfizer.[12] Besides interviews, I was able to get at Pfizer marketing efforts through a range of secondary sources (many procured from the above Pfizer representatives), including promotional materials aimed at doctors and the general public such as brochures, videos, surveys, advertisements, and website information posted on Viagra.com and Pfizer.com.

Men Consumers

The men I interviewed include those who make up the market for Viagra. These are men who have a personal investment in this product, be it psychological, emotional, financial, or some other investment. I will refer to them here as consumers. Consumers in my sample vary in ethnicity, sexual orientation, and age (ranging from seventeen to eighty-six years old). Twenty-one of the twenty-seven are older than forty years of age. The majority are middle- or upper-middle-class. All of the consumers I interviewed had purchased and/or used Viagra or other, similar products, such as penis pumps and herbal supplements promising potency. While one would assume that consumer and expert categories might overlap, only one consumer volunteered that he identified as both a medical practitioner and a consumer.

The male consumers I spoke with were a self-selected group who responded to my requests for interviews through internet postings, newspaper advertisements, practitioner referrals, senior-citizens organizations, personal contacts, and prostate-cancer support-group meeting announcements. Those consumers who volunteered for an interview generally had experience with Viagra and had an interest in sharing this experience because it had affected their lives in some way (good or bad). Others were retired and expressed interest in helping a graduate student with her project, seeming to welcome the opportunity to talk with a young person (my youth was probably evident from my voice in phone-interview situations).

I also distributed a simple one-page survey at several sites in hopes of finding people willing to agree to follow-up interviews. Surveys were distributed to seventy senior citizens enrolled in senior summer school in southern California, five men in a middle-aged men's group, and twenty members of a central California senior-citizens singles group. A total of sixty completed surveys from all sites revealed general information (through a mixture of quantitative and qualitative data) about who uses Viagra and how Viagra use has affected lives and lifestyles. Of these sixty, eleven individuals (eight females and three males) agreed to follow-up phone interviews. Thus, the survey method became an effective instrument for locating willing male and female interview subjects.

Semistructured conversational interviews of thirty to sixty minutes were primarily conducted over the phone or by e-mail (for anonymity and confidentiality reasons) with the in-person interview being the exception. Conversations with male consumers would begin with, "When did you first hear about Viagra?" This question was followed up by "What did you hear?" and "How did you come to try it?" As with my other interviews, the first half of the conversation was generally based on personal experience with the drug and sense of self, while the second half focused on reactions to more macro issues about Viagra's general popularity and meaning for men and women, and the medicalization of sex.

Women Consumers

Women have highly varied relationships to Viagra. I use the term "consumer" loosely here to represent a member of the marketplace with an investment in Viagra. While women may not invest in the product itself (or literally buy it), they may be invested in what Viagra promises or symbolizes. Thus, their relationship to Viagra varies; they are Viagra users, potential Viagra users, wives or partners of Viagra users, and Viagra commentators. Female consumers were by far the most difficult to locate because they were hard to find (male consumers at least were connected to medical networks like doctors and pharmacists), claimed to have no relationship to Viagra, or were extremely uncomfortable with the subject because of its personal nature.

While I actively sought a diverse sample of both male and female consumers, all of the women I ended up interviewing were white, heterosexual, and middle class. The majority (nine of thirteen) were culled from senior-citizens organizations, are thus over sixty-five years of age, and live in California or Florida. Six were widows, and of those, two were actively dating. The others were married, or divorced and dating. For the purposes of this study, I have focused my analysis efforts solely on the nine female senior citizens, since they were the largest group of women informants to which I had access.

While it was difficult to find women willing to speak with me directly, I *was* able to find women's voices in the media: first-person accounts of Viagra use posted on the web, *Dear Abby* letters reflecting concerns about Viagra, and an array of feature articles in magazines and newspapers penned by female journalists. One opinion piece published in a feminist monthly (and later in the *Los Angeles Times*) led me to the Working Group on Women's Sexual Problems.

My conversations with women began with, "Do you remember when/what you first heard about Viagra?" Conversations moved from the personal realm to the public realm, as I asked women to speculate on why men use Viagra, whether women would use a similar type product, and what their feelings are about the medicalization of sex and the taking of pills for sexual enhancement. Phone conversations lasted from thirty to sixty minutes. Unlike the men I interviewed, many of the older women I spoke with expressed an interest in knowing a young person's perspective on many of my own questions. Generally, I would share my own perspectives after the interview was over, and this would lead to fascinating discussions about how times have changed for women. The rapport was only helped by a level of familiarity with me—many of these women I had met while teaching senior summer school.

Critics

The group I am calling the critics is the Working Group on Women's Sexual Problems—a mixed group of clinicians, therapists, women's health advocates, and academics organized around their concerns about expanding medicine and the Viagra phenomenon and its implication for women in particular. To this day, this is the only formally organized group of Viagra critics to receive consistent media attention.[13]

I became a participant activist in this group in 1999, when I came across an article in the Boston-based feminist monthly, *Sojourner,* by Dr. Leonore Tiefer, which warned of profit-driven drug companies promoting sexual dysfunction in epidemic numbers. The article called for a "feminist action" to take place that October at the Boston Forum. When I arrived and saw Dr. Tiefer and only six other women, I realized how hard it would be to act like a fly on the wall. When it was revealed that I was the only woman in the room besides Dr. Tiefer who was able to attend the medical conferences (because of time and the affordable student registration rates), I quickly became a participant. I attended, observed, took issue with, and took part in the medical conference and the preconference feminist meetings, and quickly came to identify as a scholar-activist concerned about profit-focused, drug-company-sponsored promotion of sexual dysfunction. As other feminist activist scholars have pointed out, my feminist sympathies would have meant very little if I had not participated in meetings and mobilization efforts.[14] In total, during the period from 1999 to 2001, I participated in roughly two hundred hours dedicated to group meetings, webpage design,[15] article writing, e-mail correspondence, conference planning, and protest "actions" with the Working Group on Women's Sexual Problems campaign.[16]

Feminist Methodology and "Participant Activism"

Feminist social scientists aim to bring women into their research by resisting the questions that usually define us out of existence and asking the questions that fit the contours of our lives.[17] For example, I have asked, Where do women fit in the Viagra phenomenon? What roles do women play in it? Who benefits and who is hurt emotionally, psychologically, socially, and financially? Diverse answers to these questions can be found through fieldwork as well as through articles penned by women, *Dear Abby* letters, and online chat groups. While I started with questions about women in relation to Viagra, I quickly broadened my scope to include bringing men out regarding Viagra, realizing that one story can only be understood in relation to the other. Viagra is personal and political for men and for women, so I wanted to find out how men make sense of this phenomenon.

My project takes the form of what Dorothy Smith calls "institutional ethnography," in the sense that I am interested in interrogating one social institution in particular, Viagra, with the goal of understanding power and social relations and producing knowledge for women.[18] According to Smith, an institutional ethnography is different from traditional ethnography in its starting point, direction, and aims. One starts from the margins and moves inward, towards centers of power and administration, searching to explicate the contingencies of ruling that shape local contexts. The aim of institutional ethnography is to discover the social relations that organize a particular setting. The process of discovering how social relations work requires attending to details of interaction, as well as to otherwise taken-for-granted historical contexts.[19] In an effort to understand the social relations that underlie Viagra use and organize medicine, this project prioritizes historical context and the role of texts (e.g., promotional materials, media), and it explores the details of social interactions. I started this project with attention to social groups on the margins (feminists, women, and men claiming impotence) and moved inward to interrogate established power, the institution of medicine, and the major claims makers in the Viagra phenomenon.

Feminist ethnographers couple research with advocacy for women.[20] Smith reminds us that feminist research centered on social change must go further than simply adding to knowledge *of women*; it must also proceed with the goal of producing knowledge *for women*. At the turn of the twentieth century, there now exists a great deal of research about women by women, but very little academic research "with" and "for" women.[21] Such "action-research," which entails participatory elements, may be appealing to feminist scholars but is difficult to enact and rarely done.[22] Daphne Patai asks us to consider how our research is returned to the community. My own efforts at social change and activist research have occurred simultaneously with my data collection, as I work with other feminist academics and health advocates to educate the populace about potential dangers of medicalization by publishing articles in feminist circulars, planning conferences, and developing an informational webpage. In this way, I too play the role of knowledge producer in and around the Viagra phenomenon.

My activist-ethnographer standpoint defies traditional anthropology and sociology, where detached neutrality on the part of the researcher has historically been deemed paramount to claiming objectivity. In critiquing positivism, feminist scholars favor "rigorous subjectivity" and "passionate scholarship" over researcher neutrality and detached objectivity.[23] While I do not believe in objective research, in interview situations I found myself struggling with presenting myself as neutral, when I too have a particular stake in the Viagra phenomenon, as an activist-scholar. For example, repeatedly hearing urologists and general practitioners claim that sexual problems are organic, not psychological, cultural, relational, or social, upset me, even though I realized that they were all trained in medicine and had to make these claims to legitimate their profession.

Constructing and "Diagnosing" Social Processes

I have employed a combination of qualitative research designs in this project, including ethnography, grounded theory, and content analysis. Ethnographic methods (participant observation and interview) have enabled me to explore sexual and gendered behavior and the meaning systems underlying such behavior in a way that quantitative methods might not. As a "stranger" to the world of medicine, with no vested interest in Viagra or the outcomes of this study, I am well situated to gain a realistic, balanced perspective on the processes I have observed.[24] James Clifford posits that ethnographic methods provide unique positioning for analyzing culture and rendering it problematic:

> Ethnography is actively situated between powerful systems of meaning, posing questions at the boundaries of civilizations, cultures, classes, races, and genders. It decodes and recodes, telling the grounds of collective order and diversity, inclusion and exclusion. It describes processes of innovation and structuration, and is itself part of these processes.[25]

James Clifford warns that while ethnography may appear to be about cultural representation, it is very clearly about invention of cultures. By studying the Viagra phenomenon, I am rendering it as an object to be studied. At the same time, I am cognizant that culture is complex, fluid, contested, temporal, emergent, and not easily divorced from context.[26]

Harry Wolcott suggests that qualitative researchers strive for "rigorous subjectivity" by aiming for balance, completeness, fairness, and sensitivity in the final analysis and interpretation of data. In an attempt at such rigorous subjectivity, I have collected different types of data (observations, interviews, promotional and audiovisual materials); gathered multiple perspectives on issues and events; made a concerted effort to look for contradictory evidence; and acknowledged my own biases in this research.[27] Finally, throughout the research process, I have challenged myself to avoid falling into the trap of simplification, generalization, linearity, and objectivity.

This research follows Mitchell Duneier's model of "diagnostic ethnography" in the sense that my early immersion in "Viagra culture," including media representations and ads, conversations, and medical conferences, helped me adopt the right diagnostic tools for this research project. In *Sidewalk*, Duneier explains that instead of starting his research on the street vendors of Greenwich Village with a precise research question and theoretical perspective, he began his study with observations in the field, to get a sense of the "symptoms" that characterized his "patient" (street vendors). After "seeing and hearing things on the street" Duneier had diagnostic tools to begin asking research questions, and returned to the field to continue to understand his case.[28]

Similarly, I spent months of "preliminary research" immersing myself in chat-room conversations on the internet[29] as well as attending to Viagra news reporting, talking with people, and observing medical meetings before narrowing my project and clarifying my research questions. This early research made me appreciate the "symptoms" of a medical diagnosis as well as a larger social phenomenon, and led me to new research questions about masculinity, social problems, and medicalization. After reading in these areas of literature, as well as conducting preliminary research, I had an expanding "tool kit" for understanding culture to take into the field.[30]

My own theories about the Viagra phenomenon were progressively formulated, reformulated, and sometimes discarded during the process of data collection and analysis. This process of theory building was central to coding my field notes and interview data. Using grounded theory and a mixture of inductive and deductive reasoning, I constructed theories as the social patterns in my data became more and more visible.[31] At the same time, I tried to be aware of the silences, gaps, and inconsistencies in my data, which complicated the process of coding and analysis.

While most of my data collection methods (interviews and participant observation) can be considered ethnographic, I have also employed content-analysis methods as well as phenomenology to capture the Viagra phenomenon through cultural discourse and people's experiences. Through content analysis I have systematically examined materials such as newspaper articles, television shows, advertisements, and promotional materials centered on Viagra. This data has been coded similarly to that of my interview data and field notes.[32] Finally, in my focus on consumers' experiences with Viagra, this study partially takes the form of phenomenological research. In other words, I have attempted to understand people's perceptions, understandings, and experiences in relation to Viagra and "dysfunction."

Locating Myself in the Research

While in the field, I experienced varying degrees of self-awareness and awkwardness related to my own social location as a young white woman writing about male-oriented products and "disorders." I realized early on that if I were male, I might have had an easier time with portions of the research. Casting ethical concerns aside, I might have been able to rely on participant observation methods in the research, booking the "free consultations" that so many ads offered, expressing interest in product trials, and "passing" as a man suffering from ED just to see how people would react. In terms of getting people to speak with me, as a young woman, I had the option of fabricating a personal investment story to align myself with male interests (e.g., making up a story about my embarrassed husband who needs these products). Or I could present myself in a number of other, more truthful ways (as a curious graduate student writing about Viagra, as a woman writing a book on Viagra, or as a sociologist studying the Viagra phenomenon). I generally stayed away from fabrications, for ethical reasons, and introduced myself honestly, as a curious dissertation student. But several times men (particularly one grumpy pharmacist) asked me why I, a woman, was studying this? What did I know? Why was I interested?

The Viagra story is as much a story about upper- and middle-class masculinity as it is about femininity (and everything in between), and I have approached my research with this in mind, collecting both male and female consumer perspectives on this topic. As a financially strapped young woman (first as a graduate student and then as a new assistant professor), I was required by this project to "study up," or research those with more power and status than myself.[33] I spoke with primarily white, highly educated, well-respected medical practitioners and sexual-health experts, as well as middle-class males, the majority of whom were older than I. Many of these men are active producers of knowledge about sexual dysfunction, with formal prestige, power, and expertise. Because interviews were solicited with medical professionals because of their expertise, and often took place in their offices, the difference in status between interviewer and subject was palpable. This cut both ways. While at times I was treated condescendingly or simply ignored (in my pursuit of interviews), at other times my perceived lack of expertise worked in my favor, as doctors seemed to attempt to put their thoughts into layman's language. However, I was afforded some status as a doctoral student and was expected to know medical terminology and research.

The perceived values conflict between medical professionals and myself as an activist-scholar proved threatening to the project at times. I found myself worried that, due to my visibility as a health advocate, I would not be able to find medical professionals willing to talk. At times, I feared that my critical perspectives on the medical profession would keep me from finding interview subjects. A few high-profile medical experts who knew me to be associated with Tiefer and grassroots politics were extremely rude and brusque or simply avoided me. One Los Angeles urologist and major Pfizer spokesperson never responded to my calls, e-mails, and notes, probably because I identified as a sociologist. And others seemed to avoid me for any number of reasons, one of which could have been my visibility as a protester. Then again, many times I used my concerns and critiques instrumentally to try to elicit a critical response in practitioner interviews. If nothing else, it seemed that sharing my personal stakes and biases pushed interview subjects to think about the Viagra phenomenon in new ways.

My interviews with consumers were different, partially because status and expertise were not the subject of our conversations and most conversations took place in neutral spaces, such as coffee houses, or over the phone or by e-mail. In these conversations, while I asked for demographic information from interview subjects, such as occupation (to identify socioeconomic class) and age, I divulged very little about myself at the start of the interview, except to say that I was a researcher from the University of California.[34] This title vested me with status where my sex and perceived age did not. Furthermore, since the topic of discussion with consumers was the use of Viagra, which usually brought up issues of shame and vulnerability, I occupied a powerful position as the listener and ethnographer, just as a priest in a confessional or a therapist might. In this way I was able to use the traditional imbalance of power in ethnographic research to try to offset power dynamics in my interviews with men.

However, because power is everywhere in interaction and in the telling of sexual stories, I cannot always be sure how power plays out at any given moment. As Ken Plummer points out, power flows through interaction and the telling of sexual stories in starkly different ways, as potentially oppressive, empowering, or marginalizing.[35] Power shifts and flows depending upon who is doing the telling and who is not, which voices are granted credibility over others, what is being told and what is being left out, what is being asked or not, and who is doing the asking, to name just a few contingencies.

Sociologists and anthropologists of science and technology have employed the term "studying up" to refer to the power imbalance that takes place when interview subjects have more power, prestige, and status than the social scientist.[36] In my own interviews with consumers, because the object of our conversations was, literally, "up" (or the inability to "get it up"), power dynamics were somewhat equalized, as they were in interviews with women and feminists. In other words, while most of my male interview subjects had more formal status than I (because of their age, socioeconomic position, and sex), a relative balance of power was maintained in interviews because of the levels of vulnerability displayed by these men in relation to the subject matter.

In my own interviews, consumers generally spoke openly with me about sexuality, seeming to find me nonthreatening and trustworthy. Consumers tended to view me as both an expert and a therapist, revealing concerns and experiences they may not have told anyone else, and asking questions afterwards about whether what they felt or experienced was normal. The "openness" I believe I achieved in consumer interviews was also enabled partially by the anonymity I promised and they experienced over the phone; I did not collect last names or contact information, and promised to change all first names. Protecting the subject in this way was both positive and negative; by collecting very little contact information, I sacrificed the ability to follow up with my interview subjects, or send them transcripts or drafts to review.

My position as an outsider did work to my advantage much of the time. For example, consumers and medical professionals alike assumed that, as a woman, I was interested in hearing about or trying Viagra for women.[37] Many practitioners volunteered information about Viagra clinical trials for women without my asking. It is important to note that just as I was attempting to measure and make sense of informants' investments in the product and the phenomenon in various ways, my informants also returned the gaze, constructing, situating, and questioning my motives according to the little they knew about my identity and the assumptions they made on the basis of the way I looked, sounded, and behaved during the interview. This came through both subtly and overtly, many times surfacing in unsolicited comments related to women and Viagra. By the last phase of interviewing, I was reminded of my own shifting positionality as I began to anticipate the assumptions and questions of my interview subjects while concurrently developing and strengthening my critical perspectives. Thus, while my interviews remained similar in content and structure throughout, my personal stakes in and relationship to the project had shifted.

Sexual Stories and Trouble Finding Them

To understand how people make sense of the Viagra phenomenon, I collected a wide range of Viagra-related sexual stories. Ken Plummer's concept of sexual stories provides a model very similar to the Viagra narratives that I was looking for. Plummer defines sexual stories as "personal experience narratives around the intimate."[38] Similarly, I would define the stories I collected as personal experience narratives about Viagra use, which may or may not elicit stories about intimacy. Like sexual stories, Viagra stories are socially embedded in the daily practices and strategies of everyday life, in communities and culture, and in political and social contexts. And like sexual lives and life stories, Viagra stories are rarely neat and coherent; usually, they are messy and complex. Nonetheless, as Plummer points out, these stories perform major tasks in providing information, establishing contested territories, and clarifying boundaries.[39] Viagra narratives, like sexual stories, flow from the culture and back into it; thus they are major resources for comprehending a culture and its dynamics, values, and changes.[40] Viagra stories, like sexual stories, are not simply reflections of life but social actions embedded in social worlds, emphasizing subjecthood and agency.[41] Finally, Viagra stories are not always centered on the sexual, or intimate, itself, though they are always connected to it (for example, AIDS narratives reveal stories of illness, politics, and grief as much as sex).

Finding people willing to talk about and around Viagra posed the biggest challenge of this project. While my project was still in its formative stages, it seemed as though everyone I met had something to say about Viagra. I realized early on that no matter where I was or whom I was with, a great conversation starter was simply to mention my dissertation topic. This elicited a wide spectrum of comments and emotions, including everything from the skeptical "They let you study that stuff?" to the jolly "Wanna hear some great Viagra jokes?" to the excitable "Wow—have I got some stories for you!" I began to keep a journal filled with people's (mainly male strangers') reactions to my research topic. What surprised me the most was the fact that friends and acquaintances who knew of my research went out of their way to share extremely personal stories with me regarding their own bouts with impotence, experiments with Viagra, or sexual frustrations—stories that were unsolicited. While these stories do not come from formal interviews, this data is still sociologically interesting and important. For example, here are some responses from people who had just learned about my project:

> My machinery is fine, but I'd try [Viagra] if I had to. You never know when it's going to fail you. (middle-aged white male)

> I wonder if you could tell me—what would it do for me? (twenty-something white female)

> At this club some guy was trying to come on to me and said he had some little blue pills in his pocket! (twenty-something white female)

My marriage just broke up and it was partially over this impotence issue. Viagra wasn't working for him . . . (thirty-something white female)

Viagra? It is a product for its time. Or maybe I'll just say, It's about time. Are you studying the pandas? They are reproducing with Viagra's help! (senior white male)

When you are aging, you can choose to lead a healthy life or become decrepit. With drugs like Viagra and Prozac, you can move back into the normal range of life. (middle-aged white male)

Gauging from the sheer amount of informal Viagra storytelling I was exposed to, I wrongly assumed that finding individuals willing to sit down and talk about Viagra would not be a problem. While people may be willing to joke and quip publicly about Viagra, however, when it comes to talking seriously about their Viagra experiences, I found very few takers.

I ran ads in classified sections of weekly entertainment papers in two major southern California cities shouting out (in bold) "Viagra Stories Needed," identifying myself, and promising confidentiality. Only one person contacted me. I contacted doctors of all backgrounds, describing my project and my desire to speak with all types of practitioners on the topic of Viagra. Most practitioners stated that they had no time, and even more claimed little or no expertise in "that area." Finally, upon locating several data-rich internet chat rooms dedicated to experiences with Viagra and impotence, I posted messages introducing myself as a graduate student writing about Viagra and looking for anyone willing to converse with me on this topic. Six months later, I had one response. At one point, my most successful attempts at finding interview subjects came not from direct solicitation but through an uncle's participation in a male support group.

As I was getting increasingly frustrated with the lack of response, a colleague of mine suggested I design a short questionnaire that posed several general questions and gave respondents the option of discussing them in a brief phone interview. This, we thought, might be less threatening than just an open-ended call for interview subjects. The only problem was, Where would I hand out this questionnaire? Thinking big, and aiming for a cross-section of society, I contacted the local county fair board of directors and, after describing my project and my status, I asked what I had to do to get a table or booth at the fair from which to hand out my survey. The board president laughed and then assigned me to the designated "free speech" area outside of the fair gates, where prolifers stood, handing out Operation Rescue literature. Clearly, I was thinking too big, and while the project was admittedly controversial, it didn't seem to belong with anti-abortionists. Narrowing my focus, I contacted several luxury retirement villages and senior-citizen apartment complexes, describing my project and asking if I could post a flyer or disperse questionnaires. The minute they heard the word "Viagra," the directors of these complexes stopped me and apologetically stated that my research subject was "too private and risky" for their residents. The only exceptions to this rule were two senior citizens organizations: the senior summer school where I worked, and a senior singles organization.

In an attempt to try to find "boomers" willing to discuss Viagra, I contacted several singles organizations and clubs, describing my project and my interest in finding interview subjects. Most never responded, but in one case, the president of a fifty-five and over singles club befriended me and distributed my surveys to one hundred of her club's members. Later, when I told her that I had not received any completed surveys in the mail, she was shocked. She explained that while distributing the surveys among giggling senior citizens, she had loudly posed the question, "Why can't you all admit that you are taking Viagra?" Apparently she thought that this confrontational strategy would motivate them to fill out the survey. Earlier in the summer I had distributed one hundred surveys to my senior citizen summer school class of mostly single widows, commenting that I would love their help with my dissertation research and explaining that my research was particularly concerned with what women had to say about Viagra. Despite my pitch, a significant segment of the class wanted nothing to do with the survey. Later, among the pile of completed surveys, I found a handful of blank surveys with "NO COMMENT" written across the top. In many ways, then, my call for underrepresented voices on the topic of Viagra was met with resounding silence—perhaps reflecting generations of silence relating to sexual issues.

Despite what one would assume about the content of a Viagra interview, when I did find interview subjects, my interviews about Viagra use involved just as many narratives about sex as they did narratives regarding medicine (diagnoses), health (side effects), aging (youth ideals), gender (masculinity), and technology (pills). In fact, at some point in my data collection, I began to realize that my interview data was more focused on what my informants deemed to be problematic—namely, erectile dysfunction, lack of sexual confidence, and sometimes Viagra side effects—than on what I saw as problematic—Viagra, medicalization, age and gender ideals, intercourse-only sexual scripts, and shame. This was the case with textual data as well. While both my interview and survey questions were designed to explore all of these arenas, questions were broad and open ended, and ultimately, the data revealed what subjects brought to the table.

Interview subjects who wanted to talk about sexuality went into great detail about how, when, why, and where they use Viagra. But very few of my interviews turned into sexual life histories, probably because of a number of factors, including discomfort in talking about sex and my own labeling of my research as Viagra centered (not sexuality centered). Ironically, the closest I came to taking a sexual life history was in interviewing a gynecologist who wanted to link his sexual life history to his occupational pursuits and goals.

How was I to make sense of people's seeming unwillingness to discuss Viagra? With the help of my advisors, I analyzed the situation more closely. Was it a values conflict? Was it me? Was the fact that I am young-looking and female working against me? Was I introducing my project and myself in a threatening or intimidating manner? Or was it a demographic problem? Was I choosing the wrong avenues to pursue? Clearly, boomers would be more forthcoming with their experiences than senior citizens. But how does one find middle-aged people? Where do they all congregate?

More generally, problems associated with finding interview subjects for this project reveal much about society, and American discomfort with discussing sexuality. The individuals who did agree to speak with me were those physically, emotionally, or financially invested in the Viagra phenomenon, for one reason or another. For example, medical practitioners and therapists who claimed expertise in sexual dysfunction, or saw a good number of patients wanting Viagra, or were attempting to make sense of the Viagra phenomenon themselves, made time for me. Consumers who had something to share about Viagra—whether it was a complaint, a warning, an affirmation, jokes, or stories—responded to my ads, postings, letters, questionnaires, and referrals. Those who did talk with me ranged from the very nervous and private—these interviews generally were short and to the point— to people who were so comfortable discussing Viagra, they wanted to continue our conversation for hours. Similar to Lillian Rubin's experiences interviewing people about sexuality, my subjects welcomed the chance to process and make sense of their sexual lives and to share their sexual stories with someone they defined as an expert, someone they felt they could ask if they were normal. Who best to discuss these things with than a stranger?[42] In the end, I had a widely solicited yet self-selected pool of individuals who had something to say.

Notes

NOTES TO PREFACE

1. For more on Bazooms (pseudonym), see my article "Working for Men at the Intersection of Power, Gender, and Sexuality," *Sociological Inquiry* (66:4, 1996): 399–421.

NOTES TO CHAPTER I

1. See "Stories of the Year," *San Francisco Chronicle,* January 1, 1999, A3.

2. Viagra's was the most successful prescription drug launch in history, according to "Pfizer Now Takes Viagra Hoopla to Other Countries," *Advertising Age,* May 3, 1999, 24.

3. According to Viagra.com (June 2002),

> VIAGRA is the #1 prescribed ED treatment in the world. In the United States alone, VIAGRA has been dispensed more than 39 million times to nearly 10 million patients by more than 300,000 physicians. Around the world, 7 VIAGRA tablets are dispensed every second. Since its launch, VIAGRA is the most extensively studied ED treatment in the world and has the most real-world prescription experience of any ED therapy.

Such statistics attempt to measure Viagra use in a global context, despite undefined numbers of internet, black-market, and counterfeit sales, and no clear correlation between dispensation and use.

4. On women critically reading romance books, see Janice Radway, *Reading the Romance: Women, Patriarchy, and Popular Literature* (Chapel Hill: University of North Carolina Press, 1991). On women Star Trek fans see Constance Penley, *NASA/TREK: Popular Science and Sex in America* (New York: Verso, 1997).

5. On AIDS discourses see Steven Epstein *Impure Science: AIDS, Activism, and the Politics of Knowledge* (Berkeley: University of California Press, 1996); and Paula Treichler, *How to Have Theory in an Epidemic: Cultural Chronicles of AIDS* (Durham, NC: Duke University Press, 1999). On fetal surgery see Monica Casper, *Making of the Unborn Patient: A Social Anatomy of Fetal Surgery* (New Brunswick, NJ: Rutgers University Press, 1998). On fertility see Gay Becker, *The*

Elusive Embryo: How Men and Women Approach New Reproductive Technologies (Berkeley: University of California Press, 2000). On cosmetic surgeries see Nora Jacobson, *Cleavage: Technology, Controversy, and the Ironies of the Man-Made Breast* (New Brunswick, NJ: Rutgers University Press, 2000); and Kathy Davis, *Reshaping the Female Body: The Dilemma of Cosmetic Surgery* (New York: Routledge, 1995).

6. While Pfizer does not release information about who purchases and/or uses Viagra, it does publish information about what causes erectile dysfunction and thus the host of health problems contributing to the use of Viagra. Pfizer representative training material lists the primary causes of ED as "10–30% psychogenic and 70–90% organic." Erectile dysfunction (and thus the need for Viagra use) exists with a host of risk factors including "diseases (heart disease, hypertension, diabetes, depression), medications, lifestyle factors (cigarette smoking, increased alcohol consumption), surgery (prostectomy, urologic, pelvic, and abdominal procedures), trauma-related injuries (bicycling accidents, pelvic fractures, spinal-cord injury), hormonal factors (Peyronie's disease, priapism), and psychological and other factors (suppression and expression of anger, lack of sexual knowledge, poor sexual technique, relationship deterioration). Despite this comprehensive list, Pfizer maintains that Viagra is most effective on men with mild to moderate erectile dysfunction and least effective in severe cases of ED.

Pfizer does not release data on the racial makeup of its Viagra consumers, although we can assume from Pfizer's recent advertising campaigns that Pfizer hopes to further develop African-American, Latino, and Asian markets for their drug.

7. See, for example, Laura Mamo and Jennifer Fishman, "Potency in All the Right Places: Viagra as a Technology of the Gendered Body," *Body and Society* (7:4, 2001): 13–35; Barbara L. Marshall, "'Hard Science': Gendered Constructions of Sexual Dysfunction in the 'Viagra Age,'" *Sexualities* (5:2, 2002): 131–58; and Leonore Tiefer, "Doing the Viagra Tango," *Radical Philosophy* (92, 1998): 1–3; and "Female Sexual Dysfunction Alert: A New Disorder Invented for Women," *Sojourner: The Women's Forum*, October 11, 1999, 1.

8. To cite one example of many, in 2001, *Saturday Night Live* ran a skit in which an African-American man discussed Viagra in response to "chronic fatigue syndrome of the wang."

9. See Peter Conrad and Joseph Schneider, *Deviance and Medicalization: From Badness to Sickness*, rev. ed. (Philadelphia: Temple University Press, 1992).

10. John Bancroft, interview with author, tape recording, Boston: October 2000.

11. Since January 2001, thirty-eight states have passed "mental health parity" laws, requiring insurers to provide equal coverage for mental illness as for physical ailments. According to critics, this is not the final answer to the

problem of unequal coverage because of the many loopholes in the law. See "Mental Health Parity Laws by State," Insure.com., http://www.insure.com /health/mentalstate.html, 2003.

12. See, for example, Peter Conrad and Joseph Schneider, *Deviance and Medicalization: From Badness to Sickness,* (London: Mosby, 1980); Anne E. Figert, *Women and the Ownership of PMS: The Structuring of a Psychiatric Disorder* (New York: de Gruyter, 1996); Nora Jacobson, *Cleavage: Technology, Controversy, and the Ironies of the Man-Made Breast* (New Brunswick, NJ: Rutgers University Press, 2000); Donileen Loseke, *Thinking about Social Problems: An Introduction to Constructionist Perspectives* (New York: de Gruyter, 1999); and Amanda Rittenhouse, "The Emergence of PMS as a Social Problem," *Social Problems* (38, 1991): 412–25.

13. Leonore Tiefer, *Sex Is Not a Natural Act and Other Essays* (San Francisco: Westview Press, 1995).

14. Ibid.

15. Lawrence Diller, *Running on Ritalin: A Physician Reflects on Children, Society, and Performance in a Pill* (New York: Bantam Books, 1998).

16. Quoted in Marshall, "'Hard Science,'" 146. As Marshall points out, the history of impotence remedies also includes splints and supports, hormonal and glandular therapies, rejuvenation tonics, herbal remedies, and penile exercises. Pfizer has created its own "history" of sexual medicine. At an international conference on sexual dysfunction in 2003, Pfizer-affiliated faculty discussed the rise of sexual medicine by pointing to old-fashioned global aphrodisiacs, including oysters, rhino horns, rock salt, melted fat, and Spanish fly. By the twentieth century, this list had changed significantly to include sexual medicine in the form of psychotherapy, natural products like yohimbine, and, later, the pharmaceutical product caverject. According to Pfizer, all of these early forays into sexual medicine paved the way for the discovery of a "biochemical pathway" and a new era of drug therapy. George Nurnburg and Jeremy Heaton, "The Impact of Viagra over Five Years: Why Is It a Worldwide Phenomenon?" Paper read at Second International Consultation on Erectile and Sexual Dysfunction, Paris 2003.

17. Three-dimensional video glasses have been used in clinical trials dedicated to testing and treating sexual dysfunction. In trials testing Viagra in women, for example, volunteers would be asked to self-stimulate using a vibrator and 3-D video glasses that play erotic movies. For more on this see chapter 4.

18. In their 1999 "Let the Dance Begin" magazine ad, Pfizer Pharmaceuticals posits that their product is more "natural" than competing products. The bold text for this ad reads, "Naturally, the results have been positive." In smaller print the copy reads, "Achieve erections the natural way—in response to sexual stimulation." This is in contrast to competing products that produce erections instantly through injection or insertion of a suppository.

19. See, for example, Angela Davis, *Women, Race, and Class* (New York: Vintage, 1981); Barbara Ehrenreich and Dierdre English, *Complaints and Disorders: The Sexual Politics of Sickness* (New York: Feminist Press, 1973) and *For Her Own Good: 150 Years of the Experts' Advice to Women* (New York: Anchor, 1979); Michel Foucault, *The Birth of the Clinic: An Archaeology of Medical Perception* (New York: Vintage, 1973) and *The History of Sexuality: An Introduction* (New York: Random House, 1978); Nora Jacobson, *Cleavage: Technology, Controversy, and the Ironies of the Man-Made Breast* (New Brunswick, NJ: Rutgers University Press, 2000); Rachel Maines, *The Technology of Orgasm: "Hysteria," the Vibrator, and Women's Sexual Satisfaction* (Baltimore, MD: Johns Hopkins University Press, 1999); and Jennifer Terry, "The Seductive Power of Science in the Making of Deviant Subjectivity" in *Posthuman Bodies*, Judith Halberstam and Ira Livingston, eds. (Bloomington: Indiana University Press, 1995).

20. For a history of the ways in which the poor have been marked as disease carriers and controlled by the medical establishment, see, for example, Alan Brandt, *No Magic Bullet* (London: Oxford University Press, 1985). For a discussion of adolescent sexuality as a social problem, see Constance Nathanson, *Dangerous Passage* (Philadelphia: Temple University Press, 1991). For a discussion of AIDS as conflated with homosexuality, see Terry, "The Seductive Power of Science." For an analysis of centuries of black women's sterilization and state control of black women's fertility, see Dorothy Roberts, *Killing the Black Body: Race, Reproduction, and the Meaning of Liberty* (New York: Vintage Books, 1997).

21. The pharmacology of sex comes out of a context of medical hegemony in the late twentieth century, during which time pharmaceutical companies exercised increasing authority over areas of life, such as sexuality, not previously seen as requiring prescription drugs. Chapter 3 explores the construction of a dysfunctional male populace and the profit-driven aspects of this phenomenon.

22. Another example of how new reproductive technologies have been hazardous to women is the thalidomide tragedy of the 1960s. At this time, women in the United States and abroad learned that the thalidomide they were being prescribed for morning sickness was causing extreme birth defects. Such medical tragedies led to the implementation of medical safety rules and regulations and the empowerment of the FDA. For more on this, see Philip J. Hilts, *Protecting America's Health: The FDA, Business, and One Hundred Years of Regulation* (New York: Knopf, 2003).

23. See Lynne Luciano, *Looking Good: Male Body Image in Modern America* (New York: Hill and Wang, 2001): 97–99.

24. John D'Emilio and Estelle Freedman, *Intimate Matters: A History of Sexuality in America* (Chicago: University of Chicago Press, 1988): 339; and Elizabeth Watkins, *On the Pill: A Social History of Oral Contraceptives, 1950–1970* (Baltimore, MD: Johns Hopkins University Press, 1998): 8.

25. Watkins, *On The Pill*, 132.

26. See, for example, Anne Basalmo, *Technologies of the Gendered Body: Reading Cyborg Women* (Durham, NC: Duke University Press, 1996); Kathy Davis, *Reshaping the Female Body: The Dilemma of Cosmetic Surgery* (New York: Routledge, 1995); Sarah Franklin and Helena Ragone, "Introduction" in *Reproducing Reproduction: Kinship, Power, and Technological Innovation,* Sarah Franklin and Helena Ragone, eds. (Philadelphia: University of Pennsylvania Press, 1998); Donna Haraway, "The Virtual Speculum in the New World Order," in *Revisioning, Health and Healing: Feminist, Cultural, and Technoscience Perspectives,* Adele E. Clarke and Virginia L. Olesen, eds. (New York: Routledge, 1999); Bernice Hausman, *Changing Sex: Transsexualism, Technology, and the Idea of Gender* (Durham, NC: Duke University Press, 1995); Janice Irvine, *Disorders of Desire: Sex and Gender in Modern American Sexology* (Philadelphia: Temple University Press, 1990); and Janice Raymond, *The Transsexual Empire: The Making of the She-Male* (Boston: Beacon Press, 1979).

27. Foucault, *History of Sexuality.*

28. Greider dates the rise of Big Pharma after World War II, when drug makers weaned themselves from long-standing dependencies on German innovation and focused on research and patenting their own inventions. As a result, the pace of new drug introductions intensified and precipitated the rise of the "detail man." The goal of the detail man was to establish and reinforce brand-name loyalty. Thus, the 1950s saw the establishment of the pharmaceutical industry as we know it—characterized by heavy investment in research and promotion, high prices, and high profitability. More recently, Greider points out, the 1980s and '90s have been a period of robust revenue growth for Big Pharma with the shift in emphasis from producing a broad range of products to cashing in on a few high-margin products with huge markets. Katharine Greider, *The Big Fix: How the Pharmaceutical Industry Rips Off American Consumers* (New York: Public Affairs, 2003): 158–62.

29. See Lynn Payer, *Disease-Mongers: How Doctors, Drug Companies, and Insurers Are Making You Feel Sick* (New York: Wiley, 1992). Also see Public Citizen, "Pharmaceutical Industry Ranks as Most Profitable Industry—Again," April 18, 2002 (news release). According to this report, the pharmaceutical industry topped all three of *Fortune* magazine's measures of profitability for 2001. Pfizer led the U.S. pharmaceutical companies with $7.8 billion in profits in 2001.

As of 2000, five pharmaceutical companies accounted for one-third of all spending on drug products, and nearly as much in sales (Greider, *The Big Fix*, 166). This reflects the recent wave of pharmaceutical consolidation in an effort to gain control of the big drugs. For example, in 2000 Pfizer purchased Warner-Lambert. In 2002, Pfizer/Warner purchased Pharmacia. As a result, this company now can collect billions in revenue from the blockbusters Lipitor (cholesterol reducer from Warner-Lambert) and Celebrex (from Pharmacia).

30. The pharmaceutical industry has seen rapid consolidation since 1994, after which thirty-eight companies have merged. Gardiner Harris, "Where Are All the New Drugs?" *New York Times*, October 5, 2003.

31. Thomas Bodenheimer, "Uneasy Alliance: Clinical Investigators and the Pharmaceutical Industry," *New England Journal of Medicine* (342, 2000): 1539–44.

32. Ibid. Also see Marcia Angell, "Is Academic Medicine for Sale?" *New England Journal of Medicine* (342, 2000): 1516–18.

33. Some social scientists see the recent merging and expansion of science, medicine, and technology as signaling a new era of "biomedicalization." In a recent article in *American Sociological Review*, Adele Clarke and her coauthors argue that beginning around 1985, biomedicalization trumped medicalization through five central and overlapping processes: major political economic shifts; a new focus on health and risk and surveillance biomedicines; the "technoscientization" of biomedicine; transformation of the production, distribution, and consumption of biomedical knowledges; and transformations of bodies and identities. With these historical developments, we now live in an era of biomedicalization that is impossible to avoid, often transforming life itself. Adele E. Clarke, Janet K. Shim, Laura Mamo, Jennifer Ruth Foskett, and Jennifer R. Fishman, "Biomedicalization: Technoscientific Transformations of Health, Illness, and U.S. Biomedicine," *American Sociological Review* (68, 2003): 161–94.

34. According to a 1998 study, 70 percent of people who visit a doctor's office walk out with a prescription. Robert Rosenblatt, "Drug Firms' TV Ads Fuel Rise in Costs and Demand," *Los Angeles Times*, November 26, 1999, A46.

35. Ibid. Also see Greider, *The Big Fix*, 2003.

36. L. Bowman, "51% of U.S. Adults Take Two Pills or More a Day, Survey Reports," *San Diego Union Tribune*, January 17, 2001, A8.

37. Hilts, *Protecting America's Health*, 223. Also see Hilts for a great discussion of the Reagan era of deregulation, which contributed greatly to the rise of the pharmaceutical industry and to the weakening of the FDA.

38. Other factors contributing to increased pharmaceutical profitability include an aging populace, increased direct-to-consumer advertising, the increasing costs of prescription drugs (propelled in part by the cost of advertising), and accelerated and increased development of drugs (with fast-track approval by government regulators). Rosenblatt, "Drug Firms' TV Ads."

39. The prohibition on DTC (direct-to-consumer) advertising was lifted in August 1997.

40. For analysis of Prozac, see Dwight Fee, editor, *Pathology and the Postmodern: Mental Illness as Discourse and Experience* (Thousand Oaks, CA: Sage Publications, 2000); and Peter D. Kramer, *Listening to Prozac* (New York: Pen-

guin, 1993). For a sociological analysis of depression, see David Karp, *Speaking of Sadness* (London: Oxford University Press, 1997).

41. Viagra netted Pfizer $1.3 billion in sales in 2000. Ruth Rosen, "Orgasms for Sale," salon.com, April 30, 2002.

42. U.S. Bureau of the Census, "Demographic Profiles," *Census 2000 Gateway* (http://www.census.gov, 2000).

43. Judy Treas, "Older Americans in the 1990s and Beyond," *Population Bulletin* (50:2, 1995). Washington, DC: Population Reference Bureau.

44. John D'Emilio and Estelle Freedman, *Intimate Matters: A History of Sexuality in America* (Chicago: University of Chicago Press, 1988).

45. Andrew Cherlin, *Public and Private Families: An Introduction* (New York: McGraw Hill, 1999); and Stephanie Coontz, *The Way We Really Are: Coming to Terms with America's Changing Families* (New York: Basic Books, 1997).

46. D'Emilio and Freedman, *Intimate Matters*.

47. A majority or near majority of Americans now support antidiscrimination laws and gay rights, according to a USA Today/CNN/Gallup poll taken in May 2003. Eighty-eight percent said they favored equal rights in the workplace; 62 percent expressed support for health and Social Security benefits for gay partners; 54 percent approved of the "alternate lifestyle"; and 49 percent favored gay marriage. (An equal number opposed it.)

48. In Eric Schlosser, *Reefer Madness: Sex, Drugs, and Cheap Labor in the American Black Market* (New York: Houghton Mifflin, 2003). Schlosser writes that America is the world's largest producer of porn, producing 211 new "hardcore" videos per week, and porn revenues are currently estimated to be around eight to ten billion dollars, about the same as Hollywood's domestic box office receipts.

49. Nurnburg and Heaton, "The Impact of Viagra over Five Years."

50. For national sex research in the 1940s and '50s, see Alfred Kinsey, Wardell B. Pomeroy, and Clyde E. Martin, *Sexual Behavior in the Human Male* (Philadelphia: Saunders, 1948), and *Sexual Behavior in the Human Female* (Philadelphia: Saunders, 1953). For sex research in the 1960s and '70s, see William Masters and Virginia Johnson, *Human Sexual Response* (Boston: Little, Brown, 1966) and *Human Sexual Inadequacy* (Boston: Little, Brown, 1970). And for qualitative research on women's sexualities in the 1970s, see Shere Hite, *The Hite Report: A Nationwide Study of Female Sexuality* (New York: Dell, 1976).

51. Kinsey, *Sexual Behavior in the Human Male*.

52. Edward O. Laumann, John H. Gagnon, Robert T. Michael, Stuart Michaels, *The Social Organization of Sexuality: Sexual Practices in the United States* (Chicago: University of Chicago Press, 1994): 368.

53. Ibid., 372.

54. See D. Grady, "Sure, We've Got a Pill for That," *New York Times*, February 14, 1999; and "Sex-Study Authors Had Ties to Viagra Maker, AMA Says,"

Boston Globe, February 11, 1999, A8. Notably, a few days after these statistics were published in *JAMA,* the Associated Press reported that the authors of the article had been paid consultants to Pfizer. Viagra and sexual dysfunction emerged out of this context of increasingly privatized medical and scientific research.

55. NASCAR race car driver Mark Martin was part of Pfizer's "Tune Up for Life" health promotion project, and Earth, Wind, and Fire held a "True Blue" summer 2001 concert tour featuring male health screenings sponsored by Viagra.

56. Foucault, *History of Sexuality.*

57. Harvey Molotch would call this combination of factors that produced a product such as Viagra a "lash up." For more on this, see *Where Stuff Comes From* (New York: Routledge, 2003). The concept of "enrollment" comes from Bruno Latour and Steve Woolgar, *Laboratory Life: The Construction of Scientific Facts* (Princeton, NJ: Princeton University Press, 1979).

58. Sildenafil, the chemical in Viagra, is a phosphodiesterase-5 (PDE5) inhibitor. Phosphodiesterases are enzymes that catalyze the degradation of the cyclic nucleotides, cyclic AMP and cyclic GMP. Sildenafil actively blocks these enzymes and thus enables increased blood flow to the penis. Initially, inhibitors of PDE5 were thought to treat cardiovascular conditions, such as angina. In clinical trials, these drugs caused no cardiovascular activity, but they did have a beneficial effect on erectile function. Viagra, Levitra, and Cialis are described on their webpages as drugs that work through PDE5, which helps the smooth muscles in the penis to relax, which effectively increases blood flow, thus allowing the penis to become and stay harder longer. See Levitranews.com, Viagra.com, and cialis.com.

59. See the final chapter of this book for a discussion of the way pharmaceutical companies such as Pfizer are working to market SSRIs and PDE5 inhibitors together.

60. Currently, women are two times more likely to be diagnosed with depression than men according to the National Institute of Mental Health. This is probably due to many social factors, not the least of which is that woman are probably two times more likely to see their doctors on a regular or semiregular basis.

61. A recent survey by market research firm Insight-Express found that 80 percent of respondents were aware of the pharmaceutical phenomenon Viagra, as opposed to the 45 percent who knew Zocor, a cholesterol-lowering drug. Greider, *The Big Fix,* 87.

62. Boston and Los Angeles are both medically sophisticated urban areas with somewhat different medical scenes. Selecting these two areas allowed me to have access to a range of medical institutions, most of which are producing and profiting from the Viagra campaign.

63. In November 2000, I attended a CME (Continuing Medical Education) conference on erectile dysfunction where Pfizer representatives handed out notepads and promotional materials printed with a picture of Viagra tablets circling the globe and the words, "4 tablets dispensed every second." Clearly, Pfizer is proud of its global marketing and worldwide popularity.

64. I came to this project with research questions initially focused on profit-based sexual empowerment campaigns and women's stakes in the Viagra phenomenon, both as consumers and partners of Viagra consumers. I wondered, Can consumption practices and commodities affect social change? These questions were fueled by my past research, which interrogated various contemporary forms of sexual commodification, my investment in feminist research, and a strong concern for social inequality.

65. For more on "partial truths," see James Clifford and George Marcus, *Writing Culture: The Poetics and Politics of Ethnography* (Berkeley: University of California Press, 1986); Marjorie DeVault, *Liberating Method: Feminism and Social Research* (Philadelphia: Temple University Press, 1999); and Judith Stacey, *In the Name of the Family: Rethinking Family Values in the Postmodern Age* (Boston: Beacon Press, 1996).

66. See Warren St. John, "In an Oversexed Age, More Guys Take a Pill," *New York Times,* December 14, 2003, sec. 9, 1.

NOTES TO CHAPTER 2

1. This literature is used to train new Pfizer drug representatives, whose job requires promoting, or "detailing," drugs in personal visits to doctors' offices, often with gifts and drug samples. A Pfizer sales trainer provided the literature quoted here. Carl Elliott reports that drug detailing is the industry's most important marketing strategy. In 1999, there were eighty-three thousand drug detailers in America, dispensing eight billion dollars worth of drug samples. Carl Elliott, *Better Than Well: American Medicine Meets the American Dream* (New York: Norton, 2003): 120.

2. "Erectile disorder" as a medical diagnosis was officially entered into the *DSM IV* in 1994. See American Psychiatric Association, *DSM-IV: Diagnostic and Statistical Manual of Mental Disorders,* 4th ed. (Washington, DC: American Psychiatric Press, 1994).

3. The overwhelming majority of urologists featured in the articles I analyzed were or had been paid consultants for Pfizer. Their voices clearly overshadow the psychologists, who are, by and large, not affiliated with a pharmaceutical corporation. Only one-third of the articles feature psychologists claiming that impotence has a psychological dimension.

4. Environmental factors are generally ignored efforts to in understand the causes of impotence. For example, the fact that ancient Romans became

impotent by ingesting lead from their aqueducts is not widely acknowledged. From Elizabeth Abbott, *A History of Celibacy* (New York: Scribners, 2000).

5. Malcolm Gladwell, *The Tipping Point: How Little Things Can Make a Big Difference* (New York: Little, Brown, 2000): 18.

6. Sociologist Howard Becker's well-respected model for understanding art worlds is also helpful here in locating the important role of actors, contexts, and conventions in constructing Viagra worlds. See Howard Becker, *Art Worlds* (Berkeley: University of California Press, 1982).

7. To track the construction of a medicalized social problem and a cure, this chapter relies on content analysis of Viagra-related articles in mainstream and medical publications prior to the product's release in 1998, Pfizer promotional materials, a television documentary on "Sexual Chemistry," and my own practitioner interview data. My general searches for mainstream articles discussing Viagra prior to its debut yielded no more than twenty sources on several different databases. (In the nine months *after* Viagra's debut, over five hundred articles were written.) Of these preliminary reports, I chose ten broadly representative pieces that attempted to make sense of Viagra's origins and development. The product announcements and cover stories I analyzed came from a variety of specialty magazines, including *Insight on the News, Time* (2), *Newsweek* (2), *Fortune, Harper's Bazaar, Playboy, GQ,* and *Maclean's*. Also included in my sample are several important medically focused representations of Viagra's genesis, including a "Sexual Chemistry" documentary aired on The Learning Channel in 1999, and one article by the leading national medical journal, *JAMA,* the journal of the American Medical Association. In total, I analyzed twelve mainstream media sources for their early Viagra narratives. In addition, I looked at two specialty pieces in *Urology Times* (1997), and *Journal of Urology* (1994), as well as at Pfizer promotional and training materials, in order to track the use and evolution of the term "erectile dysfunction."

8. Raymond Rosen and Sandra Leiblum, *Erectile Disorders: Assessment and Treatment* (New York: Guilford Press, 1992): 3.

9. George Nurnburg and Jeremy Heaton, "The Impact of Viagra over Five Years: Why Is It a Worldwide Phenomenon?" Paper Read at Second International Consultation on Erectile and Sexual Dysfunction, Paris 2003.

10. William Robinson, *Sexual Impotence: A Practical Treatise on the Causes, Symptoms, and Treatment of Impotence and Other Disorders in Men and Women* (New York: Critic and Guide Co., 1912): 114.

11. See Rosen and Leiblum, *Erectile Disorders,* 11.

12. Quoted in Lynne Luciano, *Looking Good: Male Body Image in Modern America* (New York: Hill and Wang, 2001): 19.

13. Ibid., 189.

14. Leonore Tiefer and Arnold Melman, "Psychosocial Follow-up of Penile

Prosthesis Implants Patients and Partners," *Journal of Sex and Marital Therapy* (14, 1988): 184–201.

15. According to Spark's presentation at the Boston Forum, 1999, when he published his controversial article in *JAMA* in 1980 titled "Impotence Is Not All Psychogenic," he alienated his urologist and psychologist colleagues, and signaled a change in thinking about sexual problems.

16. Rosen and Leiblum, *Erectile Disorders*, 23.

17. These are results from an Academic Universe search of newspaper articles mentioning erectile dysfunction from 1970 to 2000.

18. There is an understood "split" between psychological disciplines and medical disciplines. Generally it is rare for psychologists and urologists to collaborate in publishing, or even to attend the same academic conferences. Some of the urologists I interviewed referred their problem clients to psychologists or sex therapists for help, and this is as far as collaboration usually goes. Psychiatrists, because they prescribe drugs, tend to exist on the "medical" side with urologists, and both of these groups were central in the reclaiming of erectile dysfunction, previously existing as "erectile disorder" and classified as a mental or psychological disability. For more on the disorder, see American Psychiatric Association, *DSM-IV*.

19. Quoted in Robert Aronowitz, *Making Sense of Illness* (Cambridge: Cambridge University Press, 1998): 51.

20. Talcott Parsons, *The Social System* (New York: Free Press, 1951).

21. Peter Conrad and Joseph Schneider, *Deviance and Medicalization: From Badness to Sickness*, rev. ed. (Philadelphia: Temple University Press, 1992).

22. See Leonore Tiefer, *Sex Is Not a Natural Act and Other Essays* (San Francisco: Westview Press, 1995).

23. Leonore Tiefer, "The Medicalization of Impotence: Normalizing Phallocentrism," *Gender and Society* (8, 1994): 363–77. For a critical analysis of Masters and Johnson's work see Leonore Tiefer, "Dr. Yes," http://www.nerve.com (February 27, 2001).

24. John Bancroft, interview with author, tape recording, Boston: October 2000. The majority of medical "experts" highlighted in this chapter are well-known public figures, so their names have not been changed.

25. Dr. Heiman, phone interview, tape recording, November 2000.

26. Michael Parrish, "Up, Up, and Away," *Playboy* (44, 1997): 92–99. Also see Edward Laumann, A. Paik, and R. Rosen, "Sexual Dysfunction in the United States: Prevalence and Predictors," *JAMA* (281:6, 1999): 537–44; and Pat Philips, "Reports at European Urology Congress Reflect Issues of Interest for Aging Men," *JAMA* (279:17, 1998): 1333–36.

27. The theme of male sexuality out of control is a common and notable construction in relation to male sexuality.

28. Luciano, *Looking Good*, 163.

29. David Stipp and Robert Whitaker, "The Selling of Impotence" *Fortune* (136, 1998): 114–22.

30. Parrish, "Up, Up, and Away." See the Urological Sciences Research Foundation (USRF) website for a visual dramatization of Brindley's experiment, www.usrf.org/news/030303_PDE5_Inhibitors/Brindley_clip1.html.

31. Emily Martin, *Flexible Bodies* (Boston: Beacon Press, 1994). Also see chapter 3 for more on twentieth-century cultural valuation of flexibility and "on call" bodies.

32. See Stipp and Whitaker, "The Selling of Impotence."

33. Ibid.

34. No one I spoke with had actually attended this conference, which left me wondering if this could be an urban myth. Nonetheless, the narrative of Brindley's presentation was reported on many times by various journalists and urologists.

35. John Bancroft, interview with author, tape recording, Boston: October 2000.

36. Caverject was released in 1995 and MUSE was released in 1997.

37. David Friedman, "Erections: A Real Growth Stock," salon.com (April 1998).

38. Pfizer, in a huge investment of resources, hired fifteen hundred staff developers. "Sex, Pills, and Love Potions," The Learning Channel (TLC), Granada Television Production (October 28, 2001).

39. The Nobel Prize in Physiology or Medicine for 1998 was awarded to Robert F. Furchgott, Louis J. Ignarro, and Ferid Murad for their discoveries concerning "nitric oxide as a signalling molecule in the cardiovascular system." The following year, Louis Ignarro was invited by Pfizer to speak about his prize-winning research and its relation to the new science of erections at a continuing education meeting in Beverly Hills, CA. In his talk, Ignarro admitted that he never realized the potential applications for his research in the realm of sexual medicine. Author's field notes, Sexual Medicine Symposium, Beverly Hills: November 2000.

40. According to the Discovery Health documentary, "Sex, Pills, and Love Potions," an erection is a simple mechanical event. Blood transfers from one chamber to another after brain messages release nitric oxide, which changes the tissues, allowing them to engorge with blood. The muscle retains the blood with Viagra because it delays an enzyme that works to eventually release the blood.

41. The most common penile prosthesis is an inflatable implant with a pump, although there are various models. The surgery can be costly. Despite this, sales of penile prosthetics have increased since Viagra's debut (Second international Consultation on Sexual Dysfunction, author's field notes, 2003), as have masculinity and sexuality clinics that offer these services.

42. In order to sell Viagra to doctors, Pfizer representatives are required to learn all of the elements of penile anatomy (structural, vascular, and neurological) and the latest scientific knowledge about the physiology of an erection (smooth muscle walls, artery dilation, production of nitric oxide). Thus, the "new" medicalization of sex is central to Pfizer representative training.

43. Leonore Tiefer, "Sexual Biopropaganda in the Twenty-First Century." Paper read at Women's Sexualities Conference, Indiana University, Bloomington, Indiana, November 15, 2003.

44. Leonore Tiefer, "In Pursuit of the Perfect Penis," *American Behavioral Scientist* (29, 1986): 579–99.

45. See Edward Laumann, A. Paik, and R. Rosen, "Sexual Dysfunction in the United States: Prevalence and Predictors," *JAMA* (281:6, 1999): 537–44.

46. Quoted in Jerry Adler, "Take a Pill and Call Me Tonight: Viagra's Debut Makes Medical History but It Won't Help Everyone," *Newsweek*, May 4, 1998, 48.

47. For example, see Leslie Ann Horvitz, "Can Better Sex Come with a Pill? The Nineties Impotence Cure," *Insight on the News*, 13 December, 1997, 38–40.

48. Luciano, *Looking Good*, 162.

49. Michael Cohen, James March, and Johan Olsen, "A Garbage Can Model of Organizational Choice," *Administrative Science Quarterly* (17, 1975): 1.

50. Dr. Bending, interview with author, tape recording, California: May 2000.

51. Framing erections as a "side effect" is a notable part of the Viagra origins story.

52. See Jim Kling, "From Hypertension to Angina to Viagra," *Modern Drug Discovery* (1:2, 1998): 31–38.

53. Christine Gorman, "A Pill to Treat Impotence?" *Time*, May 20, 1996, 54.

54. Bruce Handy, "The Viagra Craze," *Time*, May 4, 1998, 50–57.

55. Parrish, "Up, Up, and Away."

56. Eleven out of thirteen media reports included at least a portion of this "accidental discovery" origin tale. Reporting in *JAMA* and *Harper's Bazaar* did not include Viagra origin stories. This "accidental discovery" narrative was also recounted by several of my interview subjects, particularly those specializing in sexual medicine, and by several Pfizer sales representatives.

57. The happy-trial-subjects story gets repeated with frequency and intensity a decade later in Viagra clinical trials for men, but not in trials with women several years later. For more on happy clinical trial subjects, see Gorman, "A Pill to Treat Impotence?"; and Handy, "The Viagra Craze"; and Horvitz, "Can Better Sex Come with a Pill?" Reports of male trial subjects stealing medication can be found in Susan Vaughan, "The Hard Drug: Viagra Sex Tablet to Be Released," *Harper's Bazaar*, February 1998, 82–84; and John Leland and Andrew Muir, "A Pill for Impotence?" *Newsweek*, November 17, 1997, 62–67.

58. Notably, the last angina drug Pfizer launched was Norvasc, in 1991. It appears that with the discovery of Viagra, the push to develop a new drug for angina was shelved by Pfizer.

59. Latour and Woolgar conduct an "anthropology of science" to purposely apprehend as strange those aspects of science readily taken for granted, such as the construction of facts and knowledge in this social arena. They expose how the daily activities of working scientists lead to the construction of facts, and to the construction of order from disorder. See both Bruno Latour, *Science in Action: How to Follow Scientists and Engineers through Society* (Cambridge: Harvard University Press, 1987): 40; and Bruno Latour and Steve Woolgar, *Laboratory Life: The Construction of Scientific Facts* (Princeton, NJ: Princeton University Press, 1979).

60. See Laumann, Paik, and Rosen, "Sexual Dysfunction in the United States."

61. David McGibney, talk delivered to the Royal Society of Arts, Manufactures, and Commerce. Pfizerforum.com, 1999.

62. At a medical symposium that I attended in 2003 celebrating five years of Viagra, a Pfizer spokesperson shared that "the discovery of Viagra reflects scientific purpose and serendipity," and went on to emphasize how Nobel Prize–winning science led to current understandings of erections and Viagra.

63. Handy, "The Viagra Craze."

64. David Stipp and Robert Whitaker, "The Selling of Impotence," *Fortune*, March 16, 1998, 114–22.

65. "Sexual Chemistry," The Learning Channel (TLC), March 16, 1999.

66. Quoted in Handy, "The Viagra Craze."

67. Horvitz, "Can Better Sex Come with a Pill?"

68. "A Man Again," *Maclean's*, May 1998, 58.

69. Horvitz, "Can Better Sex Come with a Pill?"

70. Handy, "The Viagra Craze."

71. Bancroft, Ibid.

72. For more information on the Vatican's response, see Luciano, *Looking Good*, 200, or Handy, "The Viagra Craze." In addition, *Skeptic Magazine* reported that the Church of England, which owned two million pounds of stock in Pfizer, also announced its approval of Viagra. See Randy Cassingham, "Swell Idea," *Skeptic Magazine* (7:1, 1999): 6.

73. For more on FDA's expedited Viagra approval process, see Shannon Schultz et al., "Dying for Sex," *U.S. News and World Report*, January 11, 1999, 62–66.

74. Elliott, *Better Than Well*, 120. In an example of how one pharmaceutical company promoted illness to doctors in the 1960s, Elliott describes how Merck distributed a book called *Recognizing the Depressed Patient* in order to sell its new

antidepressant, amytriptaline. Elliott goes on to discuss the related expansion of psychiatry in the latter twentieth century:

> A look at the history of psychiatry in the past 40 years reveals star-tlingly rapid growth rates for a wide array of disorders—clinical depression, social phobia, obsessive compulsive disorder, panic disorder, attention deficit/hyperactivity disorder, and body dysmorphic disorder, just to name a few. . . . The lines between mental dysfunction and ordinary life are not as sharp as some psychiatrists like to pretend.

Elliott, *Better Than Well*, 233.

75. See Greider, *The Big Fix*, 118.

76. After questioning some of his impotent patients, Goldstein contends, he found a link between regular bicycle riding and impotence. *Newsweek* magazine, August 25, 1997, features Goldstein explaining that when a man uses a standard bike seat, his weight flattens the main penile artery, temporarily occluding the blood flow required for erections. Goldstein contends that, over time, this pressure can permanently damage the vessel. In the article, Goldstein advises men to stop riding altogether until a seat is proven safe. He said the ideal seat would "look like a toilet seat." In an article in the *Washington Post*, several of Goldstein's colleagues disputed his correlation between bicycling and impotence. See Roy Furchgott, "Bike Seat Link to Impotence Rests on Disputed Evidence," *Washington Post*, August 28, 2001, F1.

77. Goldstein was not the only Pfizer-funded medical investigator to promote Viagra. There were over a handful of Pfizer-funded urologist and psychiatrist claims makers from across the nation. I have chosen to highlight Goldstein because he was one of the more visible and prolific claims makers.

78. For evidence that Viagra and ED appeared in public discourse almost simultaneously, I searched the Lexis-Nexus Academic Universe for general news (newspaper) mentions of keyword "erectile dysfunction." In 1997, there were eleven newspaper stories about erectile dysfunction. In 1998, the year Viagra debuted, this number expanded to 136. Of the total media reports I analyzed, only two explored the shift in terminology from "impotence" to "erectile dysfunction," and only one set of journalists, Stipp and Whitaker, in "The Selling of Impotence," detailed the process Pfizer took to construct a dysfunctional populace and a market for its drug. In sum, Stipp and Whitaker are in the minority of ED claims makers when they suggest that the Viagra story is about achieving increased profits through increased medicalization or, specifically, recruiting influential doctors to help "redefine a condition to greatly increase the number of people afflicted." See *Fortune*, March 16, 1998, 114–22.

79. The *Diagnostic Statistical Manual for Mental Disorders (DSM-IV)* lists something similar (a mental disorder) as "male erectile disorder." See American Psychiatric Association, *DSM-IV*. The terminology was presumably changed to "dysfunction" to suggest organic causation.

80. To read more about the Massachusetts Male Aging Study, see H. Feldman, I. Goldstein, R. Krane, and J. McKinlay, "Impotence and Its Medical and Psychosocial Correlates: Results of the Massachusetts Male Aging Study," *Journal of Urology* (151, 1994): 54–61. Several years after the MMAS study, Irwin Goldstein was a planner and featured speaker at a 1992 Consensus Development Conference on Impotence, sponsored by the National Institute of Health. There, a consensus was reached to adopt a less shameful, more specific psychiatric term focused on the penis, not the man. In a rare consensus between sexologists and medical practitioners, "erectile dysfunction" was officially adopted by the medical community as the "more precise" term for erection difficulties, six years before Viagra debuted. Ironically, the term "erectile dysfunction" was precise when it came to locating the problem in the body (and nowhere else), but rather open-ended and vague on a subjective scale. For more on this consensus meeting, see J. Bancroft, "Foreword" in *Erectile Disorders: Assessment and Treatment*, Raymond C. Rosen and Sandra R. Leiblum, eds. (New York: Guildford Press, 1992); or Leonore Tiefer, "Critique of the *DSM-IIIR* Nosology of Sexual Dysfunctions," *Psychiatric Medicine* (10, 1992): 227–45.

81. At a 1992 NIH meeting, "erectile dysfunction" was defined as "the inability of the male to attain and maintain erection of the penis sufficient to permit satisfactory sexual intercourse." See "Impotence," *NIH Consens Statement* (10:4, 1992): 1–31. The *DSM-IV* defines "male erectile disorder" as "persistent or recurrent inability to attain or maintain until completion of the sexual activity, an adequate erection" (*DSM IV,* 504). Stock and Moser synthesized impotence, or ED, as "the inability to penetrate," and this definition reigns supreme in the Viagra era. Wendy Stock and C. Moser, "Feminist Sex Therapy in the Age of Viagra" in *New Directions in Sex Therapy: Innovations and Alternatives*, P. Kleinplatz, ed. (New York: Brunner-Routledge, 2001): 139–62.

82. Specifically, respondents in the Massachusetts Male Aging Study were asked five questions, including, "When you attempted sexual intercourse, how often was it satisfactory to you?" and "How often were you hard enough for penetration (entering your partner)?" In 1992, at a National Institute of Health Consensus Conference on Impotence, a collective decision was made to use the term "ED" instead of "impotence." Irwin Goldstein was a planner and speaker at this conference. For more information, see "Impotence," *NIH Consens Statement* (10:4, 1992): 1–31.

83. Quoted in Peter Conrad and Deborah Potter, "From Hyperactive Children to ADHD Adults: Observations on the Expansion of Medical Categories," *Social Problems* (47, 2000): 559–82.

84. Exploring the emergence of the diagnosis ADHD in adults, Conrad and Potter posit, "With active claims-makers, committed stake-holders, and receptive potential clients, diagnostic expansion can occur readily and with minimal opposition" (Ibid., 576).

85. Elliott, *Better Than Well*, 124.

86. Friedman, "Erections."

87. Impotence was long thought to affect ten million males. This figure appears in early product announcements for the first treatment for impotence, Caverject, in 1995.

88. Pfizer was extremely successful at presenting statistics to further claims of male vulnerability and illness and thus construct a sizable market for oral sildenafil. Social-problems theorists contend that expert "claims" often begin with dramatic examples, followed with statistics. For more on this, see Joel Best, *Images of Issues: Typifying Contemporary Social Problems* (New York: de Gruyter, 1989). Furthermore, the rhetoric of science is utilized as a legitimating strategy that can reach broad, popular audiences. For more on this see Joseph Gusfield, *The Culture of Public Problems: Drinking, Driving and the Symbolic Order* (Chicago: University of Chicago Press, 1980).

89. It is important to point out that ED is based on a subjective scale, not objective indications, as is Ray Rosen's International Index of Erectile Dysfunction, published in *Urology* (49, 1997): 822–30.

90. Pfizer training materials state, "ED, to some degree, affects approximately 30 million males in the United States." If America has a total of fifty-two million males aged forty and above, then with over half of males over forty "afflicted" by ED, Pfizer has constructed a medicalized social problem of "epidemic proportions." Pfizer Pharmaceuticals. Inc., *Viagra Treatment Participant's Guide* and *Viagra Disease Participant's Guide,* Training Materials, 2000.

91. Pfizer's informational advertisements (launched in early 1999) describe ED as "a widespread, treatable medical condition shared by approximately 30 million men in the U.S." See, for example, Pfizer Pharmaceuticals, Inc., *Get the Basics,* Fact Sheet, 1999; *Sexual Health Inventory for Men,* 1999; and *Patient Summary of Information about Viagra,* Fact Sheet, 1999, 2000.

92. Aronowitz, *Making Sense of Illness,* 178.

93. This information comes from conversations I had with Ian Osterloh, a prominent Pfizer researcher, and Edward Laumann at the Paris meetings on sexual dysfunction in 2003. Laumann and Raymond Rosen republished Laumann and Gagnon's general statistics on sexual dissatisfaction in *JAMA* one year after Viagra's release, at Pfizer's behest. The Associated Press reported Laumann's vested interests with Pfizer on February 11, 1999. "Sex Study Authors Had Ties to Viagra Maker, AMA Says," *Boston Globe,* A8.

94. Edward Laumann, interview with author, tape recording, Paris: July 2003.

95. See Irwin Goldstein, "New Field Could Open for Urologists: Female Sexual Dysfunction," *Urology Times* (25, 1997): 1.

96. In 1997, Goldstein took the next step, suggesting that females experience organic sexual dysfunction at rates even higher than males. For more on this, see chapter 5.

97. Quoted in Stipp and Whitaker, "The Selling of Impotence." The "sexual revolution" theme is repeated regularly in Viagra discourse.

98. When I asked Laumann about his consultant work with Pfizer, he responded by saying, "Look, I can't be bought for a bag of bones. . . . Every source of funding has its problems. But the data we get is what people tell us. People verify this. And I have access to the news media, so I can spin the story how I want. Physicians and previous sex researchers have theorized sex and the individual, but I believe sex is fundamentally a social thing." Edward Laumann, interview with author, tape recording, Paris: July 2003.

99. Concerns about such "uneasy alliances" between clinical investigators and pharmaceutical industries were raised in 2000 in the *New England Journal of Medicine* and in a second wave in the *British Medical Journal* in 2003. See Marcia Angell, "Is Academic Medicine for Sale?" *New England Journal of Medicine* (342, 2000): 1516–18; and Thomas Bodenheimer, "Uneasy Alliance: Clinical Investigators and the Pharmaceutical Industry," *New England Journal of Medicine* (342, 2000): 1539–44. Also see Ray Moynihan, "The Making of a Disease: Female Sexual Dysfunction," *British Medical Journal* (326, 2003): 45–47. In response to the first wave of concerns, the *Washington Post* announced new publishing guidelines in medical journals. "About 12 of the world's most prominent medical journals are issuing a joint editorial this week stating that they will reject any scientific studies that do not come with an assurance that the sponsor—whether a drug company or other organization—gave researchers complete access to the data and freedom to report the findings." Quoted in Susan Okie, "A Stand for Scientific Independence," *Washington Post,* August 5, 2001, A1.

100. Sexual impotence was ultimately constructed as a personal issue, linked to individuals' physiological problems, rather than a public issue. In this way, the professional treatment is focused on the diseased body (penis), without attention to the social, political, and environmental circumstances in which the individuals exists. Medical sociologists point out that today, responsibility for health is increasingly transferred to the individual. Pfizer promotes self-policing with its subjective "sexual health" scales, asking patients to regularly rate their own sexual satisfaction and potency. Thus, after the successful construction of a sexual social problem and a dysfunctional populace, Viagra became a personal solution for a personal problem. For more on self-policing and "healthism" see Chloe Bird, Peter Conrad, and Allen Fremont, eds., *Handbook of Medical Sociology* (Upper Saddle River, NJ: Prentice Hall, 2000); Robert Crawford, "Healthism and the Medicalization of Everyday Life," *International Journal of Health Services* (10, 1980): 365–88; and Michel Foucault, *The Birth of the Clinic: An Archaeology of Medical Perception* (New York: Vintage, 1973).

101. Quoted in Lynn Payer, *Disease-Mongers: How Doctors, Drug Companies, and Insurers Are Making You Feel Sick* (New York: Wiley, 1992): 5.

102. Ray Moynihan, "Selling Sickness: The Pharmaceutical Industry and Disease Mongering," *British Medical Journal* (324, 2002): 886–91.

103. Joel Best, *Images of Issues: Typifying Contemporary Social Problems* (New York: de Gruyter, 1989).

104. Susan Vaughan, "The Hard Drug: Viagra Sex Tablet to Be Released," *Harper's Bazaar*, February 1998, 82–84.

105. See Greider, *The Big Fix*, 94, for more on drug naming practices.

106. Quoted in Stipp and Whitaker, "The Selling of Impotence."

107. Generally, statistics reporting 60 percent to 80 percent effectiveness among clinical trial subjects are cited in these articles.

108. Handy, "The Viagra Craze."

109. For more on the placebo effect, see anthropologist Daniel E. Moerman's research, discussed in Greider, *The Big Fix*, 110–11.

110. See Brian Reid, "The Downside of Mind over Matter," *Los Angeles Times*, May 27, 2002, S5.

111. Quoted in Luciano, *Looking Good*, 200.

112. Many urologists I spoke with shared stories about how, from the minute Viagra was approved, their phone lines were jammed with requests for prescriptions.

113. Elliott, *Better Than Well*, 127.

114. The Viagra death scare appeared to last for roughly six months, until enough medical reports refuted these stories, insisting that the numbers of Viagra-related deaths were no different from general mortality rates in certain age groups. For examples of reporting on Viagra recreational use, see Lamar Graham, "Triumph of the Willy" *GQ*, December 1998, 197–218; Guy Trebay, "Longer, Harder, Faster: Partying with Viagra," *Village Voice*, November 2, 1999, 41–44; Robert Pela, "Younger Men Are Opting for the Viagra Fix—Even When It Ain't Broke," *Men's Fitness*, February 2000, 82–87; and Jack Hitt, "The Second Sexual Revolution," *New York Times Magazine*, February 20, 2000, 34–37.

115. FDA report (1998) quoted in Jay S. Cohen, *Over Dose: The Case against the Drug Companies* (New York: Putnam, 2001): 271.

116. Jay S. Cohen, author of *Over Dose: The Case against the Drug Companies*, cites an independent study of Viagra's first thirteen months on the market, published in the *Journal of the American College of Cardiology*, which revealed 1473 major drug reactions reported to the FDA, divided into deaths (over five hundred), heart attacks, cardiac arrhythmias, and strokes. Today, Pfizer and the FDA claim that Viagra has caused no more deaths than would be expected among several million men with medical problems commonly associated with erectile dysfunction, like heart disease, high blood pressure, and diabetes, who returned to engaging in sex. But Cohen remains unconvinced. He compared

mortality rates associated with the ED treatment Caverject with those of Viagra and came up with a higher death rate associated with Viagra. In addition, Cohen believes that serious side effects associated with Viagra may be related to overdosing patients in the product's first few years (58).

117. Mike Mitka, "Some Men Who Take Viagra Die—Why?" *JAMA* (283:5, 2000): 590. Evidence of the predominance of Viagra death-scare reporting can be found in the fact that a general search in Lexis-Nexis for general news articles that use keywords "Viagra" and "death" printed in major newspapers between 1997 and 2002 yielded a total of 306 articles. Two hundred sixty-two news wires were posted on this subject in these same years, and medical and health news sources on Viagra and death equaled thirty-eight. Because of this medical attention to Viagra's potential risks, in late 1998 Pfizer was required by the FDA to print in Viagra packaging a warning about priapism, heart attacks, hypertension, and "sudden cardiac death." "Health Warnings Added to Viagra Label," *Sex Weekly*, NewsRx.com, December 7, 1998, 3.

118. Pfizer was among the first to perfect the "help-seeking ad," which, according to FDA regulations, does not require a list of potential side effects and warnings associated with a product if the drug is not named in the ad. Many of Pfizer's Viagra ads (including the initial Bob Dole ads) mention the condition erectile dysfunction and flash "Pfizer" at the end of the commercial but do not list warnings and side effects. It is due to successful "branding" and "brand awareness" that ED and Pfizer have become largely synonymous with Viagra in the public imagination.

119. For Dole's urologist, who told me he was initially not notified of his patient's appearance on *Larry King Live* in early May 1998, the days following the CNN interview were frantic, with the phone ringing off the hook. I have omitted his name to protect his identity. Phone interview with author, field notes, October 2001.

120. Bob Dole was the very image of dignified but wounded virility after his election loss to Bill Clinton (Greider, *The Big Fix*, 118). While Dole acted as a "sanitizing" force, he also played up Viagra/erection humor in his later television endorsements for Pepsi, where he was depicted watching a Britney Spears video and responding by telling his dog, "Down, boy." In another Pepsi ad, Dole addresses audiences with, "Hi, I'm Bob Dole, and I've always spoken to you frankly. I'm eager to tell you about a product that helps me feel youthful and vital again. What is this amazing product? It's my faithful little blue friend, an ice cold Pepsi Cola."

As high-profile citizens, both Bob and Elizabeth Dole have been the targets of numerous jokes in relation to Bob's impotence. For example, a joke version of "Liddy Dole's Diary" on the internet has Elizabeth "bursting into tears" as she passes by the (highly phallic) Washington monument in her car.

121. According to Paul Bedard, Bruce Ausler, Thomas Omestad, and

David E. Kaplan, *U.S. News and World Report*, October 25, 1999, 5, Bob Dole received forty-five thousand dollars a week while the ad was on TV.

122. Pfizer's Viagra also won corporate sponsorship rights with professional baseball. This association with professional athletics is continuing in 2004, as Viagra competitors Levitra (Bayer and GlaxoSmithKline) and Cialis (Eli Lilly) are each the corporate sponsors of the NFL and America's Cup sailing team, in that order.

123. Brad, interview with author, tape recording, California: May 2000.

124. See chapter 7 for more on this issue.

125. Luciano, *Looking Good*, 201. Harpers estimated that the Pentagon would spend $50 million in 1999 on Viagra, www.harpers.org/pentagon.html.

NOTES TO CHAPTER 3

A version of this chapter was published in *Sexuality & Culture* (7:3, 2004).

1. Michael Kimmel, *Manhood in America: A Cultural History* (New York: Free Press, 1996).

2. In the 1970s and 1980s, gender scholars began to complicate and problematize normative (and thus prescriptive) white, heterosexual "hegemonic masculinity." For more on hegemonic masculinity, see Robert Connell, *Masculinities* (Berkeley: University of California Press, 1995). Michael Messner, *The Politics of Masculinities: Men in Movements* (Thousand Oaks, CA: Sage Publications, 1997) argues that a singular, reductionist, unified masculinity does not reflect a society in which "at any given moment there are various and competing masculinities." Responding to feminist scholarship, early masculinities scholars argued that patriarchy forces men to oppress themselves and other men. Such scholars inspired many inquiries into male competition, power struggles, and self-objectification. Joseph Pleck's *The Myth of Masculinity* (Cambridge: MIT Press, 1981) suggested that hegemonic masculinity and the promotion of unattainable ideals caused men to experience "sex role strain" in trying to attain the unattainable. In this way, Pleck sparked an interest in male confusion and "crisis" related to out-of-date, inflexible, contradictory, turn-of-the-century sex roles. Similarly, Lynne Segal, in *Slow Motion: Changing Masculinities* (London: Virago, 1990) warned that lived masculinity is never the seamless, undivided construction it becomes in its symbolic manifestation. She argued that in the late twentieth century, masculinity was not in crisis per se, but it was less hegemonic than before. While contemporary, increasingly visible and complicated masculinities can exist in tension with potentially outdated roles and expectations, this tension can also lead to confusion about manhood and how to "do" it.

3. See masculinities scholarship by Michael Kimmel and Michael Messner, for example, *Men's Lives* (Boston: Allyn and Bacon, 1995). Also see Barbara

Ehrenreich, Elizabeth Hess, and Gloria Jacobs, *Re-Making Love: The Feminization of Sex* (New York: Doubleday, 1986).

4. Today much has been written on the Promise Keepers and Christian revival masculinity movements. See, for example, *Promise Keepers and the New Masculinity: Private Lives and Public Morality*, Rhys. H. Williams, ed. (Lanham, MD: Lexington Books, 2001).

5. Kimmel, *Manhood in America*, 310.

6. Connell, *Masculinities*, 45.

7. Kimmel, *Manhood in America*, 332.

8. Connell proposes his own model, the "body-reflexive" model, in which the social relations of gender are experienced in the body and are constituted through bodily action. See Connell, *Masculinities*, 60–64.

9. See, for example, Susan Bordo, *The Male Body: A New Look at Men in Public and Private* (New York: Farrar, Straus, and Giroux, 1999); Marc Faseau, *The Male Machine* (New York: Dell, 1975); Kimmel and Messner, *Men's Lives*; and Michael Kimmel, *Manhood in America.*

10. See, for example, Annie Potts, "The Essence of the Hard-On," in *Men and Masculinities* (3:1, 2000): 85–103. Also see Leonore Tiefer, "The Medicalization of Impotence: Normalizing Phallocentrism," *Gender and Society* (8, 1994): 363–77, and *Sex Is Not a Natural Act and Other Essays* (San Francisco: Westview Press, 1995).

11. See, for example, Potts, "The Essence of the Hard-On"; Tiefer, *Sex Is Not a Natural Act*; Lynne Luciano, *Looking Good: Male Body Image in Modern America* (New York: Hill and Wang, 2001); and Barbara L. Marshall, "'Hard Science:' Gendered Constructions of Sexual Dysfunction in the 'Viagra Age,'" *Sexualities* (5:2, 2002): 131–58. Phallocentrism refers to the phallus, a male organ that symbolizes power and control.

12. See, for example, Bordo, *The Male Body.*

13. Laura Mamo and Jennifer Fishman, "Potency in All the Right Places: Viagra as a Technology of the Gendered Body," *Body and Society* (7:4, 2001): 13–35.

14. A very limited cohort of scholars, primarily historians, has written about how white men's heterosexual bodies have been normalized and naturalized and, in rare cases, pathologized. See Bordo, *The Male Body*. Also see Vern Bullough, "Technology for the Prevention of 'les maladies produites par la masturbation,'" *Technology and Culture* (28:4, 1987): 828–32; and Kevin Mumford, "Lost Manhood Found: Male Sexual Impotence and Victorian Culture in the United States," *Journal of the History of Sexuality* (3:1, 1992). Kevin Mumford explores how male impotence was medicalized, constructed, and cured historically. Starting from advertisements promising male virility and vigor, Mumford traces the "crisis of masculinity" along with modernization and the changing American conceptions of male sexuality and masculinity from the 1830s to the 1920s.

15. All names have been changed to protect the identity of my informants. The twenty-seven male consumers I spoke with are a self-selected group who responded to the interview requests I made through internet postings, newspaper advertisements, practitioner referrals, senior-citizens organizations, personal contacts, and prostate cancer support-group meeting announcements. Those consumers who volunteered for an interview generally had experience with Viagra and had an interest in sharing this experience because it had affected their lives in some way (good or bad). A group of men from a post-prostate-surgery support group agreed to speak with me over the phone under conditions of anonymity and confidentiality about their experiences dealing with surgery-induced ED. Interestingly, all had tried Viagra, and none had had any "success" with it, a fact that turned several of the interviews into "ranting" sessions, which rendered visible how emotionally invested these consumers were in Viagra's promise. Of the twenty-seven male consumers I spoke with, all but two had tried Viagra, and half of these discontinued using Viagra after the initial trial because of unsatisfactory response or preference for a different product. This "take rate" is representative of the larger population of Viagra users nationally; Pfizer's research has shown that over half of those who receive a prescription for Viagra do not request a refill.

16. In addition to being the only Viagra expert known to most men, their doctors are the only person most men feel comfortable talking to about their sexual problems.

17. I also spoke with twenty-two medical practitioners. Six of the twenty-two medical professionals I spoke with are female; sixteen are male. Eight are acclaimed experts in sexual medicine, regularly publishing and delivering lectures on female sexual dysfunction.

18. Dr. Bern, interview with author, tape recording, California: August 2000.

19. Phil, phone interview, tape recording, May 2000.

20. Byron, phone interview, tape recording, May 2000.

21. In *The Male Body*, Susan Bordo explores the link between masculinity and the phallus throughout Western history, from Roman phallic gods to St. Augustine's "lustful member" to John Bobbitt's detachable penis to Clinton's not-so-private parts (24–25). Bordo argues that for as long as we can remember, the phallus has embodied our cultural imagination, symbolic of power, permission, defiance, and performance. Annie Potts adds that medicine and sexology produce and perpetuate the idea that an erect penis signifies "healthy" male sexuality—a destructive form of hegemonic masculinity that "ignores the diversity of penile pleasures" (89).

22. The idea that female sexuality can only be awakened by (or responsive to) the male was popular in marriage manuals of the early twentieth century and currently exist in medical discourse about female sexual dysfunction. For

more on experts and female consumers' constructions of female sexuality, see chapters 5 and 6.

23. Potts, "The Essence of the Hard-On," 98. Potts argues that we need an expansive view of male sexuality that need not rely on phallic ambitions. This would require a rethinking of penis power, "a relinquishment of this organ's executive position in sex," and an "embrace of a variety of penile styles: flaccid, erect, and semiflaccid/semierect" (100).

24. For more on gender as an accomplishment, see Candace West and Don Zimmerman, "Doing Gender," *Gender and Society* (1, 1987): 125–51; and Candace West and Sarah Fenstermaker, "Doing Difference," *Gender and Society* (9:1, 1995): 8–38. Also see West and Fenstermaker, *Doing Gender: Doing Difference* (New York: Routledge, 2002).

25. See, for example, Diane Dull and Candace West, "Accounting for Cosmetic Surgery: The Accomplishment of Gender," *Social Problems* (38:1, 1991): 54–71; and Kathy Davis, *Reshaping the Female Body: The Dilemma of Cosmetic Surgery* (New York: Routledge, 1995).

26. Donna Haraway, *Simians, Cyborgs, and Women: The Reinvention of Nature* (New York: Routledge, 1991): 149.

27. See Emily Martin, *Flexible Bodies* (Boston: Beacon Press, 1994).

28. Elizabeth Grosz, *Space, Time, and Perversion: Essays on the Politics of Bodies* (New York: Routledge, 1995): 35.

29. Quoted in "One Couple Looks Back at Facing Up to ED and Ahead," *LifeDrive* magazine, Lifedrivemagazine.com, April 12, 2002.

30. See any of Goldstein's coauthored reports in the *International Journal of Impotence Research,* volumes 10, 11, 12, and 15.

31. Dr. Curt, interview with author, tape recording, California: August 2000.

32. Chuck, phone interview, tape recording, May 2000.

33. Differing markedly in age, health, and reason for using Viagra (and, less markedly, in race, occupation, and sexual orientation), my sample is representative of a diversity of Viagra users. Pfizer identifies its largest market as "men over forty years of age." Pfizer Pharmaceuticals, Inc., *Patient Summary of Information about Viagra,* Fact Sheet, 1999, 2000; and *Uncover Ed,* Pfizer Informational Brochure, March 2000. In my sample of male consumers, diseases, medications, and surgeries were the most frequently cited reasons for trying Viagra. Ten of the twenty-seven male consumers I interviewed experienced erectile difficulties after undergoing prostate surgery. Others blamed erectile dysfunction on age (four), diabetes (one), heart problems (one), and medications (two). Three consumers cited psychological (self-esteem) factors as the main cause of their erectile difficulties. Perhaps of most interest is the significant number of interviewees who denied they had erectile dysfunction (seven), and instead explained that they used Viagra as an assurance or enhancement drug. Pfizer does

not officially acknowledge or discuss this population of Viagra users in its promotional or training information, although these users may fall into the "mild ED" and "psychological and other factors" categories.

34. Nora Jacobson found this to be the case with breast implants in her book *Cleavage: Technology, Controversy, and the Ironies of the Man-Made Breast* (New Brunswick, NJ: Rutgers University Press, 2000). Some have suggested that gay males are a ready market for the "enhancement" uses of Viagra, including several of my gay interview subjects. But both gay and straight men in my interview pool expressed interest in the enhancement uses of Viagra.

35. Will, interview with author, tape recording, California: September 2000.

36. Stanford, interview with author, tape recording, California: August 2000.

37. Previous treatments for ED included a liquid injected directly into the penis, which would produce an erection for several hours (Caverject). Viagra is constructed as a superior treatment due to its simple delivery (as a pill) and production of a penis that will wait to become erect until the user is ready.

38. See Martin, *Flexible Bodies*.

39. Stu, interview with author, tape recording, California: October 2000.

40. As an interesting comparison, over-the-counter impotence product Enzyte, which debuted in 2002, promises, as a "male enhancement product," to increase penile size and confidence and well as to enhance masculinity.

41. Dr. Tobin, phone interview, tape recording, May 2000.

42. Dr. Basson, interview with author, tape recording, Massachusetts: October 2000.

43. Will, Ibid.

44. Potts, in "The Essence of the Hard-On" (94), reminds us that the true mark of therapeutic success is restoration of "phallic manhood."

45. This idea comes from Riessman, "Women and Medicalization: A New Perspective," *Social Policy* (14:1, 1983).

46. Dr. Pellis, interview with author, tape recording, California: May 2000.

47. Julia Heiman, phone interview, tape recording, November 2000.

48. Dr. Redding, interview with author, tape recording, California: May 2000.

49. Dr. Blackwood, phone interview, tape recording, May 2000.

50. Dr. Bern, Ibid.

51. Dr. Patt, interview with author, tape recording, California: October 2000.

52. Peter Conrad and Joseph Schneider, *Deviance and Medicalization: From Badness to Sickness* (London: Mosby, 1980); and Riessman, "Women and Medicalization."

53. See Edward Laumann, A. Paik, and R. Rosen, "Sexual Dysfunction in

the United States: Prevalence and Predictors," *JAMA* (281:6, 1999): 537–44; and chapter 2 on the construction of a social problem and a dysfunctional populace.

54. Dr. Golding, interview with author, tape recording, California: May 2000.

55. Dr. Loud, interview with author, tape recording, California: August 2000.

56. Dr. Cummings, interview with author, tape recording, California: August 2000.

57. Thom, phone interview, tape recording, May 2000.

58. Scott, e-mail interview, e-mail transcript, May 2000.

59. There is a long-standing struggle between therapists and practitioners to locate the source of erectile dysfunction and treat either physiological or psychological manifestations of the problem.

60. Ricardo, phone interview, tape recording, August 2000.

61. Barbara L. Marshall, "'Hard Science.'"

62. Viagra competitor Enzyte is an over-the-counter product that offers "natural male enhancement," which seems to put Viagra in the "unnatural" (synthetic) category.

63. Irwin Goldstein, phone interview, tape recording, November 2000.

64. Dr. Lee, phone interview, tape recording, May 2000.

65. Long, interview with author, tape recording, California: October 2000.

66. I never expected to be a stand-in for consumers' doctors. In these cases where consumers asked for advice, I awkwardly assured them that I was not an expert on ED, but judging from my interviews with other male consumers, their experiences sounded normal. If the side effects they mentioned sounded potentially dangerous (like heart palpitations or trouble breathing), I advised them to contact their doctors as soon as possible.

67. Interestingly, several of the men I spoke with, primarily those who had undergone prostate surgery, felt more of a stigma associated with incontinence than with impotence. This is yet another area where millions of men suffer in silence.

68. See Janice Raymond, *Transsexual Empire: The Making of the She-Male* (New York: Atheneum, 1994).

69. Fred, phone interview, tape recording, August 2000.

70. Chuck, Ibid.

71. Scott, Ibid.

72. Dave, interview with author, tape recording, California: July 2000.

73. Phil, e-mail interview, e-mail transcript, August 2000.

74. Don, phone interview, tape recording, May 2000.

75. Marvin, email interview, email transcript, August 2000.

76. Dr. Pemel, interview with author, tape recording, California: August 2000.

77. Wilshore, interview with author, tape recording, California: May 2000.

78. Pal, email interview, email transcript, August 2000.

79. Dr. Pemel, Ibid.

80. Dr. Curt, Ibid.

81. Dr. Bending, interview with author, tape recording, California: July 2000.

82. Bordo, in *The Male Body*, argues that in a culture where "big and bulky" represent male ideals, "shrinkage" is feared, as evidenced in popular culture (*Seinfeld, Boogie Nights*, etc.).

83. Bob, interview with author, tape recording, California: August 2000.

84. Dr. Pemel, Ibid.

85. Potts, "The Essence of the Hard-On," 96.

86. Ricardo, Ibid.

87. In Ricardo's case, Viagra, constructed as the miracle treatment, did not work. This may have reinforced his insecurities and sense of loss even more.

88. Irwin Goldstein, Ibid.

89. Joel, interview with author, tape recording, California: October 2000.

90. Marvin, Ibid.

91. Relationship experts have described this "delicate dance" that couples do when they are dealing with situations like sexual dysfunction. Without open communication between partners, the fear of "failure" can lead to avoidance and alienation, which can only exacerbate the problem.

92. Ten of my interview subjects experienced erectile difficulties after undergoing prostate surgery. Others blamed erectile dysfunction on diabetes, heart problems, medications, partners, or psychological factors.

93. Dr. Golding, Ibid.

94. Julia Heiman, Ibid.

95. Art, interview with author, tape recording, California: May 2000.

96. Fred, Ibid.

97. Stanford, interview with author, tape recording, California: May 2000.

98. These sociocultural explanations are very close to the explanations that senior women gave me, as discussed in chapter 6.

99. Joel, Ibid.

100. Don, Ibid.

101. Dusty, interview with author, tape recording, California: August 2000.

102. Stanford, Ibid.

103. Joel, Ibid.

104. Ollie, phone interview, tape recording, May 2000.

105. Hancock, phone interview, tape recording, May 2000.

106. Miles, e-mail interview, e-mail transcript, August 2000.

107. Stu, Ibid.

108. Ollie, Ibid.

109. Quoted in Susan Faludi, *Stiffed: The Betrayal of the American Male* (New York: Morrow, 1999): 602.

110. See Carl Elliott, *Better Than Well: American Medicine Meets the American Dream* (New York: Norton, 2003): 53.

111. Luciano, *Looking Good,* 165.

112. Wendy Stock and C. Moser, "Feminist Sex Therapy in the Age of Viagra," in *New Directions in Sex Therapy: Innovations and Alternatives,* P. Kleinplatz, ed. (New York: Brunner-Routledge, 2001): 27.

113. P. J. Huffstutter and Ralph Frammolino, "Lights! Camera! Viagra! When the Show Must Go On, Sometimes a Little Chemistry Helps," *Los Angeles Times,* July 6, 2001, A1.

114. Luciano, *Looking Good,* 204.

115. I have Michael Kimmel to thank for helping me come up with this term.

116. This phrase is borrowed from Michael Messner's *Politics of Masculinities.*

NOTES TO CHAPTER 4

A version of this chapter was published in *Sexualities* (7:3, 2004).

1. See John Leland and Andrew Muir, "A Pill for Impotence?" *Newsweek,* November 17, 1997, 62–67.

2. "Letters to the Editor," *Newsweek,* December 8, 1997, 22.

3. Permission to reprint this letter was granted by Creators Syndicate, Incorporated.

4. Permission to reprint this letter to Ann Landers was granted by The Esther P. Lederer Trust and Creators Syndicate, Inc. The "sexual stories" I collected through advice columns and interviews are personal experience narratives about Viagra use, which may or may not elicit stories about intimacy. Ken Plummer, *Sexual Stories: Power, Change, and Social Worlds* (London: Routledge, 1995): 7. For example, Viagra narratives reveal just as much about aging, science and technology, health and medicine, and gender as they reveal about sex. As sexual stories, they "flow from the culture and back into it"; thus they are major resources for comprehending a culture and its dynamics, values, and changes (176). Additionally, these stories take the form of "claims making" in the sense that these women are making claims, constructing grievances, and locating sexuality within a matrix of social problems they take issue with. For more on sexual stories, see Plummer, *Sexual Stories.* For more on claims making, see Malcolm Spector and John I. Kitsuse, *Constructing Social Problems* (New York: de Gruyter, 1977).

5. I use the term "senior" here to refer to people aged sixty-five and older. While I group these women together in this analysis (as they do), it is important

to point out that my interview subjects span two different age cohorts, or generations. A "generation cohort perspective" acknowledges differences in year of birth and historical time periods that make each of these generations and their shared histories unique. For more on generational cohorts, see Ken Plummer, *Documents of Life 2: An Invitation to a Critical Humanism* (London: Sage, 2001). The senior women highlighted in this chapter are embedded in a sociohistorical, or generational, context. Though I did not conduct life histories, we can assume several things generally about the generational histories of my interview subjects. One cohort of women currently in their eighties, including interview subjects Hilda, Doris, Pauline, and Annette, with Nora and Sally following close behind, were roughly in their late twenties and early thirties in the 1950s, when some experts estimated that half of all American women were completely nonorgasmic, or "frigid." For more on this, see Barbara Ehrenreich, Elizabeth Hess, and Gloria Jacobs, *Re-Making Love: The Feminization of Sex* (New York: Doubleday, 1986). In contrast, a cohort currently in their sixties, including Agnus and Bette, were in their twenties during what Ehrenreich, Hess, and Jacobs call the "sexual revolution for women" beginning in the mid-1960s, which was made possible by the availability of the birth control pill, the publication of Masters and Johnson's ground-breaking sex research, women's mass challenges to male-dominated heterosexual sex, "second wave" feminist organizing and lesbian liberation movements, a growing "sexual marketplace for women," and women's mass entrance into the workplace. Though it is important to place these women's stories in a specific generational context, it is clear that all of these women have witnessed (to some extent) changing gender and sexual norms, practices, and meanings during their lifetimes.

6. See chapter 3 for more on male claims making related to Viagra.

7. Aside from a narrow field of publications within sexology and gerontology, data on the sex lives of seniors in America is limited. This may be linked, in part, to erroneous assumptions that before Viagra, seniors were asexual. Unfortunately, the assumption that sexuality declines and disappears with age has led to gaps and silences in landmark national sexuality research. Research by Kinsey in the 1950s and Masters and Johnson in the late 1960s exemplifies such negligence. For more on this, see Judith A. Levy, "Sex and Sexuality in Later Life Stages" in *Sexuality across the Life Course*, Alice S. Rossi, ed. (Chicago: University of Chicago Press, 1994). Finally, this assumption may have informed the latest *Sex in America* survey (1994), which included only those aged eighteen to fifty-nine. One notable exception to this omission is Shere Hite's *Hite Report on Female Sexuality* (1976), which received questionnaire responses from women aged fourteen to seventy-eight. According to Hite, one of her major findings in this report was that age is not a factor in female sexuality or, in other words, "Older women are NOT less sexual than younger women—and they are often more sexual." See Shere Hite, *Women as*

Revolutionary Agents of Change: The Hite Reports and Beyond (Madison: University of Wisconsin Press, 1994). Thanks to Viagra and former U.S. presidential candidate Bob Dole, seniors' active sexual lives are becoming more visible, legitimate, and accepted by American society. But several of my interview subjects were eager to point out that seniors were sexually active prior to the Viagra era: "These days seniors are still falling in love and feeling young and sexually active again. Is this new? Probably not. It has probably been the case for some time now, but people didn't talk about it" (Agnus, phone interview with author, tape recording, October 2000). Here Agnus asserts that with Viagra, people are now talking about sexually active seniors, and thus bringing them into being. Furthermore, *Modern Maturity*'s survey data leaves us with questions about social and cultural meanings attached to sexuality, aging, marriage obligations, and Viagra—questions that fuel my own research and this chapter. In response to these questions, I employ my own qualitative data to help fill out and complicate limited existing survey data with discussions of pleasure, desire, and danger in the Viagra era.

8. I had taught at the senior summer school for a summer. I described my project to the directors of each of these organizations, as well as one retirement home, explaining that I was a doctoral student interested in seniors' reactions to the Viagra phenomenon. Two of the organizations allowed me to distribute a one-page survey to their members, while the latter, the retirement home, was not comfortable with the subject matter of my research, explaining that it was a "privacy issue" for their boarders.

9. It should also be mentioned that while some women were eager to talk about Viagra, several anonymous survey respondents wrote "NO COMMENT in large letters on the survey, perhaps as a way to convey their discomfort in discussing an issue they deemed personal and private.

10. For more on the complex debates surrounding the 1982 Barnard College conference called "Towards a Politics of Sexuality" and ongoing historical discussions about sexuality and feminism, see volumes edited by Ann Snitow and Christian Stansell (1983) and Carole Vance (1984) as well as historical accounts by scholars such as Duggan and Hunter (1995).

11. See Sarah Goodfellow, *The Sexual Hush: Medical and Scientific Representations of Late-Life Sexuality, 1850–1920,* Ph.D. dissertation, Pennsylvania State University, forthcoming 2004.

12. Judith A. Levy, "Sex and Sexuality."

13. Shere Hite, *Women as Revolutionary Agents of Change,* 29.

14. See Lance Morrow, *Time International,* October 18, 1999, 78.

15. All names were changed to protect my informants. All interviews took place over the phone in October and November 2000. All were conducted by the author and tape recorded.

16. Jacoby, "Great Sex."

17. Jacoby, "Great Sex." There are problems with this survey, e.g., limited reporting, small sample size, and simplistic quantitative findings.

18. Jacoby, "Great Sex."

19. Hilda's and Pauline's sexual-health concerns are not unfounded. A minority of health-centered publications have addressed the risk that Viagra may pose to women's physical health. For example, the *New England Journal of Medicine* reported six months after Viagra's debut that Viagra might be associated with health risks not only for men (heart attacks) but also for women (acute cystitis). According to a letter sent by three doctors in September 1998 to the *New England Journal of Medicine*, "More and more older women are suffering from frequent, urgent, burning urination—usually found among women half their age, usually after prolonged sexual activity." One of the doctors explained the growing prevalence of acute cystitis among women to the *New York Times*, stating, "Every one of their husbands had been treated with Viagra." In 1999, health newsletters such as *Johns Hopkins Health Insider* strongly urged women with partners on Viagra to use a lubricant, reminding readers, "Your bodies are not as pliable as they once were." See "Viagra Called Not So Hot for Female Partners," *New York Times*, October 13, 1999, A5; and Julia G. Strand, "Viagra Wives," *Johns Hopkins Health Insider*, May 1999, 2.

20. See chapter 2 for more on the "risky Viagra" framing in the media.

21. For examples of news reports on seniors and Viagra in relation to dating and divorce, see Adair Lara, "Sex, Lies, and Viagra: Dating Scene Poses a Tangle of Issues for Older Singles," *San Francisco Chronicle*, October 20, 2002, E8; and Donna Koehn "The Late Divide," *Tampa Tribune*, July 13, 2003, B2.

22. See Jon Nordheimer, "Some Couples May find Viagra a Home-Wrecker," *New York Times*, May 10, 1998; and Jane Brody, "Facing Viagra's Emotional Ripples," *New York Times*, May 26, 1998.

23. Permission to reprint this letter to Ann Landers was granted by The Esther P. Lederer Trust and Creators Syndicate, Inc.

NOTES TO CHAPTER 5

1. Through their association with sexual medicine, the "sexy" Berman sisters have become pseudocelebrities. Besides running their sexual-medicine clinic at UCLA, they have been featured in countless mainstream media publications, including a spread in *Vogue*. (See their webpage, newshe.com, for their list of media appearances.) After appearing on *Oprah* and *Good Morning America*, the Berman sisters began hosting, on the Discovery network, their own late-night talk show centered on women and health-related issues.

2. "Wives Who Don't Want Sex," *The Oprah Winfrey Show*, NBC Television, February 9, 2001.

3. The Berman sisters also used their appearance on the *Oprah* show to

introduce treatment options for female sexual dysfunction, including an FDA-approved treatment produced by one of their many pharmaceutical industry supporters. It is important to point out their affiliation because most audience members probably assumed they were neutral, unaffiliated practitioners when in truth, most public medical "experts" are increasingly affiliated with a corporation. Without laws or rules about disclosure, the public will never be aware that it is not receiving unbiased information.

4. One prominent example of this media attention was *Newsweek*'s cover story by John Leland, "The Science of Women's Sexuality: Searching for a Female Viagra," *Newsweek*, May 29, 2000, 5+. Other examples include Curtis Pesman, "Lust Lotions: Move Over Viagra—A Batch of New Women's Love Drugs Are Coming," *Glamour*, August 1999, 60; Susie Bright, "Viagra Calls II: Curse of the Trophy Wives," salon.com (July 31, 1998); Dana Hudepohl, "The Truth about Female Viagra," *Marie Claire*, October 1999, 59; Claudia Kalb, "A Little Help in the Bedroom," *Newsweek* (Special Health Issue), Spring 1999, 38–39; Carol Brietzke, "Viagra: The Female Orgasm Pill?" *Cosmopolitan*, August 1998, 111; and Marlene Cimons, "Key to Female Viagra Seems a Brain Teaser," *Los Angeles Times*, March 21, 1999, A1.

5. See Edward Laumann, A. Paik, and R. Rosen, "Sexual Dysfunction in the United States: Prevalence and Predictors," *JAMA* (281:6, 1999): 537–44. Also see Edward Laumann, R. Michael, and John Gagnon, *The Social Organization of Sexuality: Sexual Practices in the United States* (Chicago: University of Chicago Press, 1994).

6. According to *Modern Maturity*, there are ten drugs that may be available to treat women with sexual dysfunction by 2003. Five of these drugs are hormone (mostly testosterone) based, three are blood vessel dilators (like Viagra), and one emulates a brain chemical. For more on this, see Susan Jacoby, "Great Sex: What's Age Got to Do with It?" *Modern Maturity* (42:5, 1999): 41–45. In addition, implants that "deliver an orgasm at the push of a button" have been patented in the United States and are undergoing clinical trials for orgasmic dysfunction. See "Push-Button Pleasure," *New Scientist Magazine*, February 7, 2001.

7. See Malcolm Spector and John I. Kitsuse, *Constructing Social Problems* (New York: de Gruyter, 1977); Peter R. Ibarra and John I. Kitsuse, "Vernacular Constituents of Moral Discourse: An Interactionist Proposal for the Study of Social Problems" in *Constructionist Controversies*, Gale Miller and James A. Holstein, eds. (New York: de Gruyter, 1993); and Joel Best, "Rhetoric in Claims-Making," *Social Problems* (34, 1987): 101–21. On the use of "frame analysis," see Erving Goffman, *Frame Analysis: An Essay on the Organization of Experience* (Cambridge: Harvard University Press, 1974).

8. Probably because all of these players are considered "scientists," those researchers who work primarily in labs, rather than with patients, are called "basic scientists."

9. See G. J. Barker-Benfield, *The Horrors of the Half-Known Life: Male Attitudes towards Women and Sexuality in Nineteenth-Century America* (New York: Harper and Row, 1976) for more on the sexual surgeries and diagnoses used to control women in the Victorian era. For the history of women and nymphomania, see Carol Groneman, "Nymphomania: The Historical Construction of Female Sexuality," *Signs: Journal of Women in Culture and Society* (19:2, 1994): 337–69. For a general history of women, technology, and medicine, see Barbara Ehrenreich and Dierdre English, *For Her Own Good: 150 Years of the Experts' Advice to Women* (New York: Anchor, 1979); and Catherine K. Riessman, "Women and Medicalization: A New Perspective," *Social Policy* (14:1, 1983): 3–18. On technology and transsexuality, see Bernice Hausman, *Changing Sex: Transsexualism, Technology, and the Idea of Gender* (Durham, NC: Duke University Press, 1995); and Janice Raymond, *The Transsexual Empire: The Making of the She-Male* (Boston: Beacon Press, 1979). On the history of treating hysteria, see Rachel Maines, *The Technology of Orgasm: "Hysteria," the Vibrator, and Women's Sexual Satisfaction* (Baltimore: Johns Hopkins University Press, 1999).

10. For more on black women's subjugation by medicine and the history of sterilization see Dorothy Roberts, *Killing the Black Body: Race, Reproduction, and the Meaning of Liberty* (New York: Vintage Books, 1997). For more on Puerto Rican women as test subjects for the early birth control pill see Barbara Seaman, *The Doctor's Case against the Pill* (New York: Wyden, 1969); and Andrea Tone, *Devices and Desires* (New York: Hill and Wang, 2001). For research on medical prison experiments, see Allen M. Hornblum, *Acres of Skin: Human Experiments at Holmesburg Prison* (New York: Routledge, 1998). And for information on the Tuskegee syphilis experiments, see James H. Jones, *Bad Blood: The Tuskegee Syphilis Experiment* (New York: Free Press, 1981).

11. According to family practitioner Jay S. Cohen, medicine is still based on the archaic assumption that men and women are the same, even though many studies have proven that women are more sensitive to drugs and more apt to take drugs. Fifty-five percent of women take daily meds (as opposed to 37 percent of males). Dosage is estimated for the male body. And eight out of the ten drugs withdrawn from FDA since 1997 posed greater risk for women. See *Over Dose: The Case against the Drug Companies* (New York: Putnam, 2001).

12. See Heather Hartley and Leonore Tiefer, "Taking a Biological Turn: The Push for a 'Female Viagra' and the Medicalization of Women's Sexual Problems," *Women's Studies Quarterly* (31:1, 2003): 42–53.

13. Nonetheless, the 1999 conference has been "officially" constructed (by the organizers) as the "second annual" meeting because it followed a 1998 closed-door "consensus" meeting of nineteen experts on FSD.

14. In its first three years, this conference was hosted by Boston University Medical Center, specifically, Dr. Irwin Goldstein's urology research group, which includes a number of high-profile medical practitioners who receive

funding from Pfizer. Goldstein served in the capacity of president or meeting chair all three years, and because of his charisma, visibility, and vision, the conference has been colloquially referred to many times as "Irwin's conference." In 2002, the conference site changed, the name of the meeting changed, and a new Canadian meeting chair, Dr. Rosemary Basson, took over. Despite these shifts, the substance of the conference itself did not undergo significant change. Thus, while I refer to the meetings as "The Boston Forum," largely because the first three years of meetings took place in Boston. where Goldstein's research group and clinic is located, the site of the conference is currently in flux.

15. See Irwin Goldstein, "New Field Could Open for Urologists: Female Sexual Dysfunction," *Urology Times* (25:1, 1997): 2; and Irwin Goldstein, Tom Lue, Harin Padma-Nathan, Raymond Rosen, William Steers, and Pierre Wicker, "Oral Sildenafil in the Treatment of Erectile Dysfunction," *New England Journal of Medicine* (338:20, 1998): 1397–1405. Also see Laumann, Paik, and Rosen, "Sexual Dysfunction in the United States."

To understand how in flux this meeting and corresponding goals, medical fields, and terminology are, one simply can review meeting titles for the past three years. The meeting has evolved from "New Perspectives in the Management of Female Sexual Dysfunction" (1999) to "Female Sexual Function Forum: New Perspectives in the Management of Female Sexual Dysfunction" (the Boston Forum 2000, 2001) to the newly elected official (2002) organization/meeting name, "International Society for the Study of Women's Sexual Health."

16. See, for example, Anastasia Toufexis, "It Is Not All in Your Head," *Time,* December 5, 1998, 21; and David Stipp and Robert Whitaker, "The Selling of Impotence," *Fortune,* March 1998, 114–22.

17. Additionally, I conducted fieldwork in November 2000 and 2001 at a three-day pharmaceutical-funded "international symposium" in Beverly Hills, California, aimed at supplying "continuing education" to primary care physicians. This symposium is aptly named "The Pharmacologic Management of Male Sexual Dysfunction and Issues in Female Sexual Dysfunction" (I will refer to it as the Sexual Medicine Symposium), and it featured Dr. Rosemary Basson as the leading expert on FSD. While the Boston Forum focuses entirely on FSD for four days, with emphasis on the latest research trends, diagnoses, measures, and treatments, the Sexual Medicine Symposium is designed to update primary care physicians in four hours on how to generally understand and treat FSD clinically. Thus, the simplified, physician-friendly approach to FSD at the Sexual Medicine Symposium is an important contrast to the Boston Forum basic science presentations. Finally, the Sexual Medicine Symposium serves as a barometer for what physicians know and how much attention FSD is receiving in sexual-health science and medicine generally. Nonetheless, because the Boston Forum is the only international conference dedicated to FSD, this chap-

ter focuses first and foremost on my fieldwork and participant observation there.

18. The fact that the conference's name was changed to focus on "female sexual function" in 2000 and on "women's sexual health" in 2002 obscures what these meetings are truly about: "managing" and eventually treating a dysfunction.

19. In my three years of fieldwork, I have had countless informal conversations with attendees, organizers, and speakers at these conferences, and I have formally interviewed seven primary claims makers at these FSD meetings, including two past presidents of the Boston Forum and four members of the Board of Directors. All seven have been invited and paid to deliver "Grandmaster," or "State of the Art" lectures on their research at one or more meetings.

20. In response to concern about "covert" industry presence, at the most recent Boston Forum meeting a single sheet was distributed that listed presenters' affiliations. Importantly, such affiliations still were not listed in the official program, or in the actual conference presentations.

21. I have followed this group since its inception in 1999, when I responded to a "call for action" published by Dr. Leonore Tiefer in a feminist newsletter, where she called for a "feminist welcoming committee" to "challenge the pharmaceutical fashioning of female bodies" at the first annual Boston meeting.

22. Sandra Leiblum, Boston Forum grandmaster presentation, 1999.

23. Ibid., 2001. Experts such as Leiblum benefited financially from Viagra's success in many ways, as they saw their practices grow and as offers were made to collaborate with Pfizer.

24. Julia Heiman, phone interview, tape recording, November 2000.

25. Irwin Goldstein, phone interview, tape recording, November 2000.

26. Pfizer and Viagra are certainly present at the Boston Forum meetings, although sometimes covertly. For example, at the first Boston Forum meeting in 1999, Pfizer was the primary supporter of the meetings as well as the early research on FSD, countless Pfizer marketers roamed the halls, the meetings began with a Viagra joke, and the meeting organizer wore a scarf painted with mini-Viagra pills. As the framing of FSD shifted away from Viagra for women by 2001, the Pfizer presence and Viagra emphasis has diminished slightly.

27. While the Bermans' 2001 book, *For Women Only*, asserts that women's sexual problems are related to both mind and body, a close analysis of the book's content reveals an emphasis on biomedical causation and treatment models. The common "work up" for a patient at the Bermans' sexual-dysfunction clinic includes two days of physical tests, with one or two discussions of psychological issues. For critical review of this book, see Heather Hartley, "Promising Liberation but Delivering Business as Usual?" Review in *Sexualities* (5:1, 2002): 107–13.

28. Jennifer Berman, Laura Berman, and Elisabeth Bumiller, *For Women Only: A Revolutionary Guide to Overcoming Sexual Dysfunction and Reclaiming Your Sex Life* (New York: Henry Holt, 2001).

29. Julia Heiman, Ibid.

30. John Bancroft, interview with author, tape recording, Boston: October 2000. Bancroft was director of the Kinsey Institute until 2003.

31. Leonore Tiefer, Boston Forum grandmaster presentation, 1999.

32. Julia Heiman, Ibid.

33. Rosemary Basson, Professor of Psychiatry, Obstetrics, and Gynecology, interview with author, tape recording, Boston: October 2000.

34. See Berman and Berman, *For Women Only*, for a discussion of the similarities between penile and clitoral blood flow and the role of nitric oxide.

35. Quoted in Hartley and Tiefer, "Taking a Biological Turn," 46.

36. Bob Dole's urologist, phone interview with author, October 2001.

37. For a critical analysis of this "consensus conference," see Leonore Tiefer, "The Consensus Conference on Female Sexual Dysfunction: Conflicts of Interest and Hidden Agendas," *Journal of Sex and Marital Therapy* (27:2, 2002): 227–36.

38. In their official "consensus" publication in the *Journal of Urology,* they were required to disclose their affiliations in a footnote. See R. Basson, J. Berman, A. Burnett, I. Derogatis, D. Ferguson, J. Fourcroy, I. Goldstein, A. Grazziottin, J. Heiman, E. Laan, S. Leiblum, H. Padma-Nathan, R. Rosen, K. Segraves, R. T. Segraves, R. Shabsigh, M. Sipski, M. Wager, and B. Whipple, "Report on the International Consensus Development Conference on Female Sexual Dysfunction: Definitions and Classifications," *Journal of Urology* (163, 2000): 888–93.

39. Ibid.

40. Ibid., quoted on 888–90.

41. Ibid., quoted on 891.

42. Ibid.

43. The report did have one mention of the "multi-causality" of FSD, but because it played up the organic causes and future research in this arena, this one reference appears rather empty.

44. I am assuming that the phrase "turbo-charged" refers to vaginal tissues that are highly engorged with blood (the effect of oral sildenafil on rodent vaginal tissues).

45. Promotional brochure, Nexmed Pharmaceuticals, 1999. For more recent information on Femprox, see Sabra Chartrand, "The Viagra Counterpart for Women Is on the Way," *New York Times,* January 27, 2003, C7. This article reports that NexMed Inc. was awarded a patent for a cream containing the hormone prostaglandin, which causes vasodilation in women's genitalia to remedy female sexual dysfunction due to lack of arousal.

46. Roy Levin, interview with author, Massachusetts: October 2001. Rather

than testing new technologies on themselves, experts have enlisted their wives to help with the science of women's sexual problems. See later sections for discussion of the role Goldstein's wife played in his own learning about the wonders of hormonal solutions.

47. Pfizer and journalists have referred intermittently to Viagra as the "blue diamond," which makes sense since Viagra pills are blue and diamond shaped. But one cannot help but wonder if Pfizer chose blue diamond symbolism to draw on cultural associations with the rarest and most valuable blue diamond in existence, the Hope diamond.

48. Carol Brietzke, "Viagra: The Female Orgasm Pill?" *Cosmopolitan,* August 1998.

49. See, for example, Susie Bright, "Viagra Calls II: Curse of the Trophy Wives," salon.com. (July 31, 1999).

50. Many mainstream shows and commentators have coupled sexual desire with the new, "liberated," thirty-something woman.

51. Some journalists have linked the proliferation of "Samantha type" women to a greater performance anxiety among men in their thirties and forties, leading to wider use of Viagra-like drugs for assurance purposes. See, for example, Warren St. John, "In an Oversexed Age, More Guys Take a Pill," *New York Times,* December 14, 2003, sec. 9, 1.

52. One expert from the Boston Forum meetings suggested that men's sexual problems were "shake and bake" in comparison to women's.

53. Sandra Leiblum, Boston Forum grandmaster lecture, author's field notes, October 1999.

54. Rosemary Basson, Boston Forum grandmaster lecture, author's field notes, October 2001.

55. Cindy Meston, interview with author, field notes, Massachusetts: October 2000.

56. Of the numerous trials Meston was involved in in 1999, she admitted that only one had a home-measurement component.

57. Rosemary Basson, presentation at Sexual Medicine Symposium, author's field notes, Beverly Hills, CA, November 2001.

58. Julia Heiman, Ibid.

59. Bancroft 2000, Ibid.

60. John Bancroft, Jeri Loftus, and J. Scott Long, "Distress about Sex: A National Survey of Women in Heterosexual Relationships," *Archives of Sexual Behavior,* June 2003.

61. This remark is interesting because it implies that the only activists or dissidents in the medical field are feminists. In 2003, John Bancroft lived up to his promise as he signed on as an official endorser of the "New View," written by the Working Group on Women's Sexual Problems.

62. Jean Fourcroy, Boston Forum grandmaster presentation, 2001.

63. Rosemary Basson 2000, Ibid.

64. Ibid.

65. Sue Goldstein, Boston Forum Q & A, author's field notes, 2000.

66. Irwin Goldstein, Boston Forum, author's field notes, 2000.

67. Irwin Goldstein, phone interview, tape recording, November 2000.

68. Such talks included Labrie, "Androgenic Activity in the Rhesus Monkey," Boston Forum 2001.

69. Andre Guay, presentation at Sexual Medicine Symposium, author's field notes, Beverly Hills, CA, November 2001.

70. Ridwan Shabsigh, presentation at Sexual Medicine Symposium, author's field notes, Beverly Hills, CA, November 2001.

71. John Bancroft 2000, Ibid.

72. Androgens are central to testosterone production in the ovaries, adrenal glands, and peripheral tissues. Normative levels in men and women are unknown.

73. This was before hormone replacement therapy was found, in 2002, to carry risks of serious side effects, including cancer. For more on this, see the National Women's Health Network's book, *The Truth about Hormone Therapy* (Washington DC: Prima Lifestyles, 2002); and Barbara Seaman, *The Greatest Experiment Ever Performed on Women: Exploding the Estrogen Myth* (New York: Hyperion, 2003). Since this major finding, a new disciplinary caution has emerged in relation to prescribing hormones to women without prior long-term testing. Nonetheless, Goldstein remains insistent that this is the best solution to women's sexual problems.

74. Basic Scientist Abdul Traish, presentation at Boston Forum, author's field notes, 2001.

75. Andropause research is a growing field within sexual medicine that focuses on men's declining levels of testosterone in midlife.

76. Rosemary Basson, Boston Forum presentation, author's field notes, October 2001.

77. Sandra Leiblum, Boston Forum, author's field notes, 2001.

78. Jean Fourcroy, FDA Medical Officer, Boston Forum, author's field notes, 2001.

79. Julia Heiman, phone interview, tape recording, November 2000.

80. Dr. Laan, Boston Forum grandmaster presentation, October 2001.

81. Rosemary Basson 2000, Ibid.

82. See Steven Epstein, *Impure Science: AIDS, Activism, and the Politics of Knowledge* (Berkeley: University of California Press, 1996).

83. Ibid., 326.

84. Ibid., 344.

85. See Leonore Tiefer, "Female Sexual Dysfunction Alert: A New Disorder Invented for Women," *Sojourner: The Women's Forum*, October 11, 1999, 11.

86. See Dolores Kong, "Doubts Heard over Sexual Dysfunction Gathering," *Boston Globe,* October 22, 1999, B1. In the story, Kong highlights three claims-making groups, feminist health advocates, urologists, and Pfizer marketers, with differing stakes in the Boston Forum conference. Unlike the majority of media reports on FSD, this story problematizes the medicalization of sexual issues and the proliferation of Viagra-like treatments offered as a panacea.

87. To the surprise of those of us in the Working Group, the *Boston Globe* story read just as our countermovement wanted it to, with pharmaceutical companies admitting to "defining a medical condition" in order to treat it, urologists evaluating and identifying sexual problems in women, and critics concerned about medical and pharmaceutical groups constructing, defining, shaping, and "fashioning" women's sexualities. This example reveals the power journalists can have in framing FSD.

88. Leonore Tiefer, "Dangerous Outcomes List," Boston Forum handout, 2000. Today, this list, with several changes and additions, is currently highlighted on the FSD-Alert.org webpage.

89. The "New View" was first published in *Journal of Sex Research,* May 2001. See note 90 below.

90. See Leonore Tiefer, "A New View of Women's Sexual Problems: Why New? Why Now?" *Journal of Sex Research* (38:2, 2001): 89–96; and, with Ellyn Kaschak, *A New View of Women's Sexual Problems* (New York: Haworth Press, 2001).

91. Ibid.

92. In its first year, the Working Group was quite busy, doing outreach at the Boston Forum and via the internet, drafting, dispersing, and publishing the document, holding a press conference prior to the Boston Forum 2000 to introduce the "New View" to journalists, and presenting the "New View" at over ten different multidisciplinary conferences, including the Boston Forum. By the 2001 Boston Forum conference, the Working Group was publicizing its own shadow conference, entitled "The New 'Female Sexual Dysfunction': Promises, Prescriptions, and Profits," and handing out reports on the "Campaign for a New View," described as "a feminist educational campaign to resist the current medicalization of women's sexual problems" (begun in September 2000).

93. See Tiefer and Kaschak, *A New View of Women's Sexual Problems.*

94. "Sex, Pills, and Love Potions." The Learning Channel (TLC), Granada Television Production (October 28, 2001). As the opener of the documentary reveals, we must know where sexuality comes from in order to bring it back.

95. The EROS-CTD device is an exception, as the only FDA-approved treatment for FSD, but this product has not taken off, largely due to the price, limited promotion, the device's awkwardness, emphasis on blood flow only, and new industry standards set by Viagra for oral or topical treatments.

96. In early March 2004, after eight years of chemical trails Pfizer announced that it would officially halt clinical trials of Viagra in women.

97. Leonore Tiefer, interview with author, field notes, Massachusetts: October 2000.

98. Carol Queen, a nationally recognized "sexpert" from feminist sexual-products business Good Vibrations, echoes these concerns about narrow sexual standards.

99. John Bancroft et al., 2003.

NOTES TO CHAPTER 6

1. A wide range of participants attended the Paris conference. For example, I had fascinating conversations with a urologist and his wife from Syria, a basic scientist from Pfizer's research headquarters in Sandwich, England, and another scientist from Memphis who isolated the first nitric oxide molecules.

2. "Unless contraindicated, Viagra is now used as first-line therapy for ED. Of the 30 million affected men in the United States, only 8 million are being treated with Viagra. Overall, the ED market is under-penetrated, and the introduction of Cialis and Levitra could expand the market through increased awareness. In the future, PDE5 inhibitors will treat 60–80% of men who suffer from ED." See Ronald C. Renaud and Hayley Xuereb, "From the Analyst's Couch: Erectile-Dysfunction Therapies," *Drug Discovery* (1:9, 2002): 663–64.

3. Quoted from cialis.com and levitra.com (November 2003). Cialis has been dubbed by spammers as "the weekend pill" because it lasts for up to thirty-six hours.

4. By affiliating themselves with psychologists, competitors Levitra and Cialis are attempting to promote a more "holistic" type of medicine, as well as to address and include the partners of Viagra users in their marketing campaigns. This is a major shift from Pfizer's emphasis on organic factors in the solitary male body. In many ways, this is a new "broadening" or diagnostic expansion of erectile dysfunction that relocates the problem in the couple.

5. See Peg Tyre, "Viagra Babies: Older Parents, Younger Kids," *Newsweek*, January 26, 2004, 68–70.

6. Scientists and doctors are still experimenting on themselves and coming up with fascinating new discoveries. Professor Mac Hadley, a dermatologist at the University of Arizona, is working with a team of urologists to develop a drug that will affect the brain in such a way as to create erections as well as tanned skin. Hadley knows this product works because he tried it on himself: "I decided to take one of these products home to the get the project moving by experimenting on myself. I made a slight miscalculation, and the chemical was much stronger than I planned. I didn't develop a suntan right way, but I did develop an erection very rapidly. I developed an erection that lasted eight hours.

... I couldn't reduce it with ice cubes. I reached up and said, 'We're going to be very rich!'" "Sex, Pills, and Love Potions," The Learning Channel (TLC), Granada Television Production (October 28, 2001).

7. See "Viagra Gum, Double Your Pleasure?" CNN, www.cnn.com, June 17, 2003, to learn more about Wrigley's patent. In addition, Reuters reports that Chilean researchers aim to develop a new pill to combat impotence that would have the added bonus of being a male contraceptive. Such research is based on experiments with the venom of black widow spiders. See "Black Widow Spider ɪ ill the Next Viagra?" CNN, www.cnn.com, July 10, 2003.

8. See Ariel Levy, "Pill Culture Pops," *New York*, June 9, 2003, 24–29. According to one thirty-something SSRI patient featured in the cover story, "When you first notice the sexual side-effects, you're probably so depressed you just want to get better and probably don't feel much like having sex anyway. But then you start to feel better and of course you notice." The article goes on to discuss the gay party scene, where crystal and other gay party drugs inhibit sexual arousal, and it is common to use Viagra in combination with such drugs. Pfizer also appears to be promoting layering of drugs, specifically their own Zoloft (for depression) and Viagra (for arousal). In their 2003 Paris symposia, Pfizer-affiliated faculty heralded the importance of Viagra in neutralizing the common side effect of SSRIs, or antidepressants, by "bringing people back to sexual functioning."

9. To go along with the McDonaldization of medicine, and our increased accumulation of pills, Americans are now ordering "supersized" medicine cabinets. See Deborah Baldwin, "Medicine Cabinets: Walk Right In," *New York Times*, March 18, 2004, D1. Sadly, while senior citizens may be the ones taking the most pills, they are rarely represented in clinical trials or drug company studies. Perhaps in part for this reason, adverse reactions to medication is the fifth leading cause of death in the United States. See Katharine Greider, *The Big Fix: How the Pharmaceutical Industry Rips Off American Consumers* (New York: Public Affairs, 2003): 131.

10. Ken Silverstein, "Millions for Viagra: Pennies for Diseases of the Poor," *Nation*, July 19, 1999, 13–19.

11. Canadian drug industry critic Pat Mooney, writing in *World Watch*, July/August 2002, says there is a growing market for making well people better, because focusing on the sick is not profitable. People will either get well or die, neither of which is good for business. Quoted in Miriam Karmel, "A Drug for All Reasons," *Utne Reader*, July–August 2003, 16–17.

12. See Rob Walker, "Consumed Cialis," *New York Times*, February 8, 2004, sec. 9, 1.

13. Anonymous black-market dealers in China and the Philippines, interviews by author, field notes, California: 2001, and New York: November 2003.

14. Diane Toops, "Banned in Japan," *Food Processing* (62:3, 2001): 12.

15. Viacreme distributor, interview by author, email correspondence, e-mail transcript, September 2001.

16. For information on Viagra use in Egypt, see Michael Slackman, "Arousing Debate in Egypt," *Los Angeles Times,* June 17, 2002, A1. See Jack Boulware, "Bachelors Out of Luck" and "La Dolce Viagra," salon.com (July 14 and August 10, 2000) for information on Pfizer's study of Viagra use in Italy.

17. Edward Laumann, interview by author, field notes, Paris: July 2003. Laumann is a primary investigator in Pfizer's global research.

18. For more on Viagra resulting in saving endangered wildlife, see Margaret Talbot, "Viagra Saves Wildlife," *New York Times,* December 15, 2002, 6, col. 1. Also see Ilene Prusher, "Some Unexpected Relief for Endangered Species," *Christian Science Monitor,* May 29, 2001, sec. 2, 7.

19. See J. A. Getzlaff, "Giant Pandas to Be Given Viagra," salon.com (April 26, 2000).

20. See Greider, *The Big Fix,* xiii.

21. See Ray Moynihan, "The Making of a Disease: Female Sexual Dysfunction," *British Medical Journal* (326, 2003): 45–47; and Judy Peres, "Women Find Hope for Sex Dysfunction: Drugmakers Eager but Critics Skeptical," *Chicago Tribune,* December 29, 2002, 1–5.

22. Greider, *The Big Fix,* 140.

23. P. J. Huffstutter and Ralph Frammolino, "Lights! Camera! Viagra! When the Show Must Go On, Sometimes a Little Chemistry Helps," *Los Angeles Times,* July 6, 2001, A1.

24. This is especially apparent in my conversations with young males, who cite performance anxiety as a primary reason for their recreational Viagra use. One twenty-five-year-old male reported to me that the popular, nationally syndicated radio show, *LoveLine,* regularly receives calls from teenage boys wondering how Viagra will help their sexual performance (phone interview with author, field notes, July 2002).

25. Many doctors are prescribing testosterone off label, particularly as a treatment for male menopause, or "andropause." See Alix Spiegel (reporter), "Debate over Male 'Andropause,'" *All Things Considered,* NPR, February 9, 2004; Sally Lehman, "Concerns Rise as More Men Use Hormone Therapy," *Los Angeles Times,* November 3, 2003, F1.

26. See, for example Lynette Dumble, "Viagra: A Can of Worms for Women," *Global Sisterhood Network* (listserve) (October 1999).

27. Carole Vance quoted in Ann Eckman, "Making Women Visible in Post-1990 Women's Health Discourse" in *The Visible Woman,* Paula Treichler, Constance Penley, Lisa Cartwright, eds. (New York: New York University Press, 1998); and in Nancy Kreiger and Elizabeth Fee, "Man-Made Medicine and Women's Health: The Biopolitics of Sex/Gender and Race/Ethnicity" in

Women's Health, Politics, and Power: Essays on Sex/Gender, Medicine, and Public Health, Kreiger and Fee, eds. (Amityville, NY: Baywood, 1994): 11–29.

28. See cover story by Kathleen Deveny, "We're Not in the Mood," *Newsweek*, June 20, 2003.

29. Quoted from Pfizer Pharmaceuticals, Inc., *Uncover Ed*, Pfizer Informational Brochure, March 2000. It may be the case that sexual dysfunction is a symptom of a larger disease. This brochure cites Pfizer-funded research that shows correlations between ED and diabetes, hypertension, and depression, for example.

30. In her book, *Looking Good*, Lynne Luciano shows how phalloplasty first attracted thousands of men as a result of Calvin Klein's advertising campaigns in the 1980s. Calvin Klein revolutionized underwear advertising by no longer emphasizing functionality (wash- and wearability) but instead emphasizing sex appeal. Penile ordinariness became penile insufficiency, and men flocked to enhance their penises. *Looking Good: Male Body Image in Modern America* (New York: Hill and Wang, 2001): 188. Today, Viagra has made the penile implant industry lucrative again (Second International Consultation on Erectile and Sexual Dysfunction, Paris 2003).

31. According to one Pfizer representative, Viagra has also been a boon to the infertility industry, aiding both men and women with intercourse as well as conception, as Viagra has been used to thicken a woman's uterine lining in order to facilitate fertilized egg implantation (interview with author, field notes, Los Angeles: July 2003).

32. "Sex, Pills, and Love Potions," The Learning Channel (TLC), Granada Television Production (October 28, 2001).

33. Pfizer Pharmaceuticals, Inc., *Pfizer for Living*, General Mailing and Brochure, September 2003.

34. Botox was approved by the FDA on April 16, 2002.

35. See David Francis, "Facing the Challenges of World's Aging Population," *Christian Science Monitor*, April 22, 2002, 21.

36. According to Greider, *The Big Fix*, 125, the percentage of Americans sixty-five years old and older is expected to climb from 12.5 percent in 2000 to 20.3 percent in 2030. These new older generations promise to be a different, more "proactive" breed.

37. Robert Lee Hotz, "Boomers Seek Magic Bullets to Ward Off Symptoms of Aging," *Los Angeles Times*, May 13, 1998, 1.

38. Pfizer got a lot of attention for declaring Viagra the "official sponsor of Valentines Day" in 2000 and 2001. See Pfizer Pharmaceuticals, Inc., *Wishing You a Happy Valentines Day*, Advertisement, 2000. Many spin-off stories from Pfizer's ad campaign focused on Viagra as a "love drug" and recreational drug. For examples of media reporting on Viagra recreational use, see Charles

Ornstein, "Warning on Viagra's Role in STDs Is Requested," *Los Angeles Times,* March 15, 2002, B1; Jack Hitt, "The Second Sexual Revolution," *New York Times Magazine,* February 20, 2000, 34–37; and Robert L. Pela, "Younger Men Are Opting for the Viagra Fix—Even When It Ain't Broke," *Men's Fitness,* February 2000, 82–87.

39. For example, an online article entitled "Club Drugs and Sex: You Might Drop More Than E" warns that many clubgoers use Viagra and crystal methamphetamine to retain sexual excitement and erectile potential all night long, which can be dangerous in terms of HIV transmission. See Michael Luongo, www.gayhealth.com.

40. John Gallagher, "What Comes Up Must Go Down," *The Advocate,* June 28, 1998, 60.

41. Gabriel Rotello, writing for the *The Advocate,* July 7, 1999, 72, personally reported on Viagra's "less than revolutionary" effects, including pounding heart, flushed feelings, and a persistent headache the morning after.

42. With so many different online outlets and pharmacies to choose from, including counterfeit dealers, it is difficult to estimate the numbers of buyers or Viagra pills distributed.

43. For more on the FDA's decreasing regulatory power, see Philip J. Hilts, *Protecting America's Health: The FDA, Business, and One Hundred Years of Regulation* (New York: Knopf, 2003).

44. Greider, *The Big Fix,* 144.

45. Hilts, *Protecting America's Health,* 343.

46. Marcia Angell, "The Pharmaceutical Industry: To Whom Is It Accountable?" *New England Journal of Medicine* (342:35, 2000): 1902–4 and "Is Academic Medicine for Sale?" *New England Journal of Medicine* (342:20, 2000): 1516–18.

47. See, for example, these books published in the past two years: *Protecting America's Health: The FDA, Business, and One Hundred Years of Regulation; Prescription for Profits; Better Than Well: American Medicine Meets the American Dream; The Big Fix: How the Pharmaceutical Industry Rips Off American Consumers; Over Dose: the Case against the Drug Companies;* and *A New View of Women's Sexual Problems.*

48. The "No Free Lunch" website says,

We are health care providers—physicians, pharmacists, nurses, dentists, among others—who believe that pharmaceutical promotion should not guide clinical practice, and that over-zealous promotional practices can lead to bad patient care. It is our goal to encourage health care practitioners to provide high quality care based on unbiased evidence rather than on biased pharmaceutical promotion. . . . We believe that there is ample evidence in the literature— contrary to the beliefs of most health care providers—that drug companies, by means of samples, gifts, and food, exert significant influence on provider behavior. There is also ample evidence in the literature that promotional materials and presentations are often biased and non-informative. We believe that health care professionals, precisely because they are *professionals*, should not allow themselves to be bought by the pharmaceutical industry: It is time to *Just say no to drug reps* and their pens, pads, calendars, coffee mugs, and of course, lunch (not to mention dinners, basketball games, and ski vacations). For more information, www.nofreelunch.org.

49. Forthcoming articles from Annie Potts, Tina Vaares, Nicola Gavey, and Victoria M. Grace in 2003–2004 include, "Hard Sell, Soft Sell: Men Read Viagra Ads," *Media International Australia*; "'Viagra Stories': Challenging 'Erectile Dysfunction,'" *Social Science and Medicine*; and "The Downside of Viagra: Women's Experiences and Concerns," *Sociology of Health and Illness*.

50. In one ABC news show entitled "Bitter Medicine," Peter Jennings opens the show with a polemic, stating that the pharmaceutical industry is not doing enough for public health. See "Bitter Medicine: Pills, Profits, and the Public Health," *Peter Jennings Reports*, ABC, April 2002. For hidden camera exposé and analysis of pharmaceutical gifting practices, see *Primetime Thursday*, ABC, February 21, 2002.

51. In several cases, male clients sued their insurers to have Viagra covered by their plans, which eventually became standard for most large insurers. Even the Pentagon entered health insurance coverage debates, claiming that if the Veterans Affairs budget did cover Viagra, the budget would be largely eaten up. The government agreed to cover no more than six pills a month, and only for doctor-diagnosed erectile dysfunction (Luciano, *Looking Good*, 201).

52. Sonni Efron, "Japan: Women Find Viagra's Speedy OK Is Bitter Pill to Swallow," *Los Angeles Times*, January 30, 1999, 2.

53. The Japanese Ministry of Health approved Viagra in January 1999 and the birth control pill in June 1999. At that time, Japan was the only developed country that had not approved the low-dose birth-control pill. News reports cite various reasons for the delay, including concern over falling birth rates, an aging population, and concern about the health risks associated with birth-control pills. Two articles written by journalist Sonni Efron for the *Los Angeles Times* sum up the two approvals: "World Perspective: Japan: Women Find Viagra's Speedy OK Is Bitter Pill to Swallow: Female Ire over Quick Decision on Anti-impotence Drug Could Pressure Authorities to Finally Approve Oral Contraceptive" (January 30, 1999, 2). Five months later, Efron wrote, "Japan OKs Birth Control Pill after Decades of Delay: Asia: Female Contraceptive Took Thirty-Four Years for Approval, While Men Waited Only Six Months for Viagra to Go on Sale" (June 3, 1999, 1). Much of the approval pressure may have additionally come from pharmaceutical companies attempting to open new markets for their products. Also see Sharon

Moshavi, "Now for Japanese, the Pill, with a Shrug," *Boston Globe,* October 24, 1999, B1.

54. In addition, ongoing efforts have been underway by Congress and mental health advocates to pass a federal law to prohibit group health plans from treating coverage of mental health differently from coverage of medical and surgical benefits.

55. Brian Blomquist, "Where Are You Hillary?" *New York Post,* August 3, 2001, 20.

56. Cynthia L. Cooper, "Contraceptive Equity Is Now Law in Texas," Women's Enews, womensenews.com, August 31, 2001.

57. Rachel Maines, "Viagra and Vibrators: The Sexual Double Standard," Lecture, Hamilton College, NY (November 11, 2003).

58. For example, an early television ad for Sarafem, Eli Lilly's pill for premenstrual dysphoric disorder, was removed because it depicted an angry woman in a supermarket, casting doubt on what the pill was for.

59. For more on FDA guidance plan, see two articles by Pear in 2002. Robert Pear, "Drug Industry Is Told to Stop Gifts to Doctors," *New York Times,* October 1, 2002, A1, col. 5 and "Drug Makers Battle Plan to Curb Rewards for Doctors," *New York Times,* December 26, 2002, A1, col. 6.

60. See Jay Cohen, *Over Dose: The Case against the Drug Companies* (New York: Putnam, 2001).

61. For more on the controversy around direct-to-consumer advertising, see Robert A. Rosenblatt, "Drug Firms' TV Ads Fuel Rise in Costs and Demand," *Los Angeles Times,* November 26, 1999, A46; Aparna Kumar, "Doctors Split on Usefulness of Drug Advertising," *Los Angeles Times,* January 14, 2003, A12; Erin N. Marcus, "When TV Commercials Play the Doctor," *New York Times,* January 3, 2003, A21, col. 1; Alexandra Marks, "Rise of 'Ask Your Doctor' Ads: A Public Health Concern?" *Christian Science Monitor,* November 30, 2001, sec. 2, 2.

62. Alexandra Marks, "A Harder Look at Prescription-Drug Ads," *Christian Science Monitor,* April 4, 2001, 1–3.

63. Medical education run by pharmaceutical corporations is an embarrassing and upsetting state of affairs, according to former *New England Journal of Medicine* editor Arnold S. Relman. "Medical schools and other educational institutions are not teaching doctors how to use drugs wisely and conservatively. Until they insist that the pharmaceutical industry stick to its own business (which can include advertising but not education), we are unlikely to get the help we need from our doctors in controlling runaway drug expenditures." See Relman's *New York Times* editorial, "Your Doctor's Drug Problem," November 18, 2003, A25, col. 1.

64. Scholars have warned about the general overemphasis on the biotechnological "impact" in such writings on sexuality and technology, which can be taken to the point of erasing the role of human agency. See, for example, Donna

Jeanne Haraway, *Simians, Cyborgs, and Women: The Reinvention of Nature* (New York: Routledge, 1991); Jana Sawicki, *Disciplining Foucault: Feminism, Power, and the Body* (New York: Routledge, 1991). Technological developments are many-edged, Sawicki reminds us (89), for who, today, would deny women the contraceptive technologies developed in this century? To avoid overdeterminism, Sawicki suggests employing a Foucaultian analysis to view technology and medical science within a context of multiple sites of power and resistance operating within a social field of struggle (87). De Lauretis argues that while gender and sexuality may appear hegemonic, different constructions of each exist in the margins of hegemonic discourses, inscribed in micropolitical practices and local levels of resistance. See Teresa de Lauretis, *Technologies of Gender* (Bloomington: Indiana University Press, 1987).

NOTES TO EPILOGUE

1. Enzyte is a product of Lifekey Healthcare Incorporated. For more information, see Enzyte.com.

2. See Bayer Health Care and GlaxoSmithKline, "There Are Erections . . . and There Are 3D Erections," Print Advertisement, May 2003.

3. See Jane Spencer, "In Search of 'Female Viagra,' Doctors Try Antidepressants, Testosterone, Even Ritalin," *Wall Street Journal,* November 4, 2003, D1.

4. See Abraham Morgentaler, *The Viagra Myth: The Surprising Impact on Love and Relationships* (New York: Jossey-Bass, 2003).

5. Associated Press, "Ban on Impotence Drug Ads Shelves Brazil's Pele Viagra Campaign," *USA Today,* July 26, 2003.

6. See Vince Parry, "The Art of Branding a Condition," *MM&M* (*Medical Marketing & Media*), May 2003.

7. See Rob Walker, "Consumed Cialis," *New York Times,* February 8, 2004, sec. 9, 1.

NOTES TO APPENDIX

1. For more on this, see Meika Loe, "Feminism for Sale: Case Study of a Pro-Sex Feminist Business," *Gender and Society* (13:6, 1999): 705–32.

2. Initially, I had planned to center my interview efforts on a select group of entrepreneurs who literally cashed in on Viagra's success, such as business people in the exploding herbal aphrodisiac market, and individual doctors starting up "male clinics" across the country dedicated to penile surgeries and potency solutions. I theorized that this bustling "business of sex," and particularly the mass marketing of male potency, was expanding exponentially after Viagra established itself as a visible market success. After preliminary

interviews with a number of "entrepreneurs" (including one penile-enhance-ment specialist, three herbal-remedy-store managers, one black-market Viagra salesman in China, and one sexual-products-store owner), I realized that this group was not so separate from the other groups I had interviewed, particularly the medical professionals I call "experts" (many of whom worked for pharma-ceutical companies or made profits off Viagra prescriptions). Thus, in the end I concluded that aside from the consumers and critics I interviewed, everyone else seemed to be involved in the business of sex, broadly construed, and dropped the "entrepreneur" category entirely. As this study will show, "ex-perts" are generally very business oriented, and many do the work of "entre-preneurs," profiting off the Viagra phenomenon in various ways.

3. See David A. Karp, *Speaking of Sadness, Depression, Disconnection, and the Meanings of Illness* (Oxford: Oxford University Press, 1996).

4. See Edward O. Laumann, John H. Gagnon, Robert T. Michaels, and Stu-art Michaels, *The Social Organization of Sexuality: Sexual Practices in the United States* (Chicago: University of Chicago Press, 1994).

5. Interestingly, very few gynecologists were invited to or attended the early medical meetings on female sexual dysfunction, which were run by a group of urologists and psychiatrists. As I write this, I am aware that gynecolo-gists deal with increasing numbers of sexual complaints by their female pa-tients and, in response to this and changing medical treatments, have added sessions on "female sexual dysfunction" to their own annual meetings. This particular gynecologist is a unique case, as he admitted to being both a practi-tioner and a regular Viagra consumer.

6. I chose urologists randomly, expecting that they all dealt with sexuality in their practices. Several were referred to me by other medical professionals because they were conducting clinical trials related to sexual dysfunction or writing high numbers of scripts for Viagra. Psychiatrists, therapists, and sexual health experts were mostly referred because of their expertise in sexuality or sexual dysfunction.

7. For example, almost every medical practitioner and Viagra consumer I spoke with recommended I speak with the local Los Angeles expert on Viagra, Pfizer consultant Padma-Nathan. Despite my numerous attempts to contact him, he never returned my calls and told his secretary to tell me I needed to get consent from Pfizer before he would talk—a noteworthy response. I did meet him later at a medical conference, and he invited me to a Pfizer-sponsored set of meetings on erectile dysfunction but still evaded my attempts at an interview.

8. The only exception was the urologist who gave me exactly ten minutes by phone.

9. Many pharmacists and a few doctors expressed discomfort in hearing about their clients' sexual practices and experiences with Viagra.

10. For more on this, see *Primetime Thursday*, ABC, February 21, 2002.

11. For example, Kari criticized the fact that pharmaceutical companies hire representatives based on attractiveness, while admitting that doctors often respond more to the gender and attractiveness of a sales rep then to any other factor. Kellen implied that Pfizer's merger with Warner-Lambert revealed a corporation that was less about worker loyalty and voice, and more about profits. Finally, Buster was very up front about the fact that Viagra was really about sexual enhancement for men with "mild ED" over forty.

12. Kari left her job to get married and find work that was more "meaningful."

13. The Working Group campaign has been referred to in the following media: *Boston Globe, Boston Herald, New York Times Magazine, Sojourner, San Francisco Chronicle, Los Angeles Times, New Scientist, Sixty Minutes (Australia), SexTV (Canada)*, The Learning Channel, and online magazines salon.com and nerve.com.

14. See Nancy Sheper-Hughes, "The Problem of Bias in Androcentric and Feminist Anthropology," *Women's Studies* (10, 1983): 109–16.

15. Www.FSD-Alert.org is the Working Group's homepage. This website makes outreach, conference registration, and fund raising easier for the Working Group. Prior to the creation of the website, Tiefer would send out a printed packet of information on the grassroots campaign. Now, interested persons may visit the website to peruse our "New View" document, comments on our first annual conference, our list of international endorsers, the articles we have written, the press we have received, upcoming events, and related links.

16. My own commitment to this group as well as my concerns about medical-pharmaceutical efforts to capitalize on men's and women's sexual vulnerabilities have not changed. See Loe, "Feminists Fight Drug Companies over Vision of Women's Sexuality," Our Bodies, Ourselves, www.OurBodiesOurselves.org., reprinted from *Sojourner: The Women's Forum*, March 2001 and "Caution: You and Your Friends May Be Sexually Dysfunctional," *Women's Health Newsletter*, January 1, 2000, 6–7.

17. Marjorie DeVault, *Liberating Method: Feminism and Social Research* (Philadelphia: Temple University Press, 1999): 23.

18. For a summary of institutional ethnography, see Devault, "Institutional Ethnography: A Strategy for Feminist Inquiry" in *Liberating Method*, 46–54. Also see Dorothy Smith, *Writing the Social: Critique, Theory, and Investigations* (Toronto: University of Toronto Press, 1998); and Dorothy Smith, *The Everyday World as Problematic: A Feminist Sociology* (Toronto: University of Toronto Press, 1997).

19. Smith, *Writing the Social*, 49.

20. DeVault, *Liberating Method*.

21. See Francesca Cancian, "Feminist Science: Methodologies that Challenge Inequality," *Gender and Society* (6, 1992): 623–42; and Diane Wolf, *Feminist Dilemmas in Fieldwork* (Boulder, CO: Westview Press, 1996).

22. Cancian, "Feminist Science."

23. See Barbara DuBois, "Passionate Scholarship: Notes on Values, Knowing, and Method in Feminist Social Science" in *Theories of Women's Studies,* Gloria Bowles and Renate Klein, eds. (London: Routledge, 1983): 105–16; and Wolf, *Feminist Dilemmas in Fieldwork.*

24. C. J. Creswell, *Qualitative Inquiry and Research Design: Choosing among Five Traditions* (Thousand Oaks, CA: Sage, 1998).

25. James Clifford and George Marcus, *Writing Culture: The Poetics and Politics of Ethnography* (Berkeley: University of California Press, 1986): 2.

26. Clifford and Marcus, *Writing Culture.*

27. Paul D. Leedy and Jeanne Ellis Ormond, *Practical Research: Planning and Design* (Upper Saddle River, NJ: Merrill Prentice Hall, 2001).

28. Mitchell Duneier, *Sidewalk* (New York: Farrar, Straus, Giroux, 1999).

29. I decided not to analyze internet "chat" in this study, although this would be a fascinating project, particularly in terms of dialogue between men (about sex or sexual performance) and various online masculinity performances. The major difference I found between internet talk and my own interview data was the detailed descriptions of Viagra bodies found in Viagra-themed chat rooms. The anonymity of this space seems to invite such descriptions. I also witnessed quite a few self-described males, many of whom purchased Viagra through the internet, asking others for advice on how to use Viagra correctly.

30. Ann Swidler, "Culture in Action: Symbols and Strategies," *American Sociological Review* (51:2, 1986): 273–86.

31. For more on grounded theory, see Barney Glaser and Anselm Strauss, *Discovery of Grounded Theory: Strategies for Qualitative Research* (New York: de Gruyter, 1967); and Juliet Corbin and Anselm Strauss, *Grounded Theory in Practice* (Thousand Oaks, CA: Sage, 1997).

32. I followed Emerson, Fretz, and Shaw's inductive data analysis method of open coding and then more focused coding to find common themes, patterns, and linkages. Initially, this was difficult given the large number of interview transcripts I had to analyze, as well as print data. To make this process less daunting, I made separate code lists for each group of informants, and then for print media. I then constructed a combined list of forty codes—made up of those that seemed the most salient and prevalent across data groups. These forty codes were then weighted and grouped into five major thematic categories: (1) SCI, attention to science of sex, discovery, knowledge production; (2) PROB, definitions of the patient and the problem; (3) TREAT, medical treatment goals or script; (4) MED, references related to medicalization, including atten-

tion to the rise of the pharmaceutical industry, enhancement meds, pill culture, risk and regulation discourses; and (5) CULT, references to socio-cultural trends, discourse, phenomena. Coding and grouping helped immensely in organizing this analysis and drawing theory inductively from data. See R. Emerson, R. Fretz, and L. Shaw, *Writing Ethnographic Fieldnotes* (Chicago: University of Chicago Press, 1995).

33. Laura Nader, *Naked Science* (New York: Routledge, 1996).

34. At the end of interviews, I asked customers if they had anything to add, or any questions about me. Several male consumers asked further questions about my research.

35. Ken Plummer, *Sexual Stories: Power, Change, and Social Worlds* (London: Routledge, 1995).

36. See Laura Nader, *Naked Science* (New York: Routledge, 1996); and Diane Wolf, *Feminist Dilemmas in Fieldwork* (Boulder, CO: Westview Press, 1996).

37. Since beginning this project, I have experienced intense pressure to try Viagra from friends, colleagues, and interview subjects. Certainly, people would not recommend that I try an antidepressant or hair-loss pill if I were studying either. Viagra carries a stigma similar to that of both of these drugs, but also increased amounts of social cachet and public interest. *New York Times* journalist Jack Hitt, who wrote a feature story about Viagra, also expressed confusion about the pressure he felt from friends and interview subjects to try the product he wrote about. Hitt says, "I was confused. Pfizer's official pronouncements state clearly that Viagra doesn't really work on potent men." Jack Hitt, "The Second Sexual Revolution," *New York Times Magazine*, February 20, 2000, 34–37. In the same way, the official word from Pfizer is that Viagra is not effective in women. And yet, a percentage of the American public considers Viagra something that sexually active women should consider as a "fun" option. Television shows like *Sex in the City* promote this idea.

38. Plummer, *Sexual Stories*, 7.

39. Ibid., 178.

40. Ibid., 176.

41. Ibid., 17.

42. Lillian B. Rubin, *Erotic Wars: What Happened to the Sexual Revolution?* (New York: Farrar, Straus, Giroux, 1990): 16.

Index

Numbers in italics refer to a figure or its caption. For example, *184* refers to the figure appearing on page 184 or to its caption.

About the Author

MEIKA LOE was raised in Ventura, California, and received her Ph.D. at the University of California, Santa Barbara. She is currently Assistant Professor of Sociology and Women's Studies at Colgate University in New York, where she teaches courses on social problems, gender, sexuality, and medicine.